6

The RHS Encyclopedia of Practical Gardening

x 6

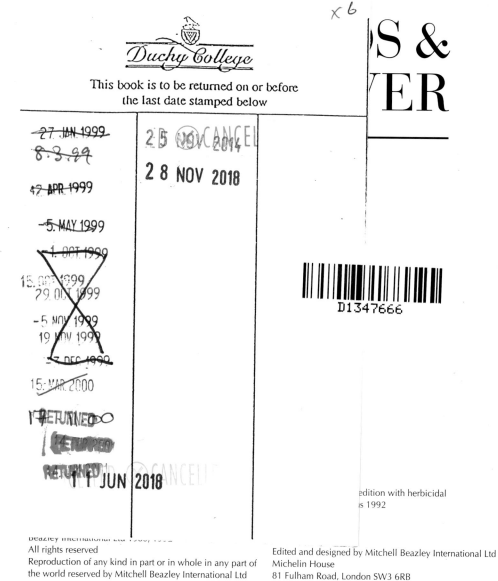

S &

ER

D1347666

edition with herbicidal
is 1992

Beazley International Ltd 1988, 1992

Edited and designed by Mitchell Beazley International Ltd
Michelin House
81 Fulham Road, London SW3 6RB
Produced by Mandarin Offset
Printed and bound in Hong Kong

Contents

**Before using any weedkiller, it is important
to read carefully the relevant parts of the
Introduction on page 5 and the points on
safety listed on pages 138–139.**

635.9647 /

Introduction 1

One of the most important aspects of gardening is routine maintenance, such as mowing grass, removing weeds and dealing with awkward inhospitable corners. Too often these simple operations are approached in a haphazard manner, with grass being neglected for perhaps several weeks in the summer before being cut, and weeds being left to grow unchecked, causing crops to suffer accordingly. The result is a garden that is not allowed to look as fresh and attractive as it would if the gardener were to adopt a more methodical approach.

The aim of this book is to provide an easily understood guide to garden maintenance. As its title implies, it is divided into three roughly equal sections. Two of these sections provide a step-by-step approach to creating and maintaining a lawn, and the prevention and control of weeds. The third section is concerned with those awkward areas in a garden where little except weeds seems to grow and, as the gardener abandons these odd corners in exasperation, increasingly become an eyesore. This section shows how these unproductive areas can be made attractive and weed-free by the planting of ground cover.

Lawns

A well maintained lawn is a valuable feature of many gardens and, as such, it is not only important to tend to the lawn to keep it healthy; its shape should also be considered. Most lawns have a standard rectangular outline which rarely complements the rest of the garden, and in almost every case a curved lawn gives the gardener greater freedom in the positioning of ornamental features and allows him to enhance the whole appearance of his garden. The lawns section begins with a detailed discussion of these considerations. The remainder of this section is concerned with creating a lawn and maintaining it once it has been established.

Creating a lawn

In these pages particular emphasis is placed on careful and thorough site preparation. Careful preparation is necessary, not only to ensure rapid and successful establishment, but also to ensure that, once laid, the lawn will not need later corrections to its level and drainage. A lawn will last for many years and any mistakes made at the beginning can only be subsequently rectified with considerable difficulty.

The section on creating a lawn also includes a discussion of the advantages and disadvantages of using seed or turf, with full step-by-step details of each technique, the problems of weeding a new lawn and the characteristics of the various lawn grasses.

Maintaining a lawn

Once a lawn has been established, it has to be maintained and the various troubles that may befall it dealt with. Many gardeners pay very little attention to their lawns, apart from applying an occasional dressing of fertilizer or raking it over in the spring. A lawn is, however, a carpet of living plants and, as with any crop, will respond strongly to regular attention. Without this attention, however, it is inevitable that one trouble or another will eventually set in.

The most important lawn operation is mowing, which is a form of pruning. Correct frequency and closeness of cut promotes the development of a dense, closely knit turf, whereas irregular and excessively close mowing encourages coarser grasses and weakens the more desirable finer ones. Regular feeding is also important since undernourished turf becomes weak and sparse, and is then more easily colonized by moss and weeds.

The final part of this section deals with lawn problems. Some can occur almost overnight, whereas others develop slowly and often remain unnoticed until the problem has become serious. All troubles affect the appearance and vigour of the turf, causing areas of discoloration or irregularity. Always keep a watch for any such symptoms and check their characteristics against those described and illustrated on pages 64–69.

Introduction 2

Ground cover

A garden is an artificial community of plants, often containing those unsuited to the type of soil or situation in which they are being grown. Many garden plants struggle for survival in poor soil, shade or very dry sites, but weeds can thrive in such conditions. Furthermore, almost all garden plants have been introduced from other climates or have been bred or selected for certain characteristics – these factors mean that such plants tend not to compete well with strong-growing weeds, which are ideally suited to their environment.

Ground cover in nature

In the wild where plant communities are natural, certain plants (or perhaps just a single plant) that are particularly suited to an environment will quite frequently become dominant and smother weaker plants. Thus, large areas of ground can become colonized by these plants to the exclusion of all others.

The success of such plants is due both to their inherent vigour and to their habit of growth. By forming a dense low canopy of overlapping leaves and branches they prevent other plants from becoming established underneath them. This is due principally to a lack of light; also any that do succeed in germinating soon die from lack of moisture and nutrients caused by the presence of the covering plants' roots.

Ground cover in the garden

In recent years gardeners have learned to imitate nature by utilizing the ground-covering properties of suitable plants for dealing with those problem areas where little except weeds will grow. Not only do cover plants keep the ground free of weeds, they also make the area attractive and have the added advantage that, once established, they require little maintenance.

The fact that ground cover plants need little maintenance means that they can also be grown by gardeners who have insufficient time, or lack the physical ability, to tend to more demanding plants, yet still wish to have a neat attractive garden.

Choosing ground cover plants

The section on ground cover lists a wide range of suitable plants. Over a hundred are included, and in each case a description of their habit and appearance is given, as well as their height, planting distance and methods of propagation. Roughly half of these plants are also illustrated. The selection of plants has been made primarily on the basis of their good ground cover qualities. It has also taken into account the wide range of conditions and situations in which ground cover may be needed, and their value as ornamental plants.

The list of plants is followed by a step-by-step section on the practicalities of growing ground cover, from planning and preparing the site through to maintenance and propagation. Various problem sites that benefit from ground cover are then discussed. To assist in the selection of the most suitable plants, charts have been provided. In extreme conditions the gardener may have a very limited choice of suitable plants. For example, on a steep dry bank it may be possible to grow only a single species such as ivy to provide functional cover. Where conditions are less severe a wider choice can be made with more emphasis placed on the ornamental qualities of the plants.

Weed control

An important prerequisite of successful gardening is to keep weeds under control. Convincing evidence can be seen of this in any garden that was once well cared for but has since been neglected; it will consist largely of weeds with perhaps a few garden plants still struggling for survival. The importance of weed control in fruit and vegetable crops can be readily seen when the quality and yield of a weed-free crop is compared to that of a crop which has had to compete with strong weed growth for light, moisture and food.

Most garden weeds are native wild plants, the most troublesome ones being those that are best adapted to survive in unfavourable conditions. Such plants are strong-growing and spread by means of creeping roots, rhizomes or freely produced seeds. Certain garden plants with these characteristics may also be regarded as weeds since they can become invasive and spread into parts of the garden where they are not wanted, especially if the soil is fertile.

The section on weed control begins by looking at the differences between annual and perennial weeds, and shows how the former tend to occur in cultivated areas whereas the latter are more typical of neglected land. It then considers the two methods of dealing with weeds; by means of cultivation and by the application of weedkillers. The advantages and disadvantages are looked at in detail, and each is discussed in turn. This section then considers how weeds should be controlled in a wide range of situations; not only are the more obvious examples such as among vegetables and flowers discussed, but there is also information on controlling weeds in pools and on paths and brickwork, clearing neglected land and how to deal with woody weeds and tree stumps. Finally, the section describes some of the most common troublesome weeds and gives specific details about how they should be controlled.

Cultural methods

In gardens it is frequently simpler and safer to remove weeds with a fork or by hand-weeding (that is, by using cultural methods) than by applying weedkillers. One important reason for this is that, in gardens, there are often many different kinds of plants growing in close association. Thus, when applying a weedkiller there may be considerable risk of spray drifting on to neighbouring plants, or of the weedkiller being absorbed by their roots while it remains in the soil, both of which can cause great damage.

A recurring weed problem can often be resolved by improved growing techniques such as feeding, mulching and pruning, or by feeding and aerating a lawn, since this encourages a stronger denser growth that will suppress weeds. It is also important to grow only those plants that are suited to the gardener's particular soil and site.

Weedkillers

Although cultural methods can be used to control any weed that may occur in a garden, there are situations where the use of weedkillers is the more practicable approach. This is especially true where physical removal of weeds is difficult, for example, in lawns, on paths and paving, in rose beds and among tree and bush fruit.

Herbicides, Fungicides, Pesticides

Read the product label before buying, and mix and apply strictly according to the manufacturer's recommendations accompanying the produce.

Weedkillers do, however, present considerable dangers if they are not stored, handled and applied sensibly and correctly. **The manufacturer's instructions accompanying a packet of weedkiller must be followed exactly. Weedkillers should be stored in a cool dark place, well away from foodstuffs, if possible in a locked cupboard where children and pets cannot reach them.** A more detailed list of points concerning safety with weedkillers is given on pages 138–139.

If weedkillers are to be used, it is important to become familiar with their mode of action, that is, whether they kill by direct contact action, by leaf absorption or by root uptake. By knowing this, the gardener can determine with reasonable accuracy whether a particular weedkiller is safe to use in a given situation. It is also important to know how long a weedkiller remains in the soil as this determines when new sowings or plantings can be made. These details are all given on pages 140–141.

If a gardener is not attracted to the idea of applying weedkillers, or if he does not feel secure in handling them, it is always possible to resort to cultural means of weed control.

Glossary 1

Aeration The process of spiking a lawn in order to allow air into the soil and relieve compaction.

Alga A primitive plant that possesses green colouring (chlorophyll) but is not differentiated into leaf, stem and root. Algae range from single-celled or thread-like organisms to seaweeds.

Annual A plant that completes its life-cycle (from germination, through growth, flowering and the development of seed, to death) within one growing season.

Axil The upper angle between a leaf or leaf-stalk and the stem from which it grows; axillary flowers or shoots arise from this point.

Bare-root plant A plant lifted from the open ground (as opposed to a container-grown plant).

Biennial A plant that completes its life-cycle within two growing seasons; developing from seed in the first season and flowering, fruiting and dying in the second.

Bract A modified, usually reduced, leaf that grows just below the flowerhead.

Broadcast To distribute seed evenly over the entire seedbed, as opposed to sowing in rows.

Bud burst The period at the end of the dormant season when new buds begin to swell and produce leaves or flowers.

Bulb An underground storage organ consisting of layers of swollen fleshy leaves or leaf bases, which enclose the following year's growth bud. Plants that grow from bulbs include onion, narcissus and tulip.

Bulbil A very small bulb, which may be formed above or below ground.

Carpeting plant A plant whose stems take root as they spread; also known as a carpeter.

Clone A plant propagated vegetatively, for example by taking cuttings. It has identical characteristics to its parent.

Clump plant A deciduous plant that grows in spring from clusters of buds or an over-wintering rosette at the top of a rootstock.

Compaction The compression of soil particles, preventing the free passage of air and moisture in the soil.

Compost, garden Decayed organic matter, formed by heaping suitable kitchen or garden refuse, which is then broken down by the action of bacteria. It can be used as a surface mulch or incorporated into the soil to improve its texture and supply nutrients.

Composts, seed and potting Mixtures of materials consisting chiefly of loam, peat, sand and fertilizers. They are used as mediums for sowing seeds and growing pot plants.

Coppice shoots Vigorous basal shoots produced by the regular pruning of a tree or shrub close to ground level.

Corm A storage organ of a plant, consisting of a short swollen stem covered with scales formed from the leaf bases. Plants that grow from corms include crocus and gladiolus.

Corymb A flat-topped flowerhead with flower stalks of variable length arising from different points on the stem; as the flowers of candytuft, for example.

Cruciferous Describes any plant belonging to the family Cruciferae. All have flowers bearing four petals arranged to form a cross. Examples include the brassicas and alyssum.

Cultivator A tool used to break up the soil surface to improve its texture. A rotary cultivator, or rotavator, has revolving tines or blades and is power-driven.

Cutting A separated piece of root, stem or leaf that has been taken in order to propagate a new plant.

Deciduous Describes a plant that loses all its leaves at the end of the growing season.

Defoliation Shedding or removal of leaves.

Die-back The death of branches or shoots, beginning at their tips and spreading back towards the trunk or stem. It may be caused by disease or poor growing conditions.

Dormant Describes a plant that is resting between periods of growth. The dormant period of most plants is usually during the autumn and winter.

Dressing A material such as organic matter, fertilizer, sand or lime that is incorporated into the soil. A top dressing is applied to the surface only, without being dug in.

Dribble bar A sealed, perforated tube attached to a watering can that enables weedkiller or other liquid to be dribbled on to the plants or soil.

Entire Describes a leaf or petal whose margins are not indented.

Evergreen A plant, usually a tree or shrub, that retains foliage throughout the year.

f Abbreviation for *forma.*

Fallowing Allowing land to remain uncropped for a period after ploughing or digging. It is often performed so that weeds may develop and be destroyed, by frequent cultivations or weedkillers, before planting.

Family A group of related genera. For example, the genera *Poa* (meadow grass), *Festuca* (fescue) and *Agrostis* (bent) all belong to the family of grasses, Gramineae.

Fertilizer Any material that is added to the soil to increase its fertility. It may be organic, such as bone meal and dried blood, or inorganic, such as sulphate of ammonia.

Foliar feed A liquid fertilizer that is sprayed on to plants and partially absorbed through the leaves.

Forma A botanical category of lower rank than variety, describing a plant that differs only slightly from the species, for example in colour.

Friable Describes a fine, crumbly soil.

Fungus Any member of a group of non-flowering plants that, since they have no green colouring (chlorophyll), cannot manufacture their own food. Therefore, they are incapable of surviving independently and live on either another living organism or on decaying organic matter.

Genus (pl genera) A group of one or more related species of plant. For example, annual meadow grass, smooth-stalked meadow grass and rough-stalked meadow grass all belong to the genus *Poa*. The first part of the Latin name of a plant denotes the genus, and the second part indicates the species.

Growing point The extreme tip of roots or shoots where new growth is generated.

Habit The natural mode of growth of a plant.

Half-hardy Describes a plant that is unable to survive the winter without protection.

Hardy Describes a plant capable of surviving the winter in the open without protection.

Herbaceous perennial *see* Perennial.

Herbicide Syn for weedkiller.

Host The plant from which a pest, fungus or other organism derives its food.

Hummock plant A plant with a short central stem and a number of low widespreading branches radiating from it. These branches may sometimes take root, in which case the plant is said to be a carpeting plant.

Humus Fertile, organic matter that is in an advanced stage of decay.

Hybrid A plant produced by the cross fertilization of two species or variants of a species.

Inorganic matter *see* Organic matter.

Lanceolate Describes a leaf that is much longer than it is wide, and is shaped like the head of a lance.

Larva The active immature stage of certain insects.

Layering Propagating by inducing shoots to form roots while they are still attached to the parent plant.

Leaching The loss of nutrients and chemicals in the soil when they are dissolved by heavy rainfall or excessive irrigation and washed away from the vicinity of plant roots.

Leaf-fall The period when deciduous plants begin to shed their leaves.

Leaf litter Partially decayed leaves, often used as a mulch.

Leaf-mould Well rotted leaves, which can be used as a mulch or added to the soil to improve its texture.

Linear Describes a leaf whose margins are more or less parallel and whose length is very much greater than its width; for example conifer leaves, grass leaves.

Loam A fertile soil with balanced proportions of clay, sand and humus.

Lobed Describes a leaf or petal whose margin is indented at one or more points; for example sycamore leaves, oak leaves.

Manure Material of animal origin added to the soil to improve its texture and provide nutrients.

Mulch A layer of organic or inorganic material spread on the soil surface around plants to conserve moisture and suppress weeds. Organic mulches also add nutrients to the soil.

Naturalized Describes plants grown in natural surroundings where they increase of their own accord and need little maintenance, for example, bulbs growing among grass. It also describes plants that have become established in an area, although they are not native to it.

Node The point on the stem of a plant from whence a leaf or leaves arise.

Nutrient A plant food.

Offset A young plant produced when a stem or short runner of the parent plant takes

Glossary 2

root. Offsets can easily be severed and re-planted as a means of propagation.

Organic matter Matter consisting of, or derived from, living organisms. Examples include farmyard manure and leaf-mould. Inorganic substances, such as sulphate of ammonia, are artificially produced or derived from minerals.

Ornamental A plant grown for its decorative qualities rather than as a commercial or food crop.

Ovate Describes a leaf that has an egg-shaped outline, with the wider half towards the stalk.

Over-wintering Passing the winter; it usually refers to the means by which an organism survives the winter. For example, certain plants over-winter as rosettes of leaves, and some insects over-winter as eggs.

Panicle A branched flowerhead with each branch having several individually stalked flowers, for example lilac.

Parasite An organism that lives upon another, to the detriment of the host, and is incapable of independent existence.

Perennial A plant that grows on from year to year. Herbaceous perennials are plants that die down to soil level in the winter and produce new growth the following spring.

pH The degree of acidity or alkalinity of soil. If the pH of the soil is less than 7, it is acid; if more than 7, it is alkaline.

Pinching (or stopping) The removal of the growing tip of a shoot, for example to encourage branching.

Pinnate Describes a leaf that comprises several pairs of leaflets borne on either side of a central stalk; for example ash leaves.

Planting mark The slight change in colour on the stem of a bare-root plant, indicating the depth at which it was formerly planted.

Procumbent Describes growth lying loosely on the soil surface.

Propagation The production of a new plant from an existing one, either sexually by seeds or asexually, for example by cuttings.

Prostrate Describes a plant with trailing shoots that spread along, or close to, the soil surface, but do not take root.

Raceme An elongated, unbranched flowerhead bearing short-stalked flowers. The tip continues to grow and produce new buds as the lower flowers open. Examples of racemose flowers include foxglove and lupin.

Rhizome A creeping horizontal swollen stem that acts as an underground storage organ and produces new shoots each season. Plants that grow from rhizomes include bearded iris.

Rhizomorph A root-like mass of fungal threads, by means of which certain fungi spread through the soil.

Rootstock The underground part of a plant from which roots and basal shoots are produced.

Rosette A small cluster of overlapping leaves radiating from the centre. It is often close to ground level.

Rotavator see Cultivator.

Runner A trailing stem that grows along the surface of the soil and takes root and forms new growth at the nodes.

Run-off When spraying, the point at which a plant becomes saturated, and further liquid runs off on to the surrounding area.

Sap The fluid in living plants that transports nutrients to various parts of the plant.

Scarifying The process of vigorously raking a lawn in order to remove thatch.

Seed dressing A pesticide or fungicide applied to seeds before sowing to protect them from pests or diseases.

Seed drill A machine for sowing seeds at regular intervals in rows.

Seed leaf (syn cotyledon) The first leaf or leaves produced by a germinated seed.

Self-sterile Describes a plant whose pollen cannot fertilize its own female parts. It must, therefore, be grown near to another plant of the same species in order to produce seeds.

Semi-evergreen Describes a plant intermediate between evergreen and deciduous. It bears foliage throughout the year, but loses some leaves during the winter.

Serrated Describes a leaf or petal having a saw-toothed margin.

Shrub A perennial plant with persistent woody stems branching from the base. If only the lower parts of the branches are woody and the upper shoots are soft and usually die down in winter, it is known as a sub-shrub.

Soakaway A natural or artificially constructed pit into which water drains.

Species An individual plant or group of plants within a genus which possess distinct and constant characteristics.

Spike An elongated flowerhead bearing stalkless flowers.

Spit The depth of a normal digging spade, roughly equal to 10 in.

Spore A simple body, by means of which non-flowering plants such as mosses, ferns and fungi reproduce.

Spot-treat To treat a small defined area or a particular plant, usually with a weedkiller, fungicide or pesticide.

spp After a genus name, indicates all species belonging to that genus.

Spray drift The dispersal of chemical sprays by the wind on to neighbouring areas where the chemical may cause damage.

ssp Abbreviation for sub-species.

Stolon A creeping stem at or just below soil level that can root at the tip to produce a new plant. A plant that has stolons is said to be soloniferous.

Stopping see Pinching.

Sub-shrub see Shrub.

Sub-soil see Top-soil.

Sub-species A category intermediate between a variety and a species.

Sucker A shoot growing from a stem or root at or below ground level, often some distance from the main stem.

Suckering plant A plant that spreads by means of underground shoots, suckers or stolons.

Sump Syn for soakaway.

Syn Abbreviation for synonym.

Systemic fungicide or insecticide A fungicide or insecticide that is absorbed into the sapstream and permeates the plant.

Tap root The primary vertical root of a plant; also any strong-growing vertical root.

Thallus The body of a primitive plant that is not differentiated into leaf, stem and root. Such a plant is known as a thallophyte.

Thatch On a lawn, a layer of dead or living organic matter, along with debris, found between the roots and foliage of the grass.

Tiller A shoot produced by a grass stolon or rhizome as it spreads along the surface of the soil.

Tilth The structure of the upper layer of the soil. A good tilth is fine and crumbly with no hard or wet lumps. It is produced by weathering or careful cultivation.

Tine The prong of a fork, rake or other tool.

Top dressing see Dressing.

Top-soil The upper layer of dark fertile soil in which plants grow. Below this lies the subsoil, which is lighter in colour, lacks organic matter and is often low in nutrients.

Transpiration The loss of water through the leaves of plants as water vapour.

Trifoliate Describes a leaf that is divided into three leaflets.

True leaves Leaves typical of the mature plant, as against seed leaves, which usually have a different appearance.

Tuber A swollen underground stem or root that acts as a storage organ and usually has buds or ''eyes'' from which new plants or tubers may develop. Plants that grow from tubers include potatoes and dahlias.

Umbel A flat-topped flowerhead in which the flowers are borne on stalks arising from the top of the main stem.

var An abbreviation for the botanical classification *varietas* (variety); it refers only to naturally occurring varieties.

Variegated Describes leaves with coloured markings, usually white or cream, due to an absence of chlorophyll.

Variety A distinct variant of a species; it may be a cultivated form (a cultivar) or occur naturally.

Weedkiller A chemical that kills plants.

Weedkiller, contact action A weedkiller that kills only those green parts of plants with which it comes into contact.

Weedkiller, residual A weedkiller that acts through the soil and remains effective for a period ranging from a few weeks (short-term residual weedkillers) to several months (long-term residual weedkillers).

Weedkiller, selective A weedkiller that kills only certain types of plant, leaving others unharmed.

Weedkiller, translocated A weedkiller that is absorbed through the leaves and stems and is rapidly carried via the sap-stream to kill the whole plant.

Wetting agent A chemical added to a liquid that is to be sprayed, in order to improve the spray's adherence to a plant.

Whorl a group of three or more leaves or flowers radiating from the same node on the stem.

Introduction/Planning a lawn 1

Introduction

Nearly every garden, regardless of its size or type, has a lawn. A well planned and maintained lawn greatly enhances the beauty of a garden, and is an attractive feature worthy of praise in its own right.

The ideal lawn is both ornamental and practical. It should be smooth, closely mown and uniform in texture and colour, with no weeds, irregular patches of coarser grass or discoloured areas of unhealthy turf. It must be able to withstand a reasonable amount of wear and tear, and be resistant to drought and waterlogging, so that it looks attractive and healthy throughout the year.

The size and shape of the lawn is, of course, largely determined by the extent of the land available. However, despite this limitation there is a great deal of scope for the amateur to create an individual and interesting design as an alternative to the traditional square or oblong stretch of grass. The shape of the lawn should complement other garden features, such as pools, trees and flower beds, yet not be so complex that it hinders mowing and maintenance. It should not extend into wet, poorly drained corners or under the dense canopy of a large tree, since most grasses will not thrive in such conditions.

Unfortunately, many amateur gardeners pay insufficient attention to the planning, preparation and maintenance of the lawn. Faults in new lawns are usually caused by factors such as inadequate preparation of the soil or site, sowing unevenly, using poor quality seed, or incorrect laying of turves. All these can result in weak, sparse growth that will be susceptible to pests and diseases, and allow mosses and weeds to take root.

Even when established, it should not be assumed that a lawn can take care of itself; it needs regular feeding, watering and maintenance in the same way as any other crop. In particular, the lawn should not be mown too closely or subjected to excessive wear and tear.

The following pages give full details of the planning and preparation of a new lawn, the various aspects of routine maintenance and the pests, diseases and problems that can occur on an established lawn, including remedial measures.

Planning a lawn

Most gardens have a fairly standard shape: they are either square or rectangular with a similarly shaped lawn enclosed by unchanging strips of flower beds. Although such a lawn is the easiest to maintain to a high standard, it does not have the most attractive of shapes and, unless the lawn complements some rectangular structure or feature such as a pool, one bounded by gentle curves is a much better proposition. A curved lawn also gives the gardener greater freedom to emphasize attractive garden features such as groupings of plants, ornaments or a pool, and to disguise unsightly features, both internal and external to the garden.

Before deciding upon the required shape and size of the lawn there are a number of points that should be noted regarding the presence of unsightly features, the growing conditions that a lawn requires and the positioning of paths. Then, bearing these points in mind, draw a sketch of the garden to ensure that the shape of the proposed lawn will permit satisfactory screening, and that paths and other points of access can be incorporated into the scheme.

Unsightly features

When planning a lawn it is advisable to take into account the positions of unsightly features, since this is the best time to take the appropriate steps to screen them from view. Such features may include the compost heap, garden shed, incinerator, greenhouse and external eyesores such as new building developments, pylons, factory chimneys and so on. All these can be screened by planting groups of suitably large shrubs or conifers in the appropriate place.

Growing conditions

The proposed lawn site should be in full sun or receive sunlight for at least part of the day. Do not extend lawns under the canopy of a tree since the soil there is usually dry, heavily shaded and dense with tree roots, and the grass will not thrive in such conditions. Avoid also wet corners; unless the area is to be drained use such corners as beds for moisture-loving plants.

Do not allow the lawn to grow right up to

A well planned garden should provide interest and variety, screen unsightly features and make the best use of potential problem areas. Here, the island bed of heathers and dwarf conifers is an attractive focal point, and the curved flower beds create an unusually shaped lawn. These beds are planted with alpines, herbaceous plants and shrubs, which, together with an ornamental conifer, screen the compost heap from view. Similarly, the vegetable garden is hidden by a low box hedge. The steep grass bank is difficult to mow and has been replaced by a terrace and rockery. Beneath the tree, ground cover has been planted since grass will not thrive there.

Planning a lawn 2

Long, narrow gardens

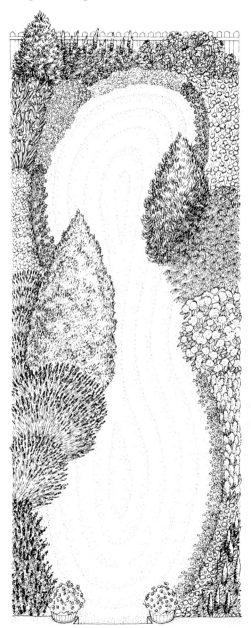

Long, narrow gardens can be disguised by indenting the lawn around groups of ornamental plants.

the foot of a wall or the edge of raised paving, since the grass cannot be mown at these places. Instead, leave a gap and surface it with gravel or plant a low-growing ground cover plant such as heather.

Paths

Before deciding upon the shape of lawn, consider the siting of paths. Avoid having a path that splits the lawn into two equal sections. If there is a central garden gate, then re-site it to one side of the lawn, where possible running the path along the shadier side of the garden. If the path is to follow the line of curve of the lawn, short-cuts across the lawn may be taken if the curve is too severe at some point. This will soon result in the turf being noticeably worn down. A useful deterrent to this is to plant thorny shrubs in a strategic position.

Access

Access to the lawn should not be restricted to a narrow strip or opening, otherwise inevitably there will be compaction and wear at that point. Where possible, allow access along one complete side or end of the lawn rather than from a single point. Ensure also that there is easy access for the mower.

Beds within the lawn

Do not plan to have flower beds in small lawns since they emphasize the smallness of the site and will create problems with mowing and edging. If some height is required on the lawn for screening purposes, plant a conifer or small deciduous tree towards one corner of the site.

Beds of perennial plants or heathers, or groups of shrubs, are acceptable in larger lawns but should be placed to one side and not positioned centrally. The shape of the bed should be informal but not sharply angled, which would hinder mowing.

Narrow strips of turf

Avoid narrow strips of turf, narrow verges and grass paths since they can be mown one way only and there will be a risk of compaction and wear. Where the inclusion of a narrow strip is unavoidable, ensure that it has a width of at least 3 ft.

Gardens with awkward shapes

There are two shapes of garden that provide particular problems when planning a lawn. These are long, narrow gardens and those that are wide but short.

To make a long, narrow garden seem shorter and wider plan the lawn to have strong curves with one or more bold indentations. Plant a small flowering tree, group of shrubs or an ornamental conifer at each of these indentations. By acting as focal points these plants will break the line of the border. They will also obscure part of the garden, which will arouse curiosity and interest in the observer and draw him forwards to explore.

This approach can also be carried out on long, narrow lawns that are already established. Such lawns may even have a path running down the middle from end to end, dividing the lawn into two even narrower segments and further increasing the apparent length of the garden. In this case, re-aligning the lawn's borders with strong curves will disguise the length and narrowness of the garden sufficiently to allow the path to be retained without spoiling the effect.

A wide, short garden can be made to appear longer by running the lawn diagonally across the garden in a sweeping curve. The eye naturally follows the longer line of the curve, especially if there is a focal point in the farthest corner, such as an attractive tree, a rock garden, a rose arbour over a garden seat or a small pond. The deeper borders formed by this design also help to make the garden seem narrower. Do not have beds or trees in the middle of the lawn because they draw attention away from the back of the garden, thereby destroying the illusion of space. An alternative method of creating depth is to grow plants on either side of the lawn that increase in height as the garden recedes.

Short, wide gardens

Short, wide gardens can be disguised by having the lawn run diagonally across the garden in a sweeping curve. The illusion is encouraged by growing tall plants at the back of the garden and shorter plants towards the front.

Preparing the site 1

When preparing a site for a lawn begin at least two to three months before the planned sowing or turfing dates. This gives sufficient time for the soil to settle and for weeds to be brought under control. For autumn sowing or winter turfing begin preparations in early summer if levelling or draining the site is going to be necessary, or if there are many weeds present. For spring sowing the draining can be done in autumn but levelling is best carried out during the summer since the soil needs to be dry.

Clearing the site
The first step is to clear away builders' rubble, bricks, discarded gravel and rubbish, if present. Remove any heaps of sub-soil left by the builders – do not spread them over the site. Next, carefully dig out any tree stumps or broken-off roots. If they are left in the soil they may become colonized by fungi, even if the pieces of wood are quite small, and in time produce unsightly and recurring crops of toadstools. If the new site is heavily infested with weeds use the appropriate weedkillers or fallow the land during the spring and summer months (see pages 162–165.

Recently vacated building sites may have been subjected to considerable soil disturbance, and in some cases much of the fertile top-soil will have been lost. First establish the nature and depth of the top-soil by making trial excavations on the nearest accessible undisturbed site. Ideally, there should be at least 9 in of top-soil, but a minimum depth of 6 in is acceptable. If there is less, purchase sufficient top-soil from a local supplier.

Grading
The term grading means the elimination of surface irregularities. This is done by relating site levels to nearby fixed levels such as house foundations, walls or paths. It is not essential to have a perfectly level site; a fall of 1:80 is quite acceptable and has the advantage of assisting surface drainage.

Grading can be expensive and on larger sites need not be necessary since a gentle slope or undulations can be visually quite pleasing.

When grading major irregularities first remove all top-soil and heap it clear of the site.

Then even out the level of the sub-soil and replace the top-soil to an even depth.

Minor irregularities can be corrected by adding a little top-soil. Do not, however, take it from higher points on the site since this may leave the top-soil very thin in places, which will cause the grass to grow irregularly. Instead, bring in top-soil from elsewhere in the garden.

Where there are steep slopes it is preferable to draw the soil forward to make a single level area since turfed banks can be very difficult to maintain. Alternatively construct two or more terraced lawns with retaining walls and connecting steps (see Box, page 20).

Levelling
Few people may take the trouble to establish the level of the site properly by using a spirit level, straight edge and pegs. Usually they rely instead on a "good eye", or pegs and garden line. However, for finer ornamental lawns and areas where games are to be played it is always advisable to do this task properly. For this, the following equipment is required: a straight-edged board about 7 ft long, a large spirit level, a tape measure or marked cane, a handful of marked pegs and a mallet. Hammer in the master peg at a selected point, leaving about 4 in of the peg above the surface. Then drive in the other pegs at 6 ft intervals to form a grid system. Establish the master peg at the required level then, working from it, adjust the other pegs with the straight edge and spirit level until they align with the master peg. Next, add or remove soil (sub-soil or top-soil) until the soil surface is level either with the top of each peg or to a predetermined peg marking. Where a slope is required, establish across-slope levels in the same manner. Down-slope levels can then be established with pegs and line or, more accurately, with a spirit level, using pairs of marked pegs at each station.

Digging
Digging serves two purposes: it allows improvement of soil texture (and hence aeration and drainage) and it relieves compaction. It is advisable to dig all lawn sites unless, of course, they have recently been ploughed. Lawn sites that have been vacated by builders

should be deeply dug because such sites almost invariably are compacted to a considerable depth.

When digging, take out a trench a spit deep, then fork over the bottom of the trench to the full depth of the fork. On heavy soils incorporate gritty material or lime-free, medium-grade sand ($1/5$–$1/2$ mm) to improve soil texture and porosity. Also add well rotted stable manure, garden compost, leaf-mould or moist granulated peat at up to 14 lb per square yard. On sandy soils improve moisture retention and encourage deeper rooting by incorporating similar dressings of organic materials. Dried sewage can also be used at up to 2 lb per square yard.

Break up organic materials when digging them in; if they are left in large lumps, surface irregularities may occur as they gradually decompose. Finely broken organic matter can also be worked into the sub-soil, but do this in moderation, otherwise settling may occur at a later date.

Soil pH

If soils are very acid (low pH) or very alkaline (high pH) some of the nutrients in the soil can become "locked up" and be unavailable to plants. The ideal pH level for most lawn grasses is between 5.5 and 6.0, that is, moderately acid – simple test kits are available for measuring the soil pH. Grasses can grow at higher or lower pH levels and it is not essential for the soil pH to be at this level, but with increasing acidity or alkalinity growth problems occur. Few lawn sites will require the pH to be altered. Possibly some heathland development sites will be too acidic for a lawn, but those developed from agricultural land almost always have a satisfactory pH value.

Where tests show that the soil is strongly acid (below pH 5) apply lime in the form of carbonate of lime (either ground chalk or ground limestone). If there is uncertainty as to how much lime is needed, apply only a moderate dressing of 2 oz per square yard on sandy soils and 4 oz per square yard on clay soils. Lime needs may vary considerably according to the texture of the soil, and very acid soils may need further treatment. Test the soil again after one or two years. Do not

Clearing the site

1 Remove any debris left by builders, such as rubble and bricks. If they have left heaps of sub-soil, remove these as well.

2 Carefully dig up and remove any tree stumps together with all their roots, including those that have broken off.

3 Test the depth of the top-soil and, if necessary, purchase sufficient to bring it up to a minimum depth of 6 in.

Preparing the site 2

over-lime, since this can lead to increased worm activity on humus-rich soils, increase the risk of disease and encourage coarse grass and weeds to establish. If in any doubt, it is preferable to seek professional advice rather than risk over-liming.

On strongly alkaline soils, the incorporation of acid peat materials will benefit early growth of seedling grasses, but it will not appreciably reduce the alkalinity of the soil.

Final preparations
The final stage of preparation is the creation of a firm, even, fine-particled soil surface. If the soil is heavy then digging may have left the surface very rough. However, if it has been subjected to a long period of weathering after digging, or if the soil is light, then the surface should be in a reasonable condition. On larger sites that have been worked with a rotary cultivator there will be few clods to break down, but the soil will have been less

thoroughly prepared than if it were well dug.

For autumn sowing, begin the final preparation of the seedbed during the summer. This will allow several weeks fallowing during which germinating weed seedlings can be killed periodically by light hoeing or spraying with paraquat/diquat. For seed sown in spring, germination will be slower and, although it is still advantageous to prepare the seedbed a few weeks in advance of sowing, the weather conditions may prevent this. In this case it is better to take advantage of favourable conditions and sow immediately after preparation. For laying turf fallowing is less important, but take advantage of favourable weather conditions for early preparation, particularly on heavier soils.

The first step is to break down clods and lumps into fine particles. On smaller sites use a heavy metal rake or a garden fork reversed. On larger sites use a rotary cultivator set to a shallow level of penetration. Breaking down

Grading major irregularities

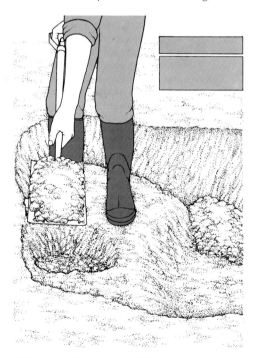

1 Dig up all the top-soil from the site and pile it up to one side, leaving just the sub-soil beneath.

2 Even out the sub-soil, filling hollows with sub-soil taken from bumps, and then replace the top-soil.

clods should be done when the soil is fairly dry since this reduces the risk of compacting the soil.

The second step is to firm, or consolidate, the soil. On smaller sites this can be done by light treading. Very short or overlapping steps are taken with body weight mainly on the heels, the ball of the foot providing balance. Alternatively, use the head of a rake. Ensure that uniform pressure is applied over the entire surface so that all soft spots are located and firmed. As with breaking down, do not firm when the soil is wet.

After firming, rake the soil level, remove stones and debris and firm again. If hollows are still present, repeat the process until the surface is uniformly consolidated and heel pressure makes only a slight indentation. Do not allow the soil to become so compressed that surface drainage is impaired. Keep a close check on the level of the site as firming progresses.

Large areas can be firmed by a roller, but this is less satisfactory than treading or using a rake since air pockets may be left, which in time may subside to leave the surface uneven.

Pre-sowing fertilizer

If a site is known to have been heavily manured and fertilized in recent years, a dressing of fertilizer is not essential. However, where there is any doubt regarding soil fertility apply the following dressing: $1/2$ oz sulphate of ammonia, 1 oz superphosphate and $1/4$ oz sulphate of potash per square yard. Rake this in thoroughly seven to ten days before sowing, if possible. However, sowing can, if necessary, be done immediately after applying fertilizer. Use the fertilizer at once – if stored it will soon set hard.

If sowing is not done immediately after applying fertilizer, give the site a final raking to remove all small stones and debris so that it is ready for sowing when planned.

Grading steep slopes

1 After removing the top-soil from the slope, transfer the sub-soil from the higher half of the slope to the lower half.

2 Level out the sub-soil and firm it. Finally return the top-soil evenly over the surface.

Preparing the site 3

Levelling the site

1 Hammer the master peg into the soil at a suitable point, leaving about 4 in of the peg showing above the surface. Then drive in the remaining pegs at 6 ft intervals to form a square grid system.

3 Add or remove soil until it is either level with the top of each peg or comes up to a predetermined marking on each peg. Ensure that all the soil has been evenly firmed before removing the pegs.

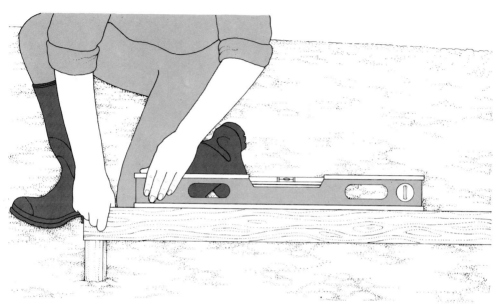

2 Adjust the height of the secondary pegs with a spirit level and straight-edged plank or board, working away from the master peg. Continue until the tops of all the pegs lie in the same horizontal plane.

Creating a sloping site

Establish the across-slope levels as above. The down-slope levels are determined by using a pair of pegs, with the soil being added or removed up to a fixed distance below the top of the down-slope peg, and to the top of the up-slope peg.

19

Preparing the site 4

Firming the soil

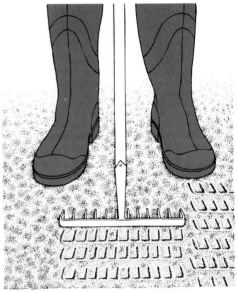

Lightly tread over the site, taking short or overlapping steps and with the weight of the body on the heels. Alternatively, firm the soil with the head of a rake. Then rake the soil level, remove any debris present and firm again.

TERRACING A STEEP SLOPE

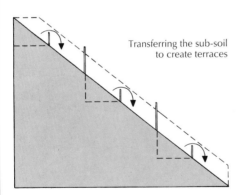

Transferring the sub-soil to create terraces

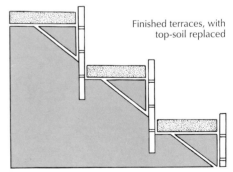

Finished terraces, with top-soil replaced

The first step is to decide how many terraces are required and to mark out their dimensions. Starting at the lowest terrace, remove the top-soil and place to one side or on the next highest level. Next, stretch a line across the terrace to divide it into an upper half and a lower half. Then move sufficient sub-soil from the upper half to bring the two halves level. Finally, replace the top-soil. If necessary, construct a re-taining wall before replacing the top-soil and beginning work on the next terrace. Do not forget to include a ramp for mowers if needed.

DRAINING

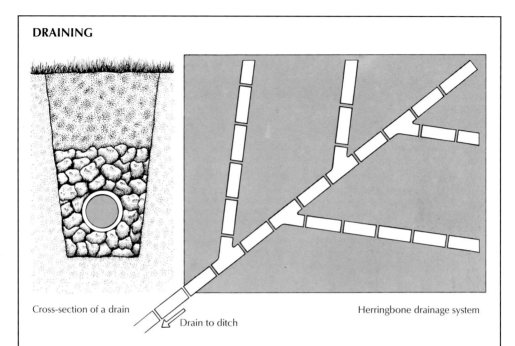

Cross-section of a drain

Drain to ditch

Herringbone drainage system

When constructing a new lawn, a thorough working of the top-soil and breaking up of the sub-soil, with textural improvement where necessary, should ensure that surplus moisture is not held at the surface. If, however, the site is known to be wet in places then some form of drainage should be installed.

For a small lawn or wet corner, a soak-away provides sufficient drainage. To build one, first dig a hole 2–3 ft square by at least 3 ft deep at the lowest part of the lawn. Fill it with clinker, broken bricks or stone to 8 in from the surface and add a 2 in layer of coarse sand, grit, or upturned turves to prevent the soil from washing through to the coarse material below. Finally, fill in the hole by adding a 6 in layer of top-soil.

A more satisfactory method of draining, though not often necessary, is tile draining. On a very wet site a herringbone or grid system may be needed, but usually a single line of drainpipes laid diagonally across the site, or through a wet section

and feeding into a sump, is sufficient. For this, use agricultural clay or 3 in diameter plastic lateral or collector pipes. If several lines are being laid, space them about 10 ft apart on heavy soils, and up to 30 ft apart on light soils. Their depth should be about 2 ft and they should have a fall of between 1:80 and 1:100. A herringbone or grid of lateral 3 in pipes should feed into a 4 in main drain laid at a depth of $2\frac{1}{2}$ ft. This in turn should be connected to a main drain or ditch – check beforehand with the appropriate authorities that this is permissible.

Pipe drainage should be installed only after the site has been levelled. Excavate the soil carefully so that, firstly, the pipes will just fit into the bottom of the hole and, secondly, the top-soil and sub-soil are kept separate. Place a small piece of turf with the grass down over the joints between the pipes, then cover with clinker or gravel to within 8 in of the surface. Finally, add a 2 in layer of coarse sand, grit or fine gravel, then replace the top-soil, discarding the sub-soil.

Lawn grasses 1

Of the many kinds of grasses that exist in nature only a few are suitable for creating lawns. The most important qualities needed in lawn grasses are that they should tolerate close mowing, drought and cold. They should also be resistant to diseases, be hard-wearing and have a naturally low-growing habit. Since no single species of grass possesses all these qualities, lawns almost invariably contain a mixture of different grasses to provide the optimum blend.

Many seedsmen supply good basic proprietary mixtures of grasses, and these are perfectly satisfactory in a wide range of conditions. If, however, problems are experienced in establishing turf from seed on the more difficult kinds of soil it could be worth while studying the qualities and preferences of the main types of lawn grasses and then over-seeding or modifying a proprietary mixture with the appropriate species or strains. New varieties having improved characteristics are introduced from time to time, and the best varieties available should be sought. They are usually the most expensive but are a worthwhile investment. Note that particular named varieties are only available commercially in large quantities.

Seed mixtures
No mixture of seeds is suited to all soils and situations, or for all purposes. The following are basic mixtures that can be used with confidence in a very wide range of conditions, but they should be modified if necessary. Smooth-stalked meadow grass, for example, dislikes wet or acid soils and on such soils can be omitted from the mixtures.

High-quality ornamental turf
80% Chewings' fescue
20% browntop bent
Sow at the rate of 1 oz per square yard. The height of cut should be 1/4–3/8 in, but it will tolerate 3/16 in.

General purpose ornamental turf
30% Chewings' fescue
25% creeping red fescue
10% browntop bent
35% smooth-stalked meadow grass
Sow at the rate of 3/4 oz per square yard. The height of cut should be 3/8–1/2 in. This mixture has ornamental quality but is harder-wearing than the first mixture and may be used for play areas.

General purpose turf
20% Chewings' fescue
20% creeping red fescue
10% browntop bent
20% smooth-stalked meadow grass
30% perennial rye grass
Sow at the rate of 1/2 oz per square yard. The height of cut should be 3/4–1 in. Since it contains rye grass, this mixture is hard-wearing and suitable for utility areas.

Banks and steep slopes
30% Chewings' fescue
45% slender creeping red fescue
20% browntop bent
5% lesser timothy
Sow at the rate of 1 oz per square yard. The height of cut should be to 1/2 in. These grasses will establish quickly, thereby preventing erosion, and, since they are low-growing, require a minimum of mowing.

Shade
All grasses grow reasonably well in light shade providing the site is prepared adequately and is fed and watered regularly. As the young grasses develop note the extent of poorer growth and, when mowing, leave the grass considerably longer over this area. In heavier shade, or if longer grass is not desired, plant ground cover plants that are tolerant of shade (see page 115).

Types of lawn grasses
Browntop bent (*Agrostis tenuis*) is a dwarf, tufted grass with short rhizomes. Bents (*Agrostis* spp) are the most tolerant of all grasses to close mowing, and browntop bent is found in most fine-lawn mixtures. It will adapt to most conditions, including soils that are acid and tend to be dry. It tolerates close mowing to 3/16 in.
Creeping bent (*Agrostis stolonifera*) is a stoloniferous species that is sometimes used in turf mixtures for playing fields on heavier alkaline soils. It is a shallow-rooting grass that lacks resistance to drought.

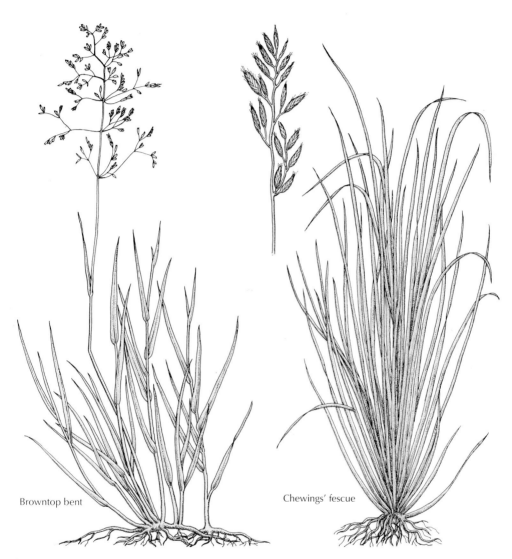

Browntop bent

Chewings' fescue

Chewings' fescue (*Festuca rubra* ssp *commutata*) has a dwarf, densely tufted habit and tolerates poor soils. It can be mown to $^3/_{16}$ in.
Creeping red fescue (*Festuca rubra* ssp *rubra*) is a hard-wearing grass with slender creeping rhizomes that is tolerant of wet, dry and cold conditions. It is, however, less tolerant of close mowing than Chewings' fescue. The strain slender creeping red fescue (*Festuca rubra* ssp *littoralis*) is better suited to close-mown turf.

Annual meadow grass (*Poa annua*) is a tufted annual or short-lived perennial weed grass that is found in many lawns,. It perpetuates itself by seeding freely and is useful in lawns subjected to hard wear.
Crested dog's tail (*Cynosurus cristatus*) has a tufted, fairly dwarf habit. It is sometimes used in fine turf mixtures, but it does not blend well. Do not mow it closer than $^3/_4$ in.
Perennial rye grass (*Lolium perenne*) is a broad-leaved species of loose, tufted habit

23

Lawn grasses 2

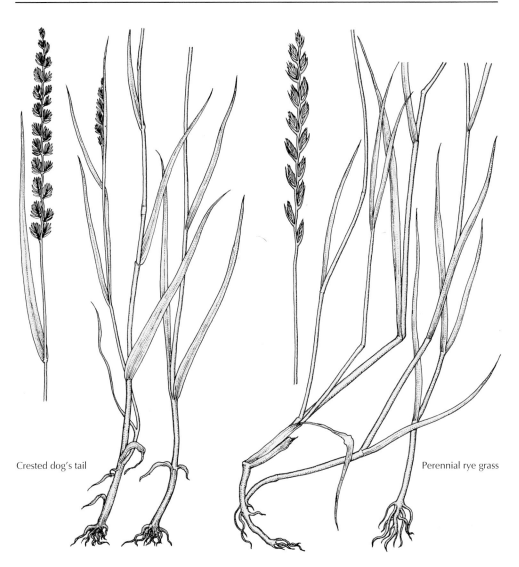

Crested dog's tail

Perennial rye grass

that grows well on almost any soil. It is particularly suited to heavier soils and is very hard-wearing. Do not mow closer than ³/₄–1 in, otherwise it will deteriorate. Some newer strains are denser and more tolerant of close mowing.

Smooth-stalked meadow grass (*Poa pratensis*) has a tufted growth with slender creeping rhizomes. It is tough and hard-wearing, but rather slow to establish. It dislikes wet, heavy or acid soils. Do not mow closer than ³/₄ in.

Rough-stalked meadow grass (*Poa trivialis*) has a loosely tufted habit with short, creeping stolons. It is more suited to wet, heavy soils than smooth-stalked meadow grass, but is less tolerant of wear and unsuitable for fine turf. Do not mow closer than ³/₄ in.

Lesser timothy (*Phleum bertolonii*) is a tufted species, with swollen basal internodes and is sometimes stoloniferous. It is hard-wearing and useful in wet, heavy conditions. Do not mow clower than ¹/₂ in.

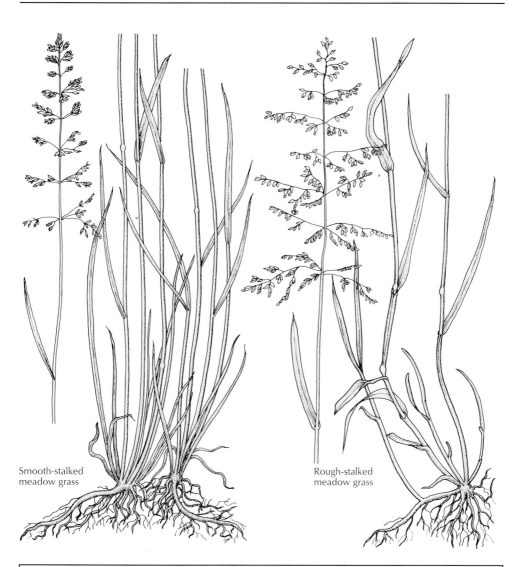

Smooth-stalked
meadow grass

Rough-stalked
meadow grass

CHOICE OF GRASSES

Grasses having the lowest growth:
Browntop bent
Creeping bent
Lesser timothy

Grasses most tolerant of close mowing:
Browntop bent
Creeping bent

Grasses tolerant of close mowing:
Chewings' fescue
Slender creeping red fescue

Hardest-wearing grasses:
Perennial rye grass
Lesser timothy
Smooth-stalked meadow grass

Seed or turf?

By far the most common methods of creating lawns in the United Kingdom are to sow seeds or lay turf. At one time turf lawns were much more common than seed lawns. However, in recent years there have been considerable improvements in the quality, variety and availability of seed mixtures, and sowing is now an increasingly popular alternative.

A point that is often overlooked when comparing seeding and turfing is that, whichever process is decided upon, the site needs to be prepared thoroughly. In particular, it is not sufficient simply to rake over the site before laying turves.

There are various factors to consider when making a choice between seeds and turf. To help the gardener decide which method to use, the various advantages and disadvantages of each are listed below.

Advantages of seed

The most important advantages that seed has over turf are that it is much cheaper to buy and there is less work involved in sowing than in laying turf. The gardener can choose a mixture of seeds to suit his or her own particular requirements or conditions, whereas with turves, the gardener has much less variety to choose from. A further advantage of seed is that it can be stored easily and will not deteriorate. Unlike turfing, sowing can, therefore, be delayed until the weather conditions are exactly right.

Disadvantages of seed

Seed takes much longer to establish than turf, and it is some months before the lawn can be used: a lawn sown in late summer will not be usable until the following June, and a spring-sown lawn will not be able to tolerate normal wear and tear until late autumn. The soil surface requires a more careful final preparation and, if the site is weedy, it must be left fallow for a time to ensure a reasonable freedom from weed seeds. These may also be carried on to the site by birds and wind, where they quickly become established and compete with the grass seedlings for water and nutrients. A lawn created from seed is more dependent on good weather for successful establishment than is a turfed lawn and, in cold damp conditions especially, is much more susceptible to disease. There is also the risk of disturbance to the seedbed from birds, cats, dogs or moles to be borne in mind. Lastly, grass seed is sown in either the spring or early autumn, which are often busy periods in the garden.

Advantages of turf

The most obvious advantage of turf is that the lawn can be created and used almost immediately, although it is advisable to allow a period for rooting into the bed before general use. Since laying turf has an instant visual effect, it is a much more attractive proposition than seeding for people moving into a newly built house with a featureless garden. Other points in favour of turfing are that it is easier to achieve a neat, well defined edge to paths and borders with turves than with seed, and turf can be laid in late autumn or winter, at which time it is too late for sowing grass seed. Another advantage of being able to lay turves in the autumn or winter is that there are few other pressing tasks in the garden at this time of year. Lastly, unlike sowing, there are no problems with birds or animals after laying.

Disadvantages of turf

Turfing is more expensive than seeding and good-quality turf is often difficult to obtain. The inexperienced buyer may fail to notice weeds, weed grasses or other defects that may be present in low-quality turf, for example, variations in thickness and shape, which will both require attention before turfing can proceed. Laying to a good standard is much more difficult than sowing, and takes both skill and time. Turf will deteriorate if a long period of bad weather prevents laying, so the operation needs to be planned well in advance. The lawn site should be completely prepared before the turves are ordered and they should be laid within two or three days of delivery, since they may deteriorate rapidly, even if they are stored carefully. Dry weather following laying also causes problems with turves. The grass dies along the joints before the turves can root into each other and the soil. This causes the turves to shrink, and crevices will soon appear between them.

STOLON LAWNS

A common method of creating lawns in warmer countries is to plant stolons. This technique can be used in temperate climates using stolons of creeping bent. To do this, chop the stolons into 2–3 in lengths and scatter them evenly over the site, ensuring that each stolon is no more than 1 in from its nearest neighbour. Cover them lightly with sifted top-soil, then lightly roll – this can be done with a rear-roller mower, holding the blades clear. Keep the site well irrigated with a lawn sprinkler; do not use a hose or watering can because their heavier spray may disturb the surface and dislodge the stolons. Mow as for new lawns raised from seed (see page 35), and when the stolons are established top-dress regularly.

Stolons should be planted in spring or early autumn during cool, moist weather.

Storing turves

Store turves for two or three days by stacking them grass upwards, three or four deep. Rolled or folded strips of turf should be similarly stacked.

For longer periods of storage, lay each turf flat in a shaded position and keep them well watered; failure to do so will cause exposed roots to dry up and shrivel.

Growing lawns from turf 1

Buying turf

Since turves are a relatively expensive means of creating a lawn, they should always be examined carefully before being purchased, and again when they are delivered. Do not hesitate to reject sub-standard turves on delivery. Failure to do so will very likely create problems both with laying the turves and with subsequent care of the lawn.

The most important points to look for are the quality of the grass, the soil and the roots, and whether there are weeds present. The grass should be uniform in appearance, with no broad-bladed coarser grasses present, and it should be suitably mown since long shaggy grass may hide defects. The soil should be loamy, not light and sandy or heavy and clayed. A clay soil, in particular, could adversely affect the lawn later on. The turves should have a good root system and a reasonable level of organic matter. If there is too little organic matter the turf may break up in handling. On the other hand, a high level may give poor rooting, which will subsequently create problems. The turves should be weed-free, or virtually so. If there are many weeds present, it indicates that the turves have been poorly managed. Such turves usually break apart when handled, and if laid, there would be immediate problems with weeds.

The last point to check is that the size and thickness of the turves should be uniform. The size of the turves may be 1 ft square, 1½ ft by 1 ft, or 3 ft by 1 ft. For the inexperienced the smallest size is the simplest to lay. Thin turf will establish satisfactorily if its quality is good and the roots are well developed, but more care is needed both when laying and with the subsequent lawn. If the turf is thicker or irregular, it will have to be trimmed to an even and satisfactory thickness. To do this lay each turf grass-side down in an open-ended box of suitable depth. Then, using a long-bladed knife, preferably one with two handles, shave off the unwanted soil.

When to turf

The best period for turfing is between October and February, though not when frost or rain is present. The advantage of turfing during this period is that newly laid turf is then rarely subjected to the stress of drying winds or hot sunshine, and it usually inter-roots before such conditions occur.

Lawns may be established satisfactorily at other periods, but in warmer, drier conditions there is increasing need for artificial irrigation. This has the disadvantage that, unless this is very carefully applied, it can affect the level of the lawn and its firmness.

Before laying

Always apply fertilizer before laying, unless the soil is already rich and well manured due to, for example, vegetables having been grown there regularly. The fertilizer encourages the turves to knit together and the roots to establish. Apply either superphosphate at 2 oz per square yard or the following mixture, which also supplies nitrogen and potash: 1 oz superphosphate, ¾ oz bone meal, ¾ oz hoof and horn meal and ¼ oz sulphate of potash per square yard. Apply the fertilizer a few days before turfing begins, and rake it well into the soil.

Lay the turves as soon as possible after they have been delivered. If laying is to be done within two or three days, the turves can be stacked grass upwards three or four deep. Strips of turf are usually rolled or folded, and can be similarly stacked.

If turves cannot be laid within this period, place them flat in a shaded site and keep them well watered otherwise exposed roots will dry up and shrivel. Before laying the turves, check each one and remove any coarse grasses or rosetted weeds.

The final step is to mark out the precise dimensions of the lawn and allow 1–2 in overlap if there is sufficient turf. This can be trimmed back when the turf is well established to leave a neat, sharp edge.

Laying turf

Begin by laying a row of turves along the most accessible side of the soil bed, using a tautly stretched garden line as a guide. Always ensure that each turf is laid as close as possible to the previous one. Lay in straight lines and do not at any time stand on the prepared bed. Work forwards facing the unturfed area, standing or kneeling on broad planks. Avoid walking on the newly laid turf by using planks as pathways. This spreads the weight and prevents depressions being formed by heavy boots or heels.

Stagger successive lines of turf by using half turves in alternate rows. The turves will then hold together more firmly when mown during the early stages of inter-rooting. If a short piece is needed to finish a row, greater stability is obtained by laying the last whole turf to the edge with the short piece fitted in behind. Keep a constant watch on the soil level and have a bucket of ordinary soil and a rake handy for adjusting minor irregularities or for packing extra soil under thin turves. Never attempt to level a piece of turf by beating it with a spade since this will cause local compaction. Instead, lift the turf, remove a little soil and then re-lay it.

After laying

When the laying has been completed, trim the turf by rolling with a light garden roller. Rolling is not essential but it will help to settle the turves. Alternatively, construct a simple turfing board by attaching a pole, such as a broom handle, to the centre of a 9 in by 15 in wooden board. Firm the turf, gently pressing down on the turfing board. Then top-dress with a sandy top-dressing mixture at 3–4 lb per square yard (see pages 46–47). This will protect the lawn from drying out and improve the level of its surface. Apply as an overall dressing, working it well into the crevices between the turves with a broom or the back of a rake. If good top-dressing materials are in short supply, fill a bucket with a mixture of sand and sifted soil, and top-dress along the crevices between turves, afterwards brushing it in.

Irrigate the new lawn thoroughly and regularly during dry periods – turf laid in the spring or summer is particularly susceptible to drying out and, if neglected, will often deteriorate rapidly.

When the grass begins to grow in spring top with the mower and from then on adopt the programme of maintenance for established lawns given on page 38.

Trimming turves

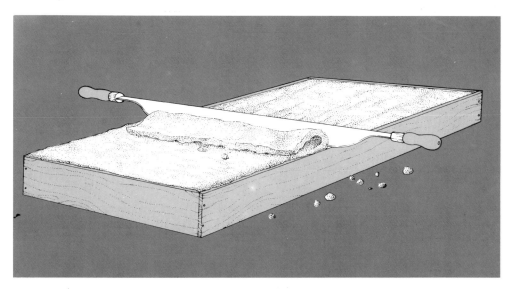

Place the turf grass-side down in a box of the correct height. Then take a knife whose blade is at least as long as the turf is wide, and pull this along the top of the box to shave off unwanted soil. If possible, the knife should have two handles.

Growing lawns from turf 2

Laying turves

1 Apply a dressing of fertilizer a few days before laying. Do not feed if the soil is already rich and well manured.

2 Rake in the fertilizer, incorporating it well into the soil.

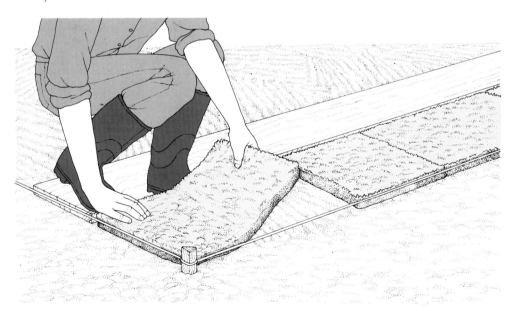

4 Lay the turves in straight lines, ensuring that each turf is as close as possible to the preceding one. If a segment of turf is needed to complete a row, lay a whole turf at the end and place the segment behind it. Allow 1–2 in overlap at the edge.

3 Mark out the exact shape of the lawn and allow for the turves to extend an inch or two beyond its edges. This can then be trimmed back after the turves have been laid and have settled down to leave a neat, sharply defined edge.

5 Stagger successive rows of turf by laying half turves. Do not walk on newly laid turf; instead lay down planks as pathways. They will spread out the weight and so avoid risk of compaction.

Growing lawns from turf 3

6 Correct irregularities in the soil level as turfing progresses. Have some soil at hand for packing under thin turves.

7 After the laying has been completed roll the lawn with a light garden roller, if one is available.

8 Apply a sandy top-dressing mixture at 3–4 lb per square yard. Distribute it throughout the lawn surface.

9 Work the dressing well into the crevices between turves, using either a broom or the back of a rake.

SEEDLING TURF

An alternative to laying turves of established grass is to lay seedling turves. These come in large lightweight rolls, about a yard thick, and are well rooted and of uniform thickness. Seedling turf is raised in special turf nurseries by one of two methods. One method uses long, polythene-lined troughs filled with water. Buoyant soil-less compost is then spread on the water, and on this is laid a thin strip of polyurethane foam upon which the grass seeds are sown. The second method is to grow the turf on a thin layer of soil-based rooting medium over a hard, impenetrable base. In the first method, the turf is held together by the foam, and in the second method by the densely intermingled roots. When laid the foam base gradually disintegrates.

Seedling turf is best laid during cool, moist conditions in spring or early autumn because it is more susceptible to cold and drought than ordinary turf. Also, it needs a period of good growing conditions in which it can quickly establish itself. Do not attempt to lay seedling turf in the summer unless it can be adequately irrigated. Give the turf an initial cut after two or three weeks, and do not cut it closer than 1 in during the first six weeks after laying. Then cut it to the appropriate height for the grass and the time of year.

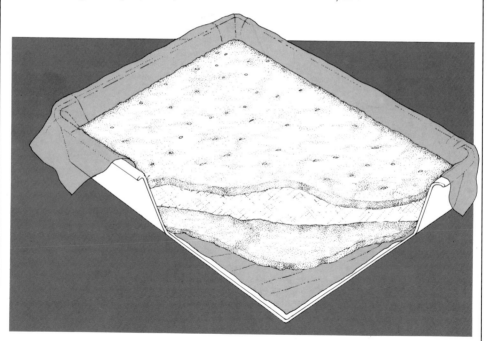

This technique can be adopted by gardeners who wish to raise small squares of turf for repair work. Line a seed box or a deep tray with polythene, then introduce a ½ in layer of well firmed seed compost and cover with a piece of cheesecloth. Add a second layer of compost and sow grass seeds on the surface at the standard rate (see page 22). Then place the box in a sunny position and keep it constantly moist. Once the seeds have germinated, feed it weekly with a liquid fertilizer. The turf will be ready for laying about three weeks after germination.

Growing lawns from seed

Sowing

Seeds may be sown either by hand or by seed drill. For hand-sowing divide the grass seeds into two equal portions, adding dry soil, if wished, to facilitate distribution. Sow half the seeds by traversing the plot lengthways, then sow the remaining half crossways. This method gives a more even coverage than a single application. Divide large areas into smaller sections or small plots marked out in square yards to facilitate accurate sowing.

If hiring a drill first ensure that it can be calibrated to apply grass seeds at the required rate. To check that a drill is applying the correct rate of seeds, mark out two separate square yard areas on a concrete or a hessian strip. Scatter 1/2 oz of seed by hand on one square, then run the drill over the other square. The density of seeds should be equal in the two squares.

Apply the seeds to the seedbed in parallel strips using the previous run's wheeltrack as a guide. Again, sow half the seed lengthways and half crossways. If space allows lay a strip of hessian along the edge of the lawn and over-run since the drill may distribute the seed unevenly when it is being turned.

Sow during a period of calm, dry weather when the surface of the seedbed is dry and soil does not adhere to boots or to the wheels of a seed drill. There should, however, be moisture just below the surface.

After sowing, lightly rake over the seedbed. Do this carefully since the seeds may not germinate if buried too deeply, and it may also make the distribution uneven. Do not roll because this tends to flatten or "cake" the surface. If after a few days there has been no rainfall then irrigate gently but thoroughly with a garden sprinkler. Do not use a hose or a coarse-rose watering can since they may re-distribute the seeds. If sparrows or other seed-eating birds are troublesome locally, use seed that has been treated with a bird deterrent. Usually a more serious problem created by birds is dust-bathing. Help to prevent this by stretching black thread 2–3 in above the seedbed. Alternatively, lay some leafless twiggy brushwood lightly over the bed after sowing.

When to sow

The two most suitable periods for sowing grass seeds are early autumn and spring. The best time for autumn sowing is early September in the warmer regions of the United Kingdom, and the end of August in colder parts. During this period the soil temperature is still high and moisture is usually plentiful, both conditions that encourage a quick

Sowing grass seeds

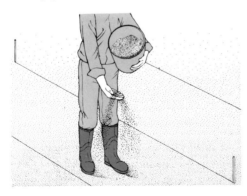

1 Divide the seeds into two halves and, if sowing by hand, broadcast one batch walking lengthways across the site and the other batch walking crossways.

2 If a seed drill is being used, lay a strip of hessian along the edge of the site and over-run. Again, sow half the seeds lengthways and the other half crossways.

germination period of seven to ten days. This enables seedling grasses to become well established before the first frosts in October or early November. Do not sow much later than these recommended times since germination may be poor and seedlings will not establish well. They may not then survive prolonged cold or wet weather.

If seed is to be sown in spring do this during April since the soil is beginning to warm up at this time and there is a full growing season ahead. Note that germination is slower at this time of year and there is a greater risk of the weather being dry than in autumn.

After germination

The soil surface is often slightly lifted at germination. Therefore, when the young grasses are about 2 in high (3 in for utility turf) lightly roll when the surface is dry using a light garden roller or a rear-roller cylinder mower with the front roller and blades lifted clear of the grass.

Two or three days later, when the grass has recovered from rolling and is growing vertically again, cut it with a sharp-bladed mower. Remove no more than about a third of the grass growth. It is preferable to use a side-wheel cylinder mower, or rotary mower since they have no front roller to flatten the grass

before cutting. If using a front-roller machine, lift or remove the front roller before mowing. After this first mow, autumn-sown turf usually needs no further mowing until the spring. With spring-sown turf progressively reduce the height of cut to the normal mowing height for an established lawn (see page 51 for details).

First season of growth

Use the lawn as little as possible during the first season of growth. If there are any surface irregularities, gradually eliminate them by top-dressing lightly with compost at intervals beginning after the first cut. Feed the lawn regularly according to seasonal requirements, and irrigate as necessary. This will quickly establish a vigorous grass coverage of sufficient density to prevent mosses and weeds from establishing.

Damping-off diseases

Fungal diseases may kill both grass seeds and young grasses. Damping off may cause young seedlings to become yellow or bronze and collapse at or near ground level, or brown shrivelled patches may occur, depending on the species of fungus responsible. At the first sign of attack water with Cheshunt compound at ½ oz in 1 gal water per square yard.

3 After sowing, lightly rake over the entire seedbed, taking care not to bury the seeds too deeply, otherwise they may not germinate.

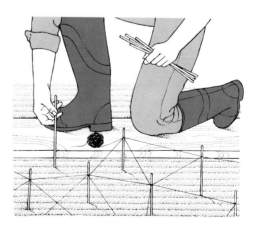

4 Prevent birds from dust-bathing by inserting small twigs or sticks at intervals in the seedbed. Then twine black thread among them 2–3 in above the soil surface.

Weed control in new lawns

In established lawns most weeds can be easily controlled by applying selective lawn weedkillers, combined with appropriate cultural measures. These weedkillers may, if used on new lawns, damage young seedling grasses before they are well established. For this reason do not use selective lawn weedkillers on newly seeded lawns earlier than three months after germination, and preferably not until at least six months have passed. However, it is important to control weeds in these early stages to prevent them competing with the young grass.

Annual broad-leaved weeds
Seeds of annual broad-leaved weeds are likely to be present on any site selected for a lawn and it is always advisable to deal with them well in advance of sowing to allow for a period of fallowing. Even so, weed seeds may still be introduced to the site unknowingly if fresh soil is used in the final stages of preparation. Seeds may also be carried in on the wind from surrounding areas. A few scattered weeds are no real cause for concern. They can be removed by hand (see below) with little effort, or left to be controlled by the mower – annuals such as groundsel, fat hen and mayweed soon die out once the grass has become strong enough for it to be mown regularly. Where strong-growing annual weeds are numerous they may smother grass growth, particularly where it is slow because of bad weather, or poor and weak because of inadequate preparation of the site. Common chickweed can be particularly troublesome since it grows strongly from very early in the year.

Grass weeds
The most troublesome weeds in new lawns are seedling perennial grasses such as cocksfoot (*Dactylis glomerata*) and Yorkshire fog (*Holcus lanatus*). In high-quality turf, perennial rye grass can also be troublesome. They are checked to some extent by frequent close mowing but tend to persist indefinitely, particularly Yorkshire fog. Seeds of coarse grasses may be present in grass seed mixtures as an impurity and it is advisable always to purchase seed of reliable quality from a reputable supplier. It is much more likely, however, that seeds were already present in the soil at the time of sowing. Annual meadow grass (*Poa annua*), a free-seeding annual grass and common garden weed, may also give trouble. It can survive close mowing to seed freely throughout the year, especially during May and June when its pale seedheads can mar the appearance of finely mown turf. Being short-lived its numbers can vary from season to season, at times leaving the turf sparser and more susceptible to invasion by moss and weeds. It is encouraged by frequent irrigation in dry weather, being shallow-rooted, and by omitting to use a grass-box when mowing. Thorough fallowing prior to sowing will minimize problems with all grass weeds.

Hand-weed in fine weather when the soil surface is firm, and not soft and wet from recent rain. If hand-weeding causes any serious disturbance to the lawn grasses, irrigate after weeding with a lawn sprinkler to resettle the grass roots.

Perennial weeds
Even after thorough preparation and removal of perennial weed growth, the deeply penetrating roots or rhizomes of some broad-leaved perennials may remain. Suitably deep cultivations during preparation should, however, ensure that little growth appears prior to mowing. Once the lawn has established, close and regular mowing combined with the use of selective lawn weedkillers will soon eradicate such recalcitrant weeds.

Newly laid turf
Do not use selective weedkillers on newly laid turf until it is well established. Purchase only good quality, weed-free turf.

GRASS WEEDS

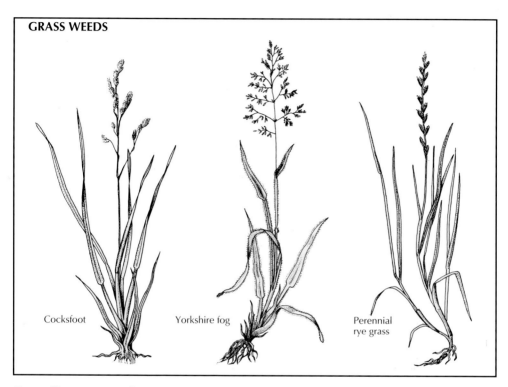

Cocksfoot   Yorkshire fog   Perennial rye grass

Controlling grass weeds

Remove grass weeds by hand-pulling, using one hand to grasp the weed and the other to press down the soil around the weed and keep it firm. This will prevent the surrounding grasses from being disturbed.

Month-by-month guide

This programme provides a useful indication of the approximate times when particular operations or treatments can be undertaken effectively. It is important for the gardener to decide firstly the precise requirements of his own lawn and secondly when the soil and weather conditions are most suitable for carrying out each operation. This programme does not give the details of these operations. For these, consult the relevant pages elsewhere in the book.

JANUARY

Remove any accumulations of dead leaves.
Check drains if water is standing on the surface for any length of time after rain, and drain persistently wet sites.
Overhaul the mower and other lawn tools before the start of the new season.

FEBRUARY

From February check regularly for signs of worm activity or unhealthy turf following mild spells. Disperse worm casts regularly.
Complete all major turfing work by the end of the month.
Apply a mosskiller in late February if weather is settled; if still cold leave until March.
Top-dress lightly if necessary.
Towards the end of the month, begin preparations for spring sowing if soil conditions and weather are suitable.

MARCH

Scatter worm casts and lightly rake to remove debris; then mow with the blade set high.
Roll before mowing if turf has been lifted by frost.
Treat against worms if they become very troublesome.
Re-align ragged lawn edges.
In southern Britain feed in late March if the weather is mild and settled.

APRIL

Increase the frequency of mowing according to the weather and grass growth.
Continue checking at intervals for signs of unhealthy turf.
Apply a spring feed in early to mid-April; a few days after feeding apply a weedkiller if necessary.
Remove patches of coarse grass and re-seed.
Seed-in sparsely grassed areas and new lawns.
Check newly turfed areas and top-dress lightly if necessary to improve levels or fill joins.

MAY

In early May adjust the mower to the summer cutting height.
Continue weedkilling; if very mossy apply a mosskiller.
From May onwards irrigation may be needed in drier periods.
During mid- to late May apply a light dressing of nitrogenous fertilizer.

JUNE

Mow frequently; if patches of creeping weeds are troublesome lightly scarify before mowing.
Continue weedkilling and irrigation as necessary.
Spike, lightly top-dress and irrigate areas that are subjected to heavy wear.

JULY

Mow regularly; scarify patches of creeping weeds and surface-running grasses before mowing.
Feed lightly early in July.
Apply weedkillers and irrigate as necessary.

AUGUST

Mow regularly.
Give a final summer feed in mid- to late August, followed by a final application of weedkiller.
In colder areas sow grass seed during late August.

SEPTEMBER

Modify the cutting height of the mower towards the end of the month, since the rate of growth is now slowing.
Examine the condition of the turf and carry out autumn renovation: scarify to remove matted growth or thatch, spike and top-dress, and seed-in sparse patches.
Apply a lawn sand to control moss. Do not use mosskillers containing sulphate of ammonia at this time of year.
With the onset of cooler, moister conditions check regularly for signs of unhealthy turf and worm activity.
In milder areas seed-in new lawn sites.

OCTOBER

Set the mower to its winter height and mow as the growth dictates during dry periods.
Switch or brush to remove early morning dew and encourage rapid drying if the weather is fine.
Spike and top-dress if unable to do so in September.
Prevent accumulation of fallen leaves because this can create conditions in which diseases may establish.
Treat against worms and leatherjackets if they become very troublesome. Lay turf lawns from this month onwards.

NOVEMBER

A final mow may be necessary, but do not attempt mowing in frosty conditions, nor when the soil is heavy after a recent fall of rain.
Continue clearing up fallen leaves.
Continue turfing when conditions are suitable.

DECEMBER

Apply lime this month if it is needed.
Continue with turfing and leaf clearance where necessary.

Table of operations

This table provides a simplified version, for quick and easy reference, of the month-by-month guide to lawn maintenance given on page 38. As stated previously, the exact timings of the various operations depend very much on the weather conditions, the state of the soil and the nature of the lawn.

In this table, heavy shading indicates that the particular operation or treatment will be necessary, or almost always so, during the period concerned. Where the shading is lighter, it indicates that the operation is optional or, in the case of treatment, that it may sometimes be necessary. For example, moss is very likely to occur in the autumn, but it may also be present in the spring.

	Sowing seed	Turfing	Feeding	Mowing	Irrigating	Scarifying	Aerating	Top-dressing	Weed control	Worm problems	Disease problems	Moss control
January		○										
February		○						○		○		○
March			○	○						●	○	○
April	●		●	●					●	●	○	○
May	○		●	●					●	○		○
June			●	●			○	○		○		
July			●	●					○			
August	○		●	●	○					○		○
September	●	○	●	●		●	●	●		●	○	●
October		●	○	○	○	●	●	●		○		○
November		●		○								
December		○										

39

Feeding

Feeding serves two important purposes. Firstly, it strengthens and thickens grass, giving it more resistance to drought, disease, weeds, moss and hard wear. Secondly, feeding maintains good colour and texture. A disadvantage of feeding is that it increases the rate of growth of grass, which therefore needs to be mown more frequently.

Spring feeding
A single annual dressing of a general lawn fertilizer containing nitrogen, phosphate and potash supplies sufficient food for most areas of turf. Apply in early spring, ideally in mild, showery, settled weather when the grass is starting to grow freely. This is usually in late March in southern Britain and early to mid-April in northern Britain. If weather conditions are unsuitable at these times, delay application for two or three weeks.

The simplest approach to feeding is to use a proprietary lawn fertilizer formulated for spring and summer use. However, different products vary widely in both analytical content and in formulation. Some are combined with weedkillers, others with a peat-based organic top dressing. The cost may also vary considerably between products. Before purchasing check the analytical content. Most lawns require fertilizers containing 5–7 per cent nitrogen, 10–15 per cent phosphoric acid and 2–4 per cent potash.

Consider also whether a product containing a weedkiller is needed. Less work is involved in applying a combined dressing but weed control may be more effective if weedkilling is attempted when grass and weeds are growing vigorously after being fed.

When applying any proprietary product use it only during the season specified, and at the dates recommended, by the manufacturer. Some saving may be achieved by making up a lawn fertilizer from basic ingredients or by having mixtures made up by a local sundriesman.

Opinions differ as to whether it is better to use only quick-acting inorganic fertilizers such as sulphate of ammonia, or slower-acting organics such as bone meal and hoof and horn meal. It may be more advantageous to use a basic mixture of quick-acting inorganics, for example when the weather conditions have delayed treatment or there has been considerable deterioration over winter. If the turf's condition is satisfactory a mixture of organic and inorganic materials is more beneficial (see Box). Where the turf has a poor colour include calcined sulphate of iron with the spring fertilizer. Apply the sulphate at the rate of $\frac{1}{5}$ oz per square yard.

Summer feeding
Nitrogen is the most important lawn nutrient, and a good level of available nitrogen is required throughout the growing season. During the late spring or summer growth may decline on lawns that have been closely mown or fed early in the spring with quick-acting inorganics. If so apply sulphate of ammonia at $\frac{1}{4}$–$\frac{1}{2}$ oz per square yard, watering thoroughly beforehand if the lawn is dry. Mix it well with 3–4 oz per square yard of sandy soil to ensure even distribution and to reduce risk of scorch. Apply two or three times during the season as necessary, but not after the end of August since this can lead to soft growth that will be susceptible to disease. Alternatives to sulphate of ammonia are dried blood or fine-grist hoof and horn meal, which are slower-acting.

Autumn feeding
Annual spring feeding supplemented by summer nitrogen usually provides ample nutrients for turf growth. However, if turf has suffered from drought or compaction, and at the end of the summer is sparse and thin, a proprietary autumn turf fertilizer can be applied in September. Apply a low level of nitrogen but a good level of phosphate and potash to encourage healthy roots (see Box).

Applying fertilizers
Apply when the grass is dry but the soil moist, preferably during cool, showery weather. Irrigate if rain does not fall within 48 hours. Do not feed during periods of drought unless it is essential; if doing so, irrigate thoroughly before feeding and lightly afterwards. Even and accurate application is important since too much fertilizer can scorch or kill turf.

Hand distribution is done by mixing the fertilizer with dry sand or sandy soil. Apply to measured strips at half the recommended rate, working lengthways across the lawn. Repeat the application working crossways.

Mechanical distribution is usually done with the standard or linear distributor. The fertilizer is carried in a hopper and distributed via a notched roller in its base. Calibrate the machine and test it carefully by running it over a newspaper or a concrete path to ensure that the fertilizer is being applied at the correct rate. Apply in parallel strips using the previous run's wheeltrack as a guideline to avoid overlapping. As with hand distribution it is preferable to apply at half the rate, going first lengthways and then crossways. There is a risk of uneven application when turning the distributor so, if space allows, lay a strip of hessian along the lawn edge and over-run.

There are also spinner-type distributors. These can be used on larger areas but deposit is uneven and requires a careful technique of partial overlapping.

Corrosion of distributors can occur rapidly as a result of the chemical action of damp fertilizers; always clean thoroughly after use.

MIXING YOUR OWN FERTILIZERS

Spring feeding
For a simple inorganic fertilizer mix:
35 parts by weight sulphate of ammonia
60 parts by weight superphosphate
 5 parts by weight sulphate of potash.

For a fertilizer containing inorganic and organic materials mix:
15 parts by weight sulphate of ammonia
15 parts by weight dried blood
40 parts by weight fine bone meal
25 parts by weight superphosphate
 5 parts by weight sulphate of potash.

Autumn feeding
For a simple low-nitrogen fertilizer mix:
25 parts by weight superphosphate
50 parts by weight fine bone meal
15 parts by weight sulphate of potash
10 parts by weight sandy soil.

Mix these fertilizers well before use. Apply them at 2 oz per square yard.

Using a distributor

Apply half the fertilizer at a time and make two journeys, one crossways and the other lengthways. If there is enough space beyond the edge of the lawn, lay a strip of hessian matting and push the distributor on to this before turning. This prevents the fertilizer from being distributed unevenly at the edge of the lawn.

Scarifying

Scarifying is the vigorous use of a rake or other tool to remove thatch from a lawn.

All established lawns have lying between the roots and foliage of the grass a layer consisting of living or dead fibrous material such as grass stems, stolons and rhizomes, together with miscellaneous debris. This material is known collectively as thatch.

Thatch is beneficial in moderation, that is up to about ½ in thick, since it reduces surface evaporation by acting as a mulch. It also gives a springy resilience to the turf and provides a degree of protection against wear. Thatch can, however, become excessively thick and impede moisture penetration to the extent that water only reaches the soil following prolonged rain or artificial watering. Fertilizers may also not be able to penetrate into the soil. In mild, wet autumns the thatch may become saturated with water, and the subsequent lack of drainage and aeration will encourage the establishment and spread of diseases. Thatch also causes the turf to become increasingly less resistant to drought and diseases.

Removing thatch

The first step in dealing with the problem of thatch is to scarify the lawn. Do this as part of the autumn programme of lawn maintenance during September when the growth of the grass is slowing down. If thatch is dense it will be necessary to seed-in after scarification. Therefore, do this early in the month to allow time for the young grasses to establish themselves before the onset of colder weather. The reason for scarifying in the autumn is that this is the time of year when the grass is thickening as new stolons and rhizomes develop and spread by rooting at the nodes. These new growths are known as tillers and are encouraged by the removal of thatch.

Do not attempt scarification in spring. This can leave the turf looking unsightly for a considerable time afterwards as there is little thickening of the turf during this period. Moreover, tillers formed in autumn may be dislodged and later sheared by the mower. Turf scarified in spring or early summer is also more susceptible to drought.

Scarify small areas of turf vigorously with a spring-tine or wire rake. The scrake, a rake-like tool but with half-moon discs instead of tines, is also an excellent tool for dealing with larger areas. When scarifying, work methodically, first lengthways and then crossways.

Preventing thatch

Excessive thatch is usually only found in long-established lawns, and routine light scarifying with a rake, stiff broom or mower-attached scarifying tool will in most cases prevent any serious build-up. Where the soil pH is on the low side top-dress regularly in the autumn with good quality loam – the loam mixes with the thatch and increases its rate of decomposition.

Thatch may become particularly troublesome in either very acid soils or wet, water-logged soils since these conditions slow down the rate of decomposition of the thatch.

If the lawn is persistently wet although the turf has been thoroughly aerated, check the land drains (see page 21).

How to scarify

Pull the scarifying tool vigorously along the surface of the lawn to pull up as much thatch as possible. It is important to keep the tool well pressed down on to the surface when doing this.

If the pH of the lawn is below about 5.5–6, which is the optimum pH level for lawns, apply a light dressing of lime during the winter. This raises the pH level slightly, encouraging microbial activity and thus increasing the rate of decomposition of the thatch. It also stimulates turf growth. Lime should, however, be applied with care since an excess reduces the quality of the turf. On lawns apply lime in the form of ground chalk or finely ground limestone.

The amount of lime needed depends on both the degree of acidity and the soil type. To raise the pH of soil by a given amount a clay soil needs more lime than a sandy soil. Apply lime only after tests have confirmed that it is necessary. If in any doubt as to the amount required apply a light dressing only, for example not more than 2 oz per square yard on light, sandy soils and not more than 4 oz per square yard on clay soils. If possible obtain professional advice.

Raking

The purpose of raking is to remove loose surface material and debris, and to control creeping weeds. It is a less vigorous operation than scarifying, and is done with an ordinary garden rake or spring-tine rake, with very little pressure being applied.

Rake at intervals in autumn to prevent the accumulation of dead leaves; if left to lie they may encourage worm activity and retain surface moisture, which helps the spread of diseases. Rake in early spring before the first mowing of the year to remove any debris left from over winter. After moss killers have been applied in autumn or early spring rake vigorously to remove the dead moss. Do not do this while the grass is growing strongly except where dealing with troublesome patches of creeping grasses, bents or procumbent weeds such as clover. In these cases rake carefully to lift up procumbent stems, then cut with a mower.

Scarifying tools

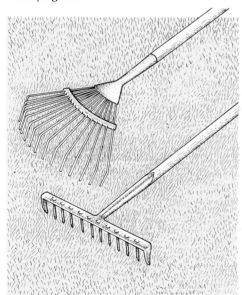

Scarifying is most commonly done with either a spring-tine rake or a garden rake.

Using a spring-tine rake

Raking is best performed with a spring-tine rake, although an ordinary garden rake may also be used. Raking is done for a variety of reasons, for example, clearing lawns of dead leaves.

Aerating

Aeration is the process of spiking a lawn to allow air into the soil. All roots of land plants require a supply of air since it assists in the uptake of water and nutrients. Where the free passage of air through the soil is impeded by the squeezing together of soil particles, the roots function poorly and the grass rapidly deteriorates. This squeezing is known as compaction.

Compaction
On lawns severe compaction is usually only localized, for example where deckchairs are used regularly or where the paper-boy and postman take their usual short cut across the turf. A degree of compaction may also be caused by the weight of the mower and its operator during the course of a season's mowing.

The effects of compaction are twofold. Firstly, by impeding the passage of air into the soil, it creates a build-up of carbon dioxide. This build-up restricts the absorption by the roots of moisture and nutrients. In hot dry weather the amount of moisture that the roots can absorb may not compensate for transpiration loss through the leaves, and the grass will weaken, in time turning brown and dying even though it is apparently well watered.

Secondly, compaction impedes the free passage of water down to the roots. Thus, the lawn owner may, when irrigating, be misled by the presence of water on the surface into thinking that he has thoroughly irrigated it when, in fact, most of the water has run off on to paths and beds. Moreover, in wet weather water may be held at the surface instead of draining away. This further impedes the passage of air, which encourages the spread of moss and the build-up of thatch.

Aeration
Few lawns require annual overall aeration; most however have some areas that do need regular attention. Aerate wherever the turf appears to be lacking in vigour, in particular children's play areas, areas that are infested with moss and where the turf turns brown during dry weather.

If a lawn is new and has been raised from seed, aerate it in the early years to encourage

good root growth and a settled crumb structure. Otherwise, if levels have been altered and clay sub-soil disturbed, or if new heavier soil was brought in, waterlogging may occur. The young grasses will then suffer accordingly.

Various tools are available for spiking. Some types do little more than prick the surface. This may be useful during the summer for breaking up light surface compaction and encouraging penetration of rain or applied irrigation. However, it is of little value for dealing with general compaction. Choose tools that give at least 3 in penetration, preferably 4–6 in. For small areas of compaction an ordinary garden fork is quite suitable. Use the fork backwards to obtain vertical penetration. Drive it in with the foot and then ease backwards and forwards fractionally. This will slightly enlarge the hole, yet allow the fork to be lifted out without disturbing the surface of the lawn. Space each

Aerating with a garden fork

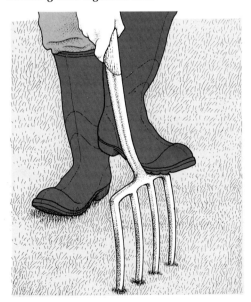

Small areas of lawns can be satisfactorily aerated with a garden fork. To do this, drive the fork backwards into the lawn to give vertical penetration, then ease it back and forth slightly before removing.

set of holes 4–6 in apart, working backwards to avoid treading on aerated turf.

If the soil is heavy or waterlogged, hollow-tine aerators give more satisfactory results. Each hollow tine removes a core or plug of soil, expelling it on to the lawn surface at the next penetration. This relieves compaction by allowing the soil to expand. The holes act as air and water channels, and stimulate new root growth. After hollow-tining sweep up the cores then top-dress with a sandy mixture and brush this into the holes. This creates permanent cores of more freely draining material in the soil. On heavier soils it should be necessary to hollow-tine only every third or fourth year, and on sandy soil the technique is of little value.

Where dealing with large-scale compaction, wheeled machines can be purchased or hired. These may be either powered or hand-propelled and usually have interchangeable, solid, hollow or flattened (wedge-shaped) tines. The latter make a narrow, elongated incision, which prunes the roots, stimulating growth.

When to aerate

In the spring and summer spike localized areas of compaction with a garden fork or solid-tine aerator. Repeat the treatment as necessary at four or five week intervals when the soil is moist, and preferably in cool, showery weather. Irrigate afterwards. Spiked rollers may be used during the summer months to break up light surface compaction and improve moisture penetration.

In September carry out deeper and more general aeration, including hollow-tining, as part of the autumn programme of renovation, scarifying first and top-dressing afterwards. Ensure that the soil is moist, since this enables the work to be done easily.

In winter carry out localized spiking where necessary to disperse standing water.

Aerating with a hollow-tine fork

Larger areas are best aerated with a hollow-tine fork on heavy soils. This tool is more efficient than a garden fork since it removes plugs of soil, which are deposited on the surface at the next penetration.

Aerating machines

Large-scale compaction can be treated with aerating machines. These machines have tines that are usually flattened and wedge-shaped, though they may also be cylindrical and solid or hollow.

Top-dressing

Top-dressing is the application of a mixture of loam, sand and well rotted organic matter to a lawn in order to even out irregularities in its surface. The term is also applied to the mixture itself. Few un-dressed lawns have a level surface. Older lawns may be uneven for a variety of reasons, for example, collapsing mole tunnels, turfing repairs, digging out weeds, children's activities and so forth. New lawns may show signs of unevenness from irregular consolidation within a few months of seeding or turfing.

The irregularities can be partly flattened by rolling but this will usually compress the soil in places, which results in poorer growth. Therefore it is better to gradually build up the level of hollows by top-dressing.

Top-dressing also improves the surface soil. On difficult soils (sands, clays and chalk) annual dressings progressively form an upper layer of better quality soil into which developing grass runners and stolons are encouraged to root, thus thickening out the turf. On heavier soils where hollow-tining has been carried out a sandy top-dressing brushed into the resultant holes considerably improves surface drainage and the general condition of the turf. Top-dressing also helps to break down thatch.

Making up a top dressing

The professional gardener often makes his own top dressing by building up alternate layers of well rotted farm manure and sandy loam soil. The heap is then left for a year or more to decompose further before use. The material is finally broken down by shredding and passing through a 1/4 in mesh sieve. It is then mixed with sharp sand as necessary until a satisfactory medium is obtained.

The amateur gardener may prefer to purchase a ready-made mixture from a local sundriesman but this is not essential since such mixtures are easily prepared. The requirements are a good loam or sandy loam soil, sand and organic material.

Loam or sandy loam soil should preferably have been sterilized to kill all weed seeds and seeds of coarse grasses. Note that sterilization is not essential since lawn weedkillers will deal with any resulting weeds, although coarse grasses can be troublesome.

Sand should be lime-free with a particle size of about 1/5–1/2 mm. Do not use builders' sand since this is usually fine-particled and often strongly alkaline.

Organic matter is usually granulated sphagnum or sedge peat but well decomposed leaf-mould or garden compost may be used. Note that the latter sometimes contains viable weed seeds if it was not sufficiently warm when decomposing.

The content of a top dressing is not critical but it should be an improvement on the soil in which the turf is already growing. A simple formula is three parts sandy loam, six parts sand and one part peat. This can be modified as necessary, for example use a lower proportion of sand on a sandy soil and a higher one on a heavy clay soil.

Sand can be used on its own as an autumn top dressing on heavy soils since it dries the soil surface and encourages better rooting of stoloniferous grasses. However, if used to excess, it can build up to form an unstable layer which will give trouble in later years.

Applying a top dressing

1 Broadcast the top dressing with a shovel, applying 4 lb per square yard. On irregular turf apply up to 6–7 lb per square yard.

Peat may also be used on its own or as the major component of a top dressing, but if used too frequently it can give rise to a spongy surface that is liable to dry out and become impervious to water.

Applying a top dressing

Broadcast the top dressing using a shovel, and then work it well into the base of the grass. Do this with the back of a wooden rake. Alternatively, construct a home-made lute using a 5–6 ft length of board attached at an angle to a long handle. With either tool push it along the surface of the lawn to clear the top dressing from the ridges and bumps and deposit it in hollows.

The rate at which the top dressing is applied depends on the condition of the lawn. An average dressing is 4 lb per square yard but on very irregular turf increase this to 6–7 lb per square yard. Be careful not to apply too much since excessive applications can smother finer grasses and in moist weather increase the risk of attack by diseases.

When to top-dress

Top-dress in early autumn as part of the autumn renovation programme. Do it after scarifying and aerating when the grass is still growing since it will then grow through the dressing. Choose a period when both the turf and the weather are dry and will remain so until the work is completed. Mow the turf short before top-dressing. Ensure that the mixture is fairly dry to facilitate spreading and levelling. Where there are minor surface irregularities apply a light, localized dressing either during February or during the late spring and summer when growth is vigorous. These should be worked in thoroughly.

It may take two or three seasons of top-dressing to achieve a smooth, level surface. Do not try to achieve perfection with a single dressing – if the grass is completely covered it may die, allowing moss and weeds to establish. Once a satisfactory surface is obtained there is no necessity for annual top-dressing unless this is justified by the nature of the soil and condition of the turf.

2 Work the top dressing well into the lawn with the back of a wooden rake.

3 A lute can also be used to work in the top dressing. Construct one by fixing a pair of poles to a 5–6 ft long plank of wood.

Irrigating

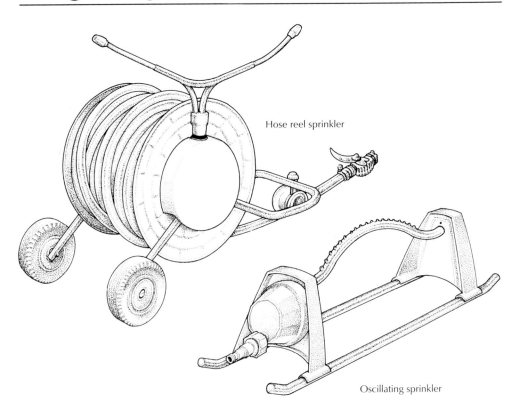

Hose reel sprinkler

Oscillating sprinkler

For most of the year there is sufficient rainfall in the United Kingdom to keep lawns well watered. Occasionally, however, there are dry periods during the spring or summer when irrigation is necessary to prevent the grass from dying back. Apart from damaging a lawn directly by causing die-back, drought also allows weeds to become dominant, for example, white clover and yarrow will survive severe drought to grow away strongly with a return to moister conditions.

Susceptibility to drought is frequently an indication that the turf is weak and under-nourished. Give attention to aerating, top-dressing, scarifying, feeding and correct mowing – all these factors contribute to the development of a deeply penetrating, more drought-resistant root system.

When to water
A lawn needs watering as soon as the symptoms of drought appear. The first signs are a

loss of resilience in the lawn and its colour becoming dull. This is followed by the leaves turning yellow and then brown. If the drought is prolonged the grass crowns shrivel, the roots become desiccated and the grass dies. In spring or summer begin looking for these symptoms after there has been dry weather for seven to ten days, ignoring occasional light showers. Most grass roots are found in the top 10–12 in of soil. The first signs of drought can usually be seen once the top 4–5 in have dried out.

The frequency of watering varies according to the type of soil. A clay soil holds considerably more water than a loam soil, which in turn holds more than a light sandy soil. Consequently a lawn on a lighter soil needs irrigating sooner and more frequently than a similar lawn on heavier soil. As a general guide, in dry sunny weather during the spring or summer a healthy, well maintained lawn on an average loam soil needs

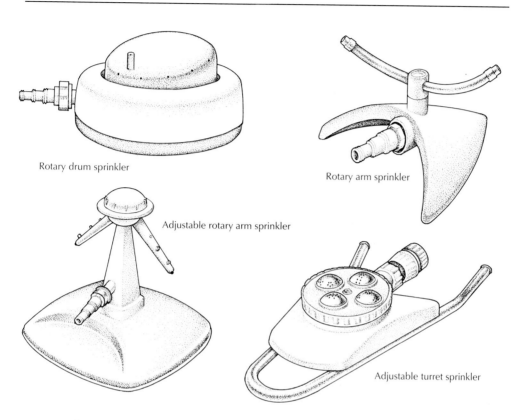

Rotary drum sprinkler

Rotary arm sprinkler

Adjustable rotary arm sprinkler

Adjustable turret sprinkler

watering about once every seven days.

Lawns may be watered at any time of the day but avoid hot sunny weather as this may cause the soil to dry rapidly to a hard crust. If the soil is too dry for water to seep through use a proprietary soil penetrant or bio-degradable wetting agent. On small areas washing-up liquid will aid penetration, but do not use one that contains bleach since this will damage the lawn. If the surface is very dry or compacted spike it beforehand to improve moisture penetration.

How much to apply

Frequent light watering is bad for a lawn since it encourages shallow-rooting and the development of mosses and pearlwort. Frequent heavy watering can also be harmful because it encourages moss and turf diseases. Always apply at least 2 gal of water per square yard (approximately $1/2$ in) and preferably 4–4$1/2$ gal per square yard.

Methods of application

Watering cans are impractical except on extremely small areas.

Hose pipes can be used for small lawns, and are particularly useful in awkward places such as banks. Apply as a fine spray with an adjustable nozzle attachment.

Perforated plastic tubes are useful for grass paths and awkward places but give a less even application than sprinklers.

Sprinklers may be either static, rotary-armed, pop-up or oscillating. The first three types of sprinkler cover a circular area whereas the oscillating type covers a rectangular area. The latter is, therefore, more economical and the problem of overlap, which occurs with other types, is avoided. Some oscillating types are adjustable to give angled coverage or changeable spray patterns. Pop-up sprinklers are installed below the surface of the lawn. They are lifted up and set in motion by the pressure of the water.

Mowing 1

The purpose of mowing a lawn is to keep the grass short enough to be neat and attractive, but without hindering its ability to grow strongly. Mowing a lawn too close weakens the grass and allows moss and lawn weeds to become established. On the other hand, where lawns are allowed to grow too long, coarser grasses become increasingly dominant and finer grasses deteriorate. The best approach is to mow regularly but not too closely. Apart from keeping the grass to a reasonable length, it encourages tillering, which increases the density of the turf, and deters moss and weed development. Further advantages of this approach are that the yield of mowings is lower and the turf quicker and easier to mow if the grass is mown regularly rather than sporadically.

Height of cut
The most suitable height of cut is determined by the kind of grasses present, the time of year and by the function of the lawn. During late spring to early autumn the finest quality ornamental turf should be cut to $1/4$–$1/2$ in. On average lawns cut the grass to a height of $1/2$ in, on utility lawns with rye grass cut to 1 in and on paddocks and areas of rough grass cut to $1^1/2$–2 in. Leave the grass slightly longer during hot dry weather unless the turf can be irrigated adequately.

During autumn to early spring, when growth is slow, increase the height of cut by $1/4$ in. This leaves the turf less open to moss and weed infestation. Where the soil is moist and soft adjust the height of cutting to compensate for any sinking of the mower's wheels or rollers.

Do not cut any turf to below $3/16$ in because all grasses are weakened when cut below this level. On the other hand, lawn turf should not be allowed to grow longer than $1^1/2$ in since above this height coarser grasses begin to dominate over the finer grasses.

Frequency of mowing
Once the most suitable height of cut has been established, mow with sufficient frequency to keep the grass as close to the desired height as is practicable. Increase or decrease the frequency of mowing according to the rate of growth. This varies from season to season, and may be influenced by factors such as weather conditions, feeding, irrigation, the varieties of grass being grown and the general health of the turf itself.

Fine lawns should be mown at intervals of two to three days. Mow average lawns at least every seven days and preferably at intervals of three to five days. For other turf mow at least once every seven days. Never allow the turf to grow long then cut it very short on the pretext that it saves time.

Removing the mowings
Most gardeners remove the mowings from a lawn, usually by means of a grass-box. There are a number of reasons for doing this. In wetter weather mowings cling to the surface, impeding aeration and becoming increasingly unsightly as they slowly decompose. Seeds of weeds and annual meadow grass are scattered and will infest other areas, as will severed stems of white clover and speedwell. Leaving the mowings on the lawn also encourages worm activity and the mowings make the turf softer and lusher. In milder, moister autumns, this causes the lawn to be more susceptible to diseases, many of which thrive in such conditions.

There are, however, some advantages in leaving the mowings on the lawn. Firstly, mowing is less arduous without a grass-box. Secondly, the mowings act as a mulch, increasing drought resistance and deterring moss. As they decompose, they return nutrients to the soil to give a greener, lusher turf. Nevertheless under normal conditions always remove the mowings from the lawn. Return them only in hot dry conditions when irrigation is not available.

After gathering the mowings do not simply lump them on to the compost heap. Grass mowings contain a high percentage of moisture, and if heaped when they are still fresh they decompose into a green-black glutinous mass. Small quantities can be added to the compost heap when fresh as long as they are layered thinly with other garden waste. Larger quantities should be dried before composting. Do this either by spreading them out thinly, or by making a loose heap of the cuttings and turning it frequently.

HEIGHT AND FREQUENCY OF CUT

This chart indicates the height and frequency to which different quality lawns should be cut for the period late spring to early autumn. The figures given are only a rough guide, and should be varied according to the weather and the state of the turf. Outside this period the height of cut should be increased by ¼ in.

Type of lawn

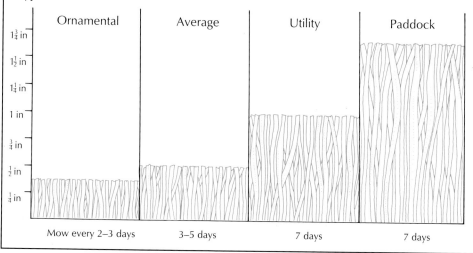

	Ornamental	Average	Utility	Paddock
	Mow every 2–3 days	3–5 days	7 days	7 days

$1\frac{3}{4}$ in
$1\frac{1}{2}$ in
$1\frac{1}{4}$ in
1 in
$\frac{3}{4}$ in
$\frac{1}{2}$ in
$\frac{1}{4}$ in

Composting mowings

Small quantities of mowings can be added to the compost heap in thin layers, which should be alternated with other refuse.

Dry large quantities before composting by spreading them out thinly, or by making a loose heap and forking it over.

51

Mowing 2

Mowing problems

Ribbing is a series of narrow, parallel strips of alternating longer and shorter grass. This effect occurs with cylinder-bladed mowers that have a low cylinder speed and a low number of blades, which cause them to give few cuts in relation to distance travelled. Ribbing may also occur when the grass is too long for the mower setting; if this is so, increase the height of cut.

The washboard effect is the occurrence of irregular waves or corrugations; the grass alternates from long on the crest of each wave to short between crests. It is caused by the grass always being mown in the same direction and usually occurs where powered mowers are used. Change the mowing pattern and vary the direction of mowing with successive cuts.

Lacerated grass or uneven cutting are caused by having blunt or incorrectly set blades, or by the mower having a damaged bottom plate. Check the mower and adjust or repair it as necessary.

Scalping occurs where there are surface irregularities. Increase the height of cut and improve the level of the lawn: correct minor irregularities by top-dressing and major ones by lifting the turf and adding or removing soil as necessary.

HOW TO MOW

1 Always plan the direction of mowing to minimize overlapping, reversing and abrupt changes of direction, since these will all increase compaction and wear.

2 Mow when dry. Wet mowings clog the machine and grass-box, and lengthen the mowing time. During the autumn and spring mow on sunny days in the early afternoon when the grass has dried. If dew is heavy disperse it two or three hours before mowing using a supple bamboo cane, rake or besom.

3 Scatter worm casts before mowing.

4 During the colder months, do not top when cold winds are blowing. The leaf-tips may be wind-scorched and seared, and remain unsightly until the next cut.

5 If the grass contains weeds or unwanted surface runners, rake it occasionally before mowing to lift unwanted growth.

6 Move steadily forward if using a hand-propelled mower. Repeated backward and forward movements result in an uneven cut.

7 Always mow at right-angles to the line of the previous mow since this helps to control weed grasses and bents and to smooth out irregularities in the mowing.

SEASONAL GUIDE TO MOWING

March: top with the blade set ¼ in higher than the summer height of cut.

April: increase frequency according to the weather and growth of the grass.

May–August: adjust to summer heights and frequencies.

August–September: reduce frequency as growth rate slows.

Late September: adjust to the autumn height of cutting.

October–February: occasional topping may be necessary during mild winters.

Producing a banded finish

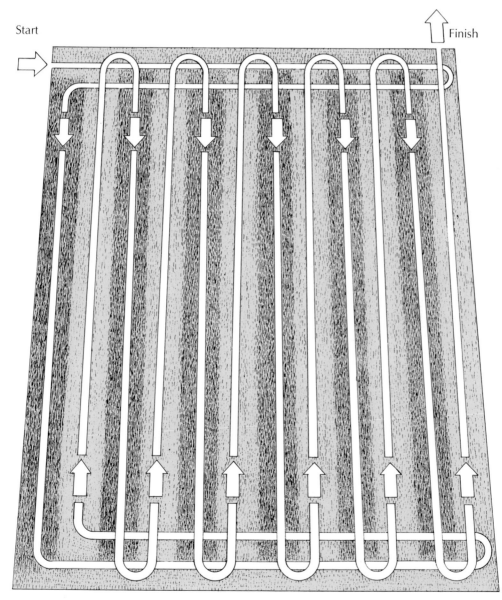

Start

Finish

A neat, banded finish of contrasting light and dark strips can be obtained by using a mower with a rear-mounted roller. Work across the lawn and mow each succeeding parallel strip in the opposite direction to the previous one.

53

Mowers 1

All lawn mowers cut grass by either of two methods. One is to trap the grass between a fixed blade and a moving blade. Mowers that use this method are known as cylinder mowers since the moving blades are arranged cylindrically. The other method has a blade rotating parallel to the lawn. These mowers are known as rotary mowers. Modern rotary mowers give a neat finish, and have the advantage that they can cut grass to any height. However, cylinder mowers are superior since their scissor-like action gives the finest finish to a lawn.

An important consideration when buying a mower is the width of cut since, obviously, the wider the cut the less the time taken to mow a given area. Usually a 12–14 in width of cut is satisfactory for smaller lawns. As a rough guide it should take about 30 minutes to cut 500 sq yd with a 12 in width of cut, 1,000 sq yd with a 16 in width of cut, or 1,500 sq yd with a 24 in width of cut.

Cylinder mowers

These have a number of narrow spiral blades arranged cylindrically around a central shaft. As the blades rotate the grass is caught between the rotating blade and the fixed bottom blade and sheared scissor-fashion. The fineness of cut is related to the number of blades on the cylinder and to the gear ratio. The number of blades varies from three to 12, depending on the size and type of the mower. The greater the number of blades the more cuts the mower gives per yard. For example a mower with four blades gives 30–40 cuts per yard, whereas 12 blades gives 140–150 cuts per yard.

It is important to check cylinder mowers periodically to make sure that the cylinder blades are set correctly with respect to the fixed blade. Do this by inserting a piece of paper between the cylinder and the fixed bottom blade. Then turn the cylinder by hand. If the blades are correctly set the paper will cut cleanly at all points along the cylinder. If it is not cutting correctly adjust either the cylinder or the bottom blade.

The various types of cylinder mower are discussed below.

Hand-driven mowers usually have cutting cylinders 12–14 in wide. The simplest and cheapest are those that have side wheels with no front roller. These models are useful for cutting new lawns and longer grass, and for controlling creeping weeds and bents. However, they do have a number of disadvantages. The wheels may cut into the lawn if wet. It is difficult to mow to the edge of the lawn and to cut the grass close to obstacles if there is a front-mounted grass-box. Models with rear-mounted boxes are available but these are often less manoeuvrable and the grass-box fails to gather as much grass as one that is forward-mounted. There are also models on the market that have the cutting cylinder driven by a large rear-mounted roller. These give an attractive banded finish (see page 53) and, since the weight of the machine is spread over the length of the roller, they can cut to the edge of the lawn.

Petrol-driven mowers are heavier than hand-driven types but the effort of mowing is considerably reduced. Indeed, for larger lawns some sort of powered mower is essential. The width of the cutting cylinder ranges from 12–36 in and trailer seats are available on some larger machines. Professional gardeners often use a four-wheeled triple-cylinder model. These are ridden and resemble a small tractor. Certain models of petrol-driven mower include a ribbed rear roller, which gives them better traction in wet conditions.

Mains electric mowers are powered by heavy duty electric motors and tend to be small. On some machines the motor drives both the wheels and the cylinder. On others, just the wheels are power driven. They usually have a cylinder width of 12–14 in. These machines are light to handle but require an easily accessible three-pin power socket. Ensure that there is sufficient length of cable to reach all areas to be mown. It is advisable to develop a good mowing pattern since this avoids having to move the cable frequently. Always stop the engine and remove the plug lead before clearing or adjusting the blades. These last points also hold for mains electric rotary mowers.

Battery electric mowers incorporate a motor and a 12 volt battery. They are heavy machines but easy to operate. The area of lawn that can be cut on a single charge is related to the battery size and the width of cut. Before buying such a machine calculate the lawn area then check the details of performance given by the manufacturer to ensure that there is sufficient battery capacity to cut the lawn on a single charge. Some models have built-in trickle chargers, others have separate chargers for use when the battery runs down. Remember to keep the battery cells topped up with distilled water and to place the battery on charge after use.

Rotary mowers

Rotary mowers have a cutting device rotating at high speed under a protective canopy. The device is either a bar with sharpened edges or a disc with two to four small blades, which may be either fixed or hinged.

Rotary mowers can be dangerous if not used correctly. Always switch off the engine and remove the plug lead, or disconnect the power supply, before touching the blades. Always remove stones and debris before mowing, and never leave the machine unattended with the engine running.

All rotary mowers are powered by petrol or mains electricity. The various types are discussed below.

Petrol-driven mowers usually have a width of cut of 10–21 in. Larger models are ridden and have twin mowers mounted at the front or in the middle. These give mowing widths of up to 50 in. Most larger models are propelled via the rear land wheels, but there are also front-wheel and rear-roller drive models. The latter provide the banded effect of cylinder mowers. Most petrol-driven rotary mowers have grass-boxes. These are usually rear-mounted. Some machines create a strong vacuum when mowing. This lifts the grass for a cleaner cut, draws up debris from below the level of the blade and transfers it to the grass-box.

Mains electric rotary mowers work on the same principle as mains electric cylinder mowers, and have the same advantages and disadvantages. There are various types available, giving a width of cut up to 18 in. They include machines with rear-roller drive, and those with built-in automatic release and rewind cable drum.

Air-cushion mowers have a fan mounted on the crankshaft to build up air pressure under the canopy and lift the machine clear of the ground. They are ideal for cutting banks, and are light and easily stored. The disadvantages of these machines are that they are awkward to move when stopped and they do not collect the mowings. They are driven by either petrol or mains electricity. Some air-cushion mowers have a life of only two to three years if they are used regularly.

Adjusting the height of cut

With most cylinder mowers this is done by adjusting the front roller. To check the height of cut stand the mower on a raised surface. Lay a straight edge against the underside of the front and rear rollers and measure the distance between the straight edge and the fixed bottom blade. This distance is equal to the height of the cut. When altering the height of cut use a fixed or adjustable gauge to ensure accuracy.

Rotary mowers are adjusted by raising or lowering the land wheels. This is usually done by a simple lever action or by moving the rotating disc up and down on its drive shaft. Air-cushion mowers are adjusted by varying the number of spacers between the impellor fan and the cutting blade.

Maintenance

After mowing, use a stiff brush, or a garden hose, to remove caked earth and mowings from the rollers, cutting cylinders and blades, and from under the canopy of rotary mowers. Then wipe the cutting blades with an oily rag, and oil or grease in accordance with the manufacturer's instructions.

In autumn, clean and oil blades, gears, bearings and chain drives, as applicable, and sharpen all cutting edges and blades, not forgetting the bottom blade on cylinder mowers. Then slacken off the cutting cylinder, drain the petrol tank and clean the sparking plugs. Alternatively, have the machine overhauled professionally. Remove the batteries, charge them and then keep them in warm conditions. Finally, store the mower in a dry environment, making sure that it is well away from any corrosive fertilizers or chemicals such as weedkillers.

Mowers 2

TYPES OF MOWERS

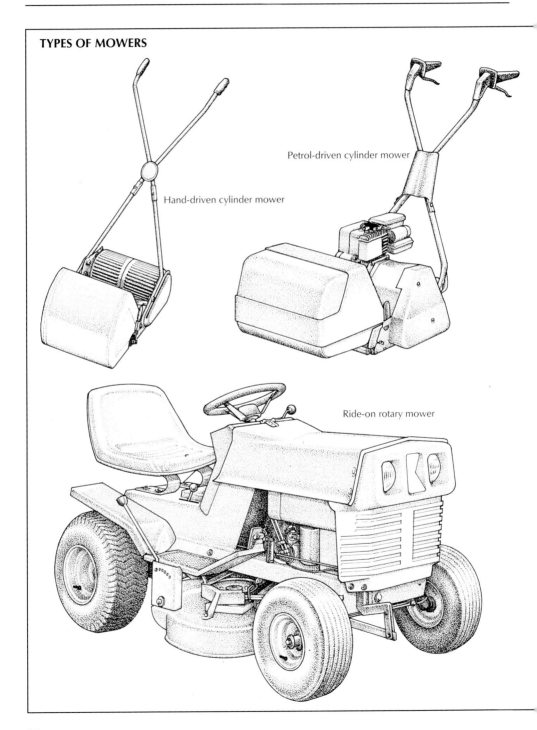

Hand-driven cylinder mower

Petrol-driven cylinder mower

Ride-on rotary mower

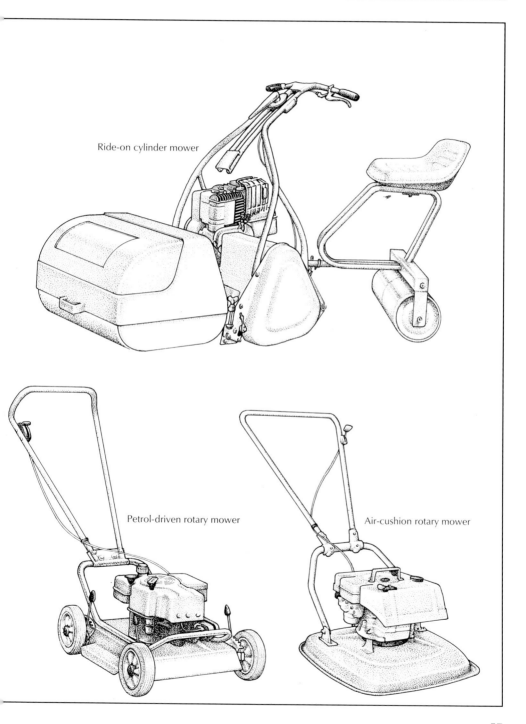

Ride-on cylinder mower

Petrol-driven rotary mower

Air-cushion rotary mower

Other lawn tools

Maintaining lawn edges

To keep lawn edges in good condition there are two tasks that should be carried out – the edges need to be kept straight and the grass there has to be cut with special tools. Straightening lawn edges should be done after the first spring cut. For this, use either a half-moon turf-cutting tool or a sharp spade. To obtain a straight edge, use a straight, sturdy plank, at least 6 ft in length. Over longer distances a tautly fixed garden line may be used. Never cut the edge of a lawn vertically, always cut it at a slight angle away from the bordering ground.

Where the edges crumble easily or are breaking down under heavy wear, insert edging strips. These also have the advantage of checking the spread of creeping grasses from the lawn into borders. Insert them carefully and ensure that the top edge of the strips lies below the level of the mower blades (see also the section on repairing broken edges, page 72).

There are two types of tools available for cutting lawn edges: edging shears and lawn edge trimmers.

Edging shears are similar to hand shears but have 3 ft long handles attached at right-angles to the blades. This enables the user to trim lawn edges while standing upright. Some edging shears have a grass-catching attachment fixed to the bottom blade. This is useful where the edges are raised and unimpeded, but it can be troublesome where the edges are overhung by foliage or lie close to walls or paving.

Lawn edge trimmers may be either manual or powered. Manual types cut by means of a disc of sharpened spokes that rotate against a fixed blade and shear off protruding grass as the user pushes it along the lawn edge. Electric or battery-powered edgers consist of a vertically fixed blade with two cutting edges rotating at high speed under a protective casing. They perform best on firm soils.

Sweeping leaves

Always remove leaves from the lawn as soon as possible. If they are allowed to accumulate and decay, the turf becomes weakened through lack of light and air, which increases the risk of disease and moss infestation, and

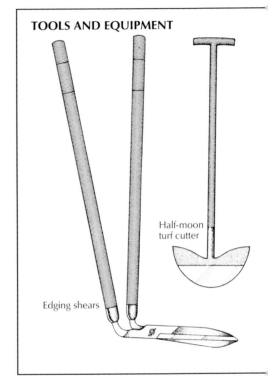

TOOLS AND EQUIPMENT

Half-moon turf cutter

Edging shears

encourages worm activity in the lawn.

For large areas it is best to remove leaves with a leaf sweeper. This machine picks up leaves with a revolving brush and deflects them into a collecting bag suspended from the push-bar of a wheeled frame. Some models can be folded for storage. There are also dual-purpose vacuum-bag models which can be used for both collecting leaves and sweeping paths.

For smaller areas most lawn rakes will deal with leaves quite efficiently and economically. Some types have pick-up mechanisms that allow the leaves to be transferred easily to a wheelbarrow or truck.

Rolling

Rolling is an essential operation where a true surface already exists but firmness is required; for example on cricket pitches or bowling greens. However, in normal circumstances the regular passage of the mower provides all the consolidation necessary and a roller is

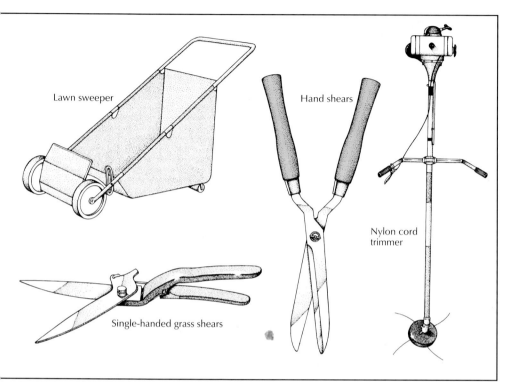

Lawn sweeper

Hand shears

Nylon cord trimmer

Single-handed grass shears

not an essential requirement for lawn owners. Very occasionally though, an established lawn may be lifted sufficiently by frost action to require the use of a roller in early spring.

If it is thought that rolling is necessary, roll when the soil is moist but the surface dry. Remove all stones and scatter worm casts before rolling. The roller weight should not exceed 2 cwt. A heavier roller may compress the soil too much and cause grass growth to be impaired.

Grass trimmers and shears

Many lawns contain awkward corners that cannot be reached by the mower and are therefore difficult to cut. One solution to this problem is to eliminate such corners. Alternatively, there are a number of tools available for this job.

Hand shears are the simplest of these tools. There are lightweight, spring-loaded models for use one-handed, some types having adjustable blades for horizontal or vertical use. There are also rechargeable battery-powered models available. More sophisticated are long-handled trimmers, which obviate the necessity of bending or kneeling, and miniature rotary-bladed trimmers that run on wheels or skis and are powered by an electric motor. The main disadvantages of hand shears are that it is difficult to obtain a neat finish and it takes a long time to cut even relatively small areas.

Nylon cord trimmers are powered by battery or mains electricity. The grass is cut by means of a short length of nylon cord that protrudes from beneath the protective hood and whirls around at high speed. The cord may be in a spool or in short lengths. It can wear rapidly if in frequent contact with obstacles, such as walls or trees. Always protect your eyes when using these tools. Nylon cord trimmers give a rapid cut and are useful where the grass is not too dense. However, wear and tear on the machine may be rapid if it is used frequently for cutting large areas or coarse, dense grass.

Weed control in lawns

The weeds most troublesome in established lawns are the low-growing perennials of creeping or rosette-type growth, such as clovers, speedwell, daisy and plantain, which can adapt to or are unaffected by regular close mowing.

Sowing or laying clean turves on a thoroughly cleaned and fallowed site will ensure a weed-free start (see pages 14–21). Regular mowing with a grass-box, careful feeding and attention to irrigation will keep the turf densely leaved and healthy, making it difficult for weeds to establish themselves.

Weeds may reach the lawn in various ways: as seeds blown by the wind; carried by birds; brought in on muddy footwear, machinery or tools; or concealed in unsterilized soil or badly made compost used for top dressing. Runners may be introduced on borrowed mowers or fertilizer spreaders, or they may encroach from weedy paths or flower beds.

Always use a grass-box when mowing since this minimizes the spread of lawn weeds. Sections of runners of certain weeds can regrow if not removed from the lawn, while the seeds of lesser yellow trefoil, which seeds freely, are easily scattered.

Hand-weeding with a hand fork or grubbing tool is a useful approach when dealing with scattered weeds, but it is essential to firm the surrounding turf carefully after extracting each weed. Hand-weed only during good growing conditions in spring when the grass will grow quickly to fill in the bare patches. Later in the year, when there are drier conditions, slower grass growth and more weed seeds, there is a much greater risk of bare patches being recolonized by weeds – or moss if a wet period follows a long spell of warm, dry weather. If large numbers of weeds are present in the lawn then hand-weeding is no longer practicable and weedkillers must be used.

Weedkillers

Lawn sands containing sulphate of ammonia and sulphate of iron are occasionally advocated for spot treatment of lawn weeds. They have a burning or caustic effect when sprinkled on flattened leaves and into the crowns of rosette weeds. The high localized nitrogen source also inhibits clovers and trefoils when it reaches their roots. But there is often strong weed regrowth, and lawn sand has now been largely superseded by selective lawn weedkillers.

These do not harm narrow-bladed erect grasses but kill or check broad-leaved weeds. Some weeds can be killed by a single treatment, others may need several.

Most proprietary brands of lawn weedkiller contain two or occasionally three active ingredients, such as mecoprop, MCPA or 2,4-D. A product with two different active ingredients will give control of a wider range of weeds than a product containing a single ingredient. To decide which is best, list the different kinds of weeds in the infested lawn. Then check the proprietary mixtures and choose one that carries the manufacturer's recommendations for use in controlling the listed species.

If some weeds are not killed by the first application, repeat the treatment after four or five weeks. Some weeds may survive a second treatment. If so, confirm their identities then check the most effective means of control (see pages 181–185). This may indicate the need to change to a different weedkiller or suggest some cultural measure that will help to weaken or check its spread.

Form and methods of application

Most lawn weedkillers are sold in concentrated liquid form, to be applied after dilution with water. Read the product label before buying, and mix and apply strictly according to the manufacturers' recommendations accompanying the product. Some lawn fertilizers incorporate weedkillers in dry form, which allows the two operations of feeding and weedkilling to be combined into one.

Lawn weedkillers are also available in aerosol or solid stick form for spot-treating isolated weeds. Some aerosols have the advantage that they leave a foam marker which persists for some time after weed treatment. Although spot treatment is a more economical approach than overall spraying where few weeds are involved, there may often be some localized temporary scorching of the grass since it is difficult to gauge the amount being applied.

Apply lawn weedkillers from spring to late

summer, ideally during fine warm conditions when the soil is thoroughly moist and grass growth is vigorous. The weedkiller is then rapidly translocated throughout the weed and the vigorously growing grass will fill in the space as the weed dies. Apply a nitrogenous fertilizer one or two weeks before the weed-killer is used to encourage recovery of the turf. Then apply the weedkiller evenly with the aid of canes and twine.

Spot-treating weeds

Spot treatment with a lawn weedkiller in aerosol or solid stick form is a simple and economical method of control if there are only a few isolated weeds present.

HOW TO USE LAWN WEEDKILLERS

Do not apply in the cold earlier months of the year or during drought when there is little growth.

Do not apply immediately before rain, otherwise much of the weedkiller may be washed into the soil.

Do not apply when windy, otherwise the spray may be carried to affect nearby garden plants. If this does happen, spray the plants immediately with large amounts of clean water.

Do not apply immediately before mowing, or much of the treated leaf surface may be removed before the weedkiller can reach the roots. Allow three or four days where possible before resuming mowing.

Do not apply at a rate stronger than that recommended by the manufacturer. Too high a concentration may kill weed foliage before the weedkiller can reach the roots, and this would allow the weed to revive. It may also cause the grasses to be badly damaged.

Do not mow immediately before weed-killer application or there will be a much-reduced leaf-surface area to receive and absorb the weedkiller.

Do not use fresh mowings as mulches for at least two weeks following treatment of lawns. Freshly treated mowings can be composted but the compost should not be used for at least six months.

Moss control in lawns

Of the hundreds of mosses found in temperate climates relatively few are troublesome as lawn weeds. Of these the most common are the following. *Hypnum cupressiforme* (and its forms) has yellow to golden-green trailing stems, and often colonizes large areas. *Brachythecium rutabulum,* with bright green, creeping, irregularly branched stems, is common in poorly drained lawns. *Ceratodon purpureus,* with short erect stems and densely tufted growth, is often found on poor, acid, heathland soil. *Bryum argenteum* is a cushion-type moss which has an attractive silvery sheen to its foliage.

Contrary to widespread opinion, the presence of moss in a lawn does not necessarily show the need for lime, for example, mosses such as *Hypnum cupressiforme* var *lacunosum* naturally inhabit chalk grassland. Other species are natural to all forms of grassland. Moss colonizes lawns for various reasons. Poor fertility or weakness of the turf due to attacks by pests or diseases, lack of aeration, bad drainage, excessive shade or mowing too closely will all result in weak, sparse turf that allows moss to establish.

Moss can be temporarily controlled by using mosskillers but, unless the reason for infestation is established and then corrected, moss will return. Examine the lawn and identify factors causing weak growth. Feed regularly if previous feeding has been sporadic. Top-dress regularly to improve moisture retention if the soil is light and sandy; irrigate regularly and thoroughly if the lawn is prone to drought. Aerate if surface drainage is impeded and carry out deep spiking if there is compaction through heavy usage. Watch for signs of waterlogging during the winter months and, if necessary, check and clear existing pipe drainage systems or install a new system. Do not set the mower blades too low; close and frequent mowing can weaken grass, letting weeds and moss establish themselves. On very acid soils a light winter application of lime in the form of ground chalk or ground limestone will slightly reduce acidity and usually discourage the mosses present. First determine by soil testing that liming is likely to be beneficial since excessive use of lime, or use when not required, can improve conditions for coarser grasses,

clovers and other weeds while suppressing growth of the finer-leaved, more desirable grasses. If lime is necessary, apply at 2 oz per square yard (see page 43).

Where moss is troublesome in turf under trees there is often little that can be done. Lifting the tree canopy by removal of the lower branches will let in more light but turf growth may remain poor and sparse if the soil is light, dry and full of roots. A permanent solution to this problem is to replace the turf with ground cover (see page 114).

Moss spores, which are released during the summer, may allow moss to spread on lawns where the grass is weak and sparse. The spore-producing bodies develop well above the level of the moss foliage and on a well mown lawn are unlikely to survive to maturity; mosses can, however, reproduce from vegetative cells and the simple act of mowing or raking can spread moss about the lawn. When mowing always use a grass-box to collect mowings, and rake inwards towards the centre of moss patches.

Mosskillers

Moss grows most strongly during cool moist conditions in the autumn and spring and these are the best periods for applying chemical mosskillers. Lawn sands consisting of sulphate of ammonia, sulphate of iron and lime-free sand have been used to kill moss for many years and are still a useful means of control. Proportions vary in proprietary mixtures. A suitable formula is three parts sulphate of ammonia, one part calcined sulphate of iron and ten parts medium grade lime-free sand (not builders' sand). Apply at 4 oz per square yard during fine weather, ideally on a moist, dewy morning with a fine day ahead. Water the lawn 48 hours later if there has been no rain. One to two weeks later carefully rake out the blackened dead moss. Lawn sand is not a long-term control but it does stimulate grass growth, especially when applied in spring.

Dichlorophen and chloroxuron are effective chemical mosskillers and the active ingredients in some proprietary lawn moss eradicants. They are marketed as concentrated liquid formulations. Apply with a watering can as in illustration (a).

Moss control programme: autumn

a

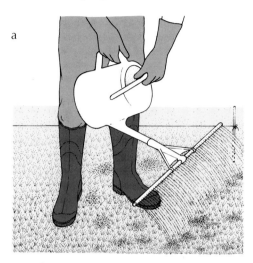

b

In early September apply a mosskiller, using a watering can with dribble bar (a). A week or two later rake out blackened and dead moss. Then apply an autumn turf fertilizer (b), followed by a top dressing of six parts sand, three parts sandy loam soil and one part granulated peat; apply it at the rate of 4 lb per square yard. If necessary, seed-in bare patches at 1 oz per square yard, then rake in.

Moss control programme: spring

c

d

In mid- to late March, apply a mosskiller during fine weather. One or two weeks later, rake out the dead moss, taking care not to disturb any young, developing stoloniferous grasses (c). Feed the lawn with a general lawn fertilizer. Then apply a light top dressing at the rate of 2–3 lb per square yard (d). As with the autumn programme, seed-in any bare patches at 1 oz per square yard and rake in.

Lawn pests

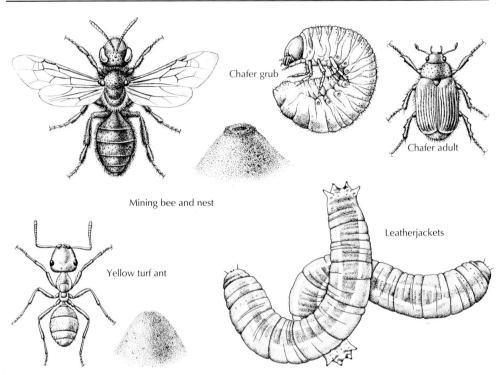

Chafer grub

Chafer adult

Mining bee and nest

Leatherjackets

Yellow turf ant

Lawn pests fall into two categories: those that feed on grass roots from below, thus weakening the turf; and those that leave a deposit of earth on the surface, which mars its appearance and hinders mowing.

Root-eating pests
Leatherjackets (*Tipula* spp) are grey, legless larvae of crane flies. The adults emerge and lay their eggs in the lawn in late summer. The larvae hatch in autumn and feed beneath the lawn over winter. The damage that they cause is first noticed during the following summer when irregular patches of yellow turf appear. These are most noticeable during dry periods.

The presence of larvae is often indicated by starlings feeding on the lawn. Check that larvae are present either by careful forking or by soaking a patch of lawn with water and covering it with sacking overnight to bring the larvae to the surface. Control them by watering with carbaryl, preferably during late September or October when the larvae are still small. Alternatively, apply carbaryl during mild, humid weather in early spring.

Chafer grubs (*Phyllopertha horticola*) are usually less numerous and less troublesome than leatherjackets. They have brown heads, creamy-white sickle-shaped bodies and three pairs of legs. The adults are large brown beetles and emerge in late May or early June to lay their eggs. Control the grubs by treating the turf with carbaryl in late May or June.

Earth-depositing pests
Earthworms (*Allolobothora* spp) feed on decaying organic matter and do not directly damage the turf. However, some species do cause indirect harm by depositing small heaps of muddy soil, called worm casts, on the lawn surface. Apart from being unsightly, these casts make the surface uneven and, if they become flattened may suppress the growth of finer grasses, leaving the turf sparser and liable to weed and moss infestation. Scatter the casts with a besom or a supple bamboo cane when they are dry and easily crumbled. Remove all mowings from the lawn since their presence en-

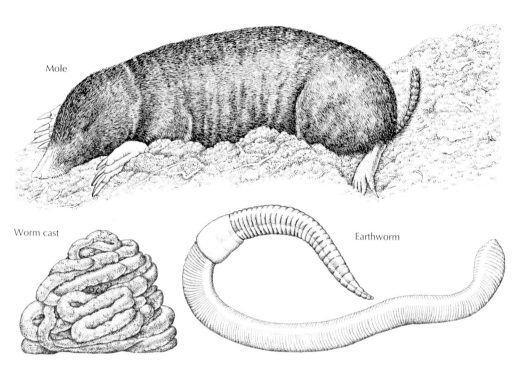

Mole

Worm cast

Earthworm

courages worms, as does liming. Casting is usually most troublesome during the autumn and early spring. These are also the best periods for worm control since the worms are then near the surface. Control them by watering the turf with carbaryl in the evening. This kills worms below the surface.

Moles (*Talpa europaea*) are solitary creatures that live in tunnels, feeding on worms and insects that fall in. The earth from the tunnels is deposited on the surface as molehills. On lighter soils the tunnels frequently collapse, leaving the lawn surface uneven. Moles also make shallow runs just below the surface, the soil being pushed up to form a ridge. Moles can cause considerable damage to newly seeded lawn sites and, if active nearby, should be dealt with before sowing.

The best method of controlling moles is to trap them. Use the Duffus trap for surface runs and the caliper type for deeper runs. When setting traps disturb the run as little as possible and after setting cover them with a pot or sacking to exclude all light. Smokes

may give some relief, but they usually only drive the mole away for a time, rather than killing it.

Ants (*Lasius* spp) can be troublesome in lawns since they deposit mounds of fine soil particles on the surface while they are building their nests. These mounds can be unsightly and make mowing difficult. Control them by applying ant powder or liquid to the nests. Alternatively apply HCH.

Mining bees (*Andrena* spp) nest in the soil and are solitary, with each female building a nest for herself. They are active in the spring and early summer. The nest consists of a vertical shaft up to 12 in deep, with side chambers in which the eggs are laid. The excavated earth forms a small conical mound, similar to the deposit from an ants' nest but with an entrance in the centre of the mound.

Mining bees are the same size as honey bees but have hairy bodies and do not sting. Since they are pollinating insects they are useful in the garden, but on lighter sandy soils they may be sufficiently numerous to become a temporary nuisance.

65

Lawn diseases 1

The most common symptom of an unhealthy lawn is discoloration of the turf. In most cases this is due to a cultural problem such as drought, poor aeration or build-up of thatch. There are, however, several diseases also causing this symptom that can kill, weaken, or disfigure large areas of turf. Therefore, it is very important to determine as early as possible whether discoloration is caused by a cultural problem or by a disease. If it is the latter then apply the recommended control measures as soon as possible.

Fungal diseases

Fairy rings are caused by certain soil-borne fungi. They show as one or more bands of lush dark green turf. These bands may be continuous or broken. During the summer and autumn, rings of spore-bearing toadstools or puffballs appear if the conditions are damp. The various fungi differ slightly in their symptoms. Some produce rings of toadstools without the rings of lusher grass; others a single ring of luxuriant grass.

The most troublesome and disfiguring species is *Marasmius oreades*. Its rings are composed of an outer and inner zone of vigorous dark green grass with a strip of brown, dead turf or bare soil between them. A dense mat of fungal threads permeates the soil, usually to a depth of 9 in, occasionally to 18 in. These threads are responsible for the death of the middle zone of grass from drought and starvation since they prevent water from reaching the roots.

To prevent new infections, rake up and burn toadstools and ensure that none of the matted turf and soil containing fungal threads is allowed to contaminate the rest of the lawn. If feasible, mow the area of infected grass separately and burn the cuttings. Wash the lawn mower with a garden disinfectant so as to prevent further spread of the fungus.

Fairy rings, particularly those due to *Marasmius oreades,* are very difficult to treat chemically, but some control may be achieved by applying certain formulations of dichlorophen with a label recommendation for this purpose.

For a fairy ring in the centre of a large lawn, employ the services of a professional gardener or contractor, with the appropriate certificates for usage, to use a commercial product for the control of the fungus, or better still, to strip and burn the turf to a distance of 30 cm outside the visually affected zones and treat the soil with a formalin solution before re-laying with fresh turf or re-sowing.

Fusarium patch (*Micronectriella nivalis,* syn *Fusarium nivale*) is a serious turf disease that occurs during mild moist conditions, usually during spring and autumn. It is also known as snow mould since it sometimes occurs after snow has fallen, particularly where the turf has been trodden on. The disease is first seen as small irregular patches of yellow grass which later turn brown and die. The spots may also enlarge and coalesce. In moist weather a white or pale pink cotton-like fungal growth may be noticeable around the perimeter of each discoloured patch.

Attacks are more likely to occur where there is poor aeration or following late summer feeding with nitrogenous fertilizers. Therefore do not feed with nitrogenous fertilizers later than August. There are a number of other measures that help to prevent the disease. Keep the grass as dry as possible by dispersing heavy morning dew with a besom or sack. Mow the lawn regularly, and scarify and aerate it to at least 3 in during September. Encourage free movement of air by removing overhanging bedding plants or other vegetation that are preventing the lawn from drying out. Finally, try not to tread on a snow-covered lawn.

To control apply fungicides containing benomyl, carbendazim or thiophanate-methyl.

Red thread (*Corticium fuciforme*) is a common fungal disease and can occur at any time of the year, but it is most troublesome during late summer and autumn. Also known as corticium disease, it causes patches of grass to turn a pinkish colour, particularly after rain or dew. These patches may persist and later turn white. Pink horn-like branching growths of fungus appear among the grass attached to leaves and stems, often binding them together. These growths can be quite gelatinous in humid conditions. They later dry and become brittle, and are then easily detached and carried by foot or mower to spread the infection. Red thread usually develops where

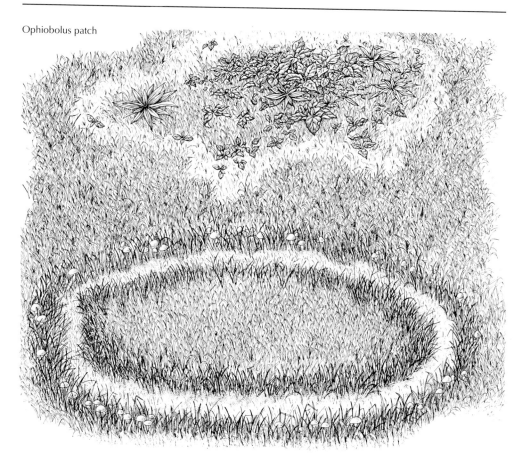

Ophiobolus patch

the turf is poorly aerated and low in vigour, particularly if it is deficient in nitrogen. The disease is unsightly but rarely kills grasses outright. Sometimes it persists for only a short time and bleached patches usually recover if the turf receives attention.

Feeding the lawn with sulphate of ammonia during spring and summer to improve the nitrogen level of the soil is often sufficient to control red thread. Scarify if there is a build-up of dead matter and aerate with hollow-tine tools. If the disease persists, apply those fungicides recommended for fusarium patch.

Dollar spot (*Sclerotinia homoeocarpa*) may be seen at any time of the year but is usually encountered during humid weather in late summer. It appears as small golden-brown or straw-coloured circular patches, 1–2 in in diameter. In heavy attacks the small patches may coalesce.

To control dollar spot apply those fungicides recommended for fusarium patch. In addition feed with sulphate of ammonia during the spring and summer to improve the nitrogen level of the soil and encourage vigour in the turf.

Lawn diseases 2

Lichen (*Peltigera canina*)

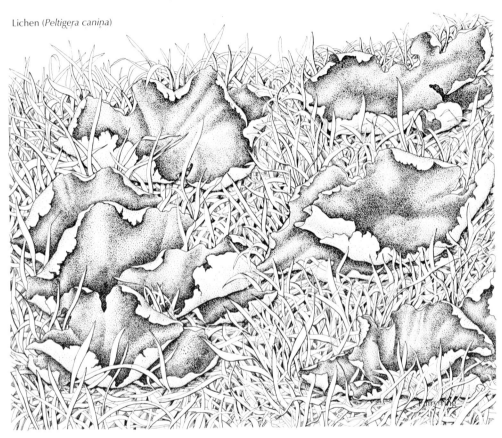

Ophiobolus patch (*Gaeumannomyces grami-nis* var *avenae,* syn *Ophiobolus graminis* var *avenae*) occasionally occurs on lawns during late summer or autumn. It shows as circular straw- or bronze-coloured depressions a few inches in diameter. These increase in size year by year and the central area where the grass has been killed becomes progressively colonized by weeds and coarser grasses. The disease is encouraged by wet conditions, high soil pH and heavy liming.

To control it, re-turf if the affected area is small. Help to prevent this disease by en-suring good drainage and aeration, and feed-ing with sulphate of ammonia during the spring and summer.

Toadstools may develop year after year if the soil underneath contains much woody debris. To control them, strip the turf and remove all debris. Toadstools may also occur scattered randomly on a lawn. Control these by sweeping them up.

Lichens, moulds and algae
Lichens are frequently mistaken for fungi, but are actually a combination of a fungus and an alga. They consist of overlapping leaf-like structures growing horizontally in the turf.

The commonest lichen to affect lawns is *Peltigera canina.* It is variable in colour, being a very dark green when moist and changing to grey-green or brown in dry weather. The upper surface of the lichen has a leathery tex-ture and the lower surface is spongy and white. Other species of *Peltigera,* differing in colour and appearance from *P. canina,* also occur in lawns, particularly in Scotland. Lichens flourish in poorly drained soil but

Fusarium patch (see page 66)

Toadstools
(*Marasmius oreades*)

MISCELLANEOUS PROBLEMS

Fertilizer scorch occurs as irregular patches of brown or blackened turf. It appears a few days after feeding and is caused by an excessive application of fertilizer or turf sand, or by applying them in dry weather. Always apply fertilizers and turf sands strictly according to the recommendations, and avoid overlap. Check the setting of spreaders before use.

Spilt fuel or oil causes small irregular brown patches. Check the mower for leaking carburettor or fuel pipes, and never refuel or attempt maintenance with the mower standing on the lawn.

Bitch urine damage occurs as small dead patches surrounded by a ring of dark green grass. Aerate damaged turf and water thoroughly and regularly to minimize the damage and encourage grass to recolonize affected patches. Damage can be avoided by watering the area copiously immediately after contamination has occurred.

Buried debris often causes irregular patches of yellow or brown grass since it impedes root development. Strip back the turf to remove the debris. Then add fresh soil to restore the level, and replace the turf.

may occur on well drained turf if there is surface compression with stickiness after rain. They are often found under trees since they favour shade and impoverished soil.

To control lichens, rake out growths and treat affected areas with a proprietary product containing dichlorophen. If iron sulphate is used to control moss it should give incidental control of the lichen. Give attention to drainage, aeration and feeding to prevent them recurring.

Blue-green algae and gelatinous lichens are usually dark green to black in colour. They are identified by the formation of a slippery gelatinous layer on the lawn. They appear on turf whose surface is continually damp from poor drainage, compaction or drips.

To control them apply a proprietary product containing dichlorophen. If iron sulphate is used on the lawn to control moss it should give incidental control of the growths. After application check for blocked drains or compaction, and drain or spike the lawn accordingly.

Slime moulds are organisms intermediate between bacteria and fungi. Their colour is white to yellow and they produce small grey fruiting bodies which release masses of purple-brown spores. They occasionally seem to be smothering grass, particularly in late spring or early autumn following heavy rain. The growths are superficial, although very unsightly, and do not harm the grass.

Once the spores have been released the growths usually disappear fairly rapidly of their own accord. Nevertheless, it is worth while hastening the process by washing the spore masses away with a stream of water.

Renovation: neglected lawns

When faced with the prospect of reclaiming a neglected lawn the first step is to examine the turf carefully. If coarse grasses and troublesome weeds or mosses are predominant reclamation may not be possible. In this case the best policy is to destroy the old lawn and make a new one. If, however, there is a pre-dominance of finer grasses with patches of coarser grasses and weeds present, then reclamation can be carried out.

The best time to begin renovations is in spring because there will then be several months of active growth ahead. If faced with a neglected lawn in late spring or summer

Programme of renovation

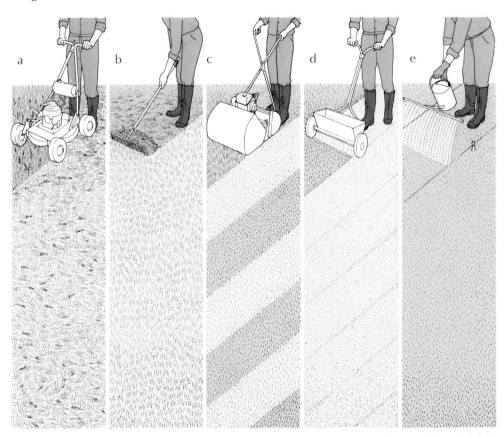

The first step is to cut back the lawn in spring to about 2 in from soil level (a). This removes dead grass, weed stalks and seedheads, leaving the grass fresher in appearance. For this first cut use a rotary-bladed mower, which can be hired, or use shears if the area is small. Do not mow too closely at this stage since this can weaken the grass and make it liable to infestation from weeds and moss. After mowing rake thoroughly to remove the cuttings and any accumulated dead material and debris present on the lawn (b).

Leave the lawn for a week or so and then mow with a cylinder mower (c), setting the blades as high as possible. Progressively reduce the height of the blades over the following two to three weeks to re-establish normal levels of cut and frequency (see also page 50). Then feed with a general purpose spring turf fertilizer (d). Apply a weedkiller follow the recommended programme below, but do not apply weedkillers or feed with fertilizers high in nitrogen after August. If the work is to start in late autumn cut the lawn back to 2 in but do not attempt to reduce it to normal levels until spring because this would weaken the turf and leave it more susceptible to infestation from weeds and mosses. After cutting back scarify the lawn to remove dead material and debris. Then spike where necessary and apply an autumn turf fertilizer. The following spring continue the process of reclamation with the recommended programme given below.

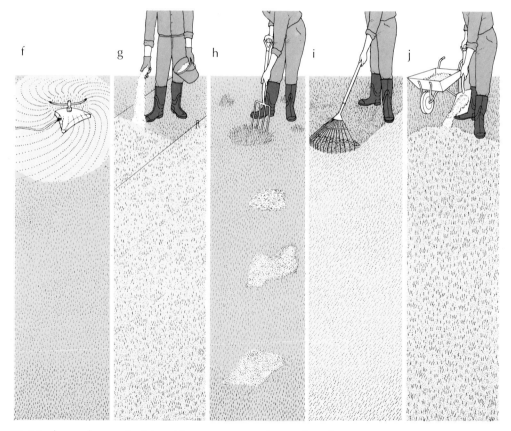

10–14 days afterwards (e), taking care to avoid any recently seeded areas.

During April seed-in any bare patches or sparsely grassed areas, and do not neglect irrigation (f) during dry periods.

In early July feed with sulphate of ammonia (g) to keep the grass growing strongly. Do not do this earlier than five to six weeks after applying the general turf fertilizer dressing. Re-examine the lawn in late August or early September for signs of unhealthy turf and worm activity.

In early September fork out patches of coarse grass (h) and re-seed. In colder areas do this in late August. During early to mid-September scarify and aerate where required (i). Then top-dress (j) and apply an autumn turf fertilizer. This completes the programme of renovation. The following spring resume a normal programme of maintenance.

Renovation: lawn repairs 1

All repairs should be carried out during cool, moist weather in autumn or spring since this is when the lawn is most able to recover rapidly. In many cases, re-turfing or re-seeding will be necessary. When doing this ensure that the turf or seed used is of the same quality as the existing grass.

Broken edges
First, mark out a square of turf that encloses the damaged edge. Cut this free and slide it away from the rest of the lawn until the damaged part of the turf lies completely beyond the edge of the lawn. Then trim off the broken edge cleanly and fill the gap, either with a small piece of turf or by adding soil and then sowing grass seeds. Alternatively, after cutting out the damaged turf, reverse it so that the broken edge faces inwards towards the lawn. Add soil to fill the gap created by the broken edge and then sow grass seed. This approach does require, however, that the turf be cut very accurately to a square or rectangle.

Bare patches
These may develop following various forms of physical disturbance or damage. Examples include excessive wear, compaction, weed removal, bitch scald, oil drip or fertilizer spillage. Always attempt to identify the cause of damage before repairing, otherwise the problem may well recur. To repair the damage remove the smallest square of turf that encloses the affected patch. Then break up the soil surface with a fork, apply a fertilizer and lay new turves. Alternatively, after removing the affected square add ordinary top-soil to restore the level and then sow grass seed, lightly raking until most of it is covered.

Thin, sparse turf
Poor turf growth is usually caused by compaction, poor aeration, malnutrition or drought. These problems can be rectified by scarifying, aerating, feeding or irrigating the affected turf, as necessary. If, however, these measures fail to improve the turf, then poor drainage or excessively acid soil conditions may be responsible.
Poor drainage is indicated by water remaining at or near the surface, even after spiking

and hollow-tine aeration has been carried out. If this occurs the drainage system is likely to be blocked or silted up. Check for the presence of overgrown outfalls in nearby ditches, and clear them of all debris. If the outfalls are clear try to locate and clear the main drain by digging a narrow trench across the wettest section of the lawn.
Excessively acid soil can cause some nutrients to become chemically "locked" in the soil and so be unavailable to plants. If tests show that the soil pH is below 5 apply a light dressing of lime in the form of calcium carbonate (either ground chalk or ground limestone) during the late autumn or early winter. Apply it at 2 oz per square yard. However, lime is slow to penetrate into the soil and the subsequent increased surface alkalinity can encourage worms and the growth of coarser grasses and weeds. If in any doubt about whether lime should be applied, seek professional advice.

Coarse grasses
Coarser grasses are usually less susceptible to drought and compaction than the finer grasses, and become more prominent and unsightly as the lawn declines in vigour.

The most satisfactory approach is to remove coarser patches of grass in spring or autumn, and re-turf or re-seed with a suitable grass seed mixture.

Failing that, the best way to weaken, and eventually kill, coarser grasses is by regular mowing. Before mowing, lightly brush or rake the lawn. Alternatively, fit a rotating brush attachment to the mower. Creeping stems of coarse grasses will be lifted, which allows them to be more readily severed by the mower blades. The spread of small patches of coarse grasses can be checked, and their growth weakened, by slashing them periodically with an edging tool or spade, making parallel cuts about an inch apart.

The most common coarse grass is annual meadow grass. Discourage it by regular feeding to promote vigour in the more desirable grasses. Lightly rake patches of this grass, or use a drag-brush, during May and June to lift the seeding heads before mowing. For a description of annual meadow grass, see page 23.

Repairing broken edges

1 Mark out a square piece of turf enclosing the broken edge and cut the turf free with a half-moon tool.

2 Use a spade to lift the turf slightly and sever it from the underlying roots and soil.

3 Slide it forwards until the damaged part of the turf lies beyond the border of the lawn.

4 With the half-moon tool trim off the broken edge so that it is flush with the border of the lawn.

5 Fill the gap left by the broken edge, either by laying a small piece of turf or by adding soil and sowing seed.

Renovation: lawn repairs 2

Replacing bare patches

1 Mark out the smallest square of turf that encloses the bare patch, and cut it out and remove it.

2 Break up the underlying soil surface with a hand fork or garden fork.

3 Cover the patch with turves and apply a sandy top-dressing mixture, brushing it into the crevices.

4 The exposed area may also be renovated by adding top-soil and then sowing grass seeds.

BUMPS AND HOLLOWS

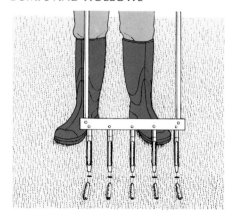

Bumps show as bare or sparsely grassed patches where the grass has been killed or weakened by being repeatedly cut too close by the mower. Eliminate minor bumps by hollow-tining at intervals until the site is level (see page 45). For larger bumps cut through their centre with a spade or turf-cutting tool. Peel back the two flaps of turf and remove some soil. Replace the flaps and fill the cracks with sifted soil or a sandy top-dressing mixture. If much soil has to be removed there is a danger that there will be too little top-soil remaining. check this and, if necessary, remove the sub-soil to a depth of 6 in, replacing with top-soil.

Hollows show as patches of grass that are lusher, greener and longer than the rest of the lawn. They may be caused by the gradual decomposition of bulky organic matter, inadequate firming when the lawn was created, or they may be caused by the action of moles. Eliminate minor hollows by periodically applying a light top-dressing adding no more than 1/2 in at any one time. Where the hollows are larger or deeper, cut the turf and roll it back in sections. Add ordinary top-soil in layers, firming each layer and checking its level with a levelling board. When the level has been restored, replace the turf, check the level again and then dress the cracks with sifted soil or a sandy top-dressing mixture. Where there are considerable surface irregularities, it will take some time to even out all of them. In this case raise the height of mowing until the modifications have been completed.

Introduction

Ground cover is the utilization of ornamental plants to provide a low canopy of foliage that is sufficiently dense to prevent weeds from establishing beneath it. Planting ground cover enables a gardener to overcome two commonly encountered problems: what to do with those parts of the garden where few plants except weeds will survive, and how to keep a garden looking neat when there is insufficient time for routine maintenance such as weeding and mowing.

Obvious problem sites that benefit from ground cover are deep shade under trees, steep dry banks, areas where the drainage is poor, and open ground or bare patches of earth between plants, for example in shrub borders. All these areas can quickly become colonized by weeds, but this can be avoided by planting low-growing ground cover plants since, once established, they compete for moisture and nutrients, and block the light. This prevents weeds from growing beneath the canopy of their foliage. On uneven areas such as steep banks, planting ground cover instead of grass saves time-consuming and arduous mowing.

There is no straightforward division between plants that are suitable for use as ground cover and those that are not. As with all other plants, success often depends on careful site preparation, planting and maintenance during the early stages of growth when the plants are trying to establish themselves in difficult conditions. However, the following general considerations should be borne in mind when selecting ground cover plants for the garden.

Choose plants that have a low, spreading habit and are sufficiently dense to suppress germinating seedlings and invasive weed growth. They should require little maintenance and be relatively permanent, that is, able to survive in good condition for at least five years. Annuals and biennials are not suitable because they need to be replaced frequently. Similarly, many herbaceous perennials are unsuitable because, although they provide dense cover in the summer, they die down in the autumn allowing weeds to become established. Lawn grass provides good cover, but it needs a lot of maintenance and is not weed free.

The specific cultural conditions where the ground cover is to be planted should also be taken into account. The plants must be able to tolerate the growing conditions of the particular site, for example, shade, dryness, coastal exposure or alkaline soil. They must also be hardy enough to survive the winter in that locality.

The best plants are fast growing and vigorous, and will provide a good cover at economical spacings within one or two years of planting. Some slower-growing evergreens need two seasons to provide a complete cover unless they are planted at half the recommended distances, but this is, of course, expensive.

Finally, one of the most important aspects influencing the choice of plants is their appearance. They should have an attractive shape and colour with good foliage. Decorative flowers or fruits are a further advantage.

The following pages give details of plants that are suitable for use as ground cover. They are divided into four groups according to characteristics such as speed of growth, density of cover and habit of growth of the plants. This last characteristic is described by the following terms:

Clump plants are always deciduous and grow in spring, either from winter buds or from rosettes that have over-wintered.

Colonizers are grouped as either carpeters or suckers.

Carpeters are plants that take root from their nodes as these spread outwards, that is, they take root from above ground.

Suckers spread by means of underground shoots, suckers or stolons.

Hummock plants have a low central stem from which radiate a large number of branches. The stems may occasionally root down, and the plant becomes a carpeter.

Where references are made to the approximate height of the plants, this is the height when not in flower. The recommended planting distances should give 75–100 per cent cover in one to two years, but this is only a rough guide since soil, situation and climate may considerably affect the rate of growth. The various methods of propagating individual plants are also indicated. For a general discussion on propagation, see page 113.

Clump plant (*Brunnera macrophylla*)

Carpeter (*Hedera helix* var *hibernica*)

Suckering plant (*Omphalodes cappadocica*)

Hummock plant (*Arabis albida*)

Specific plants: group one

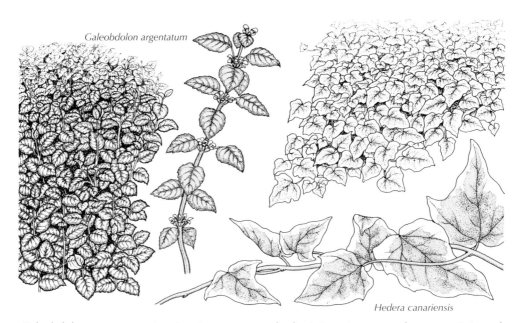

Galeobdolon argentatum

Hedera canariensis

Galeobdolon argentatum (syn Lamium galeobdolon 'Variegatum')
Height: 6–9 in
An herbaceous perennial that is best grown in cool, moist conditions, such as under trees or larger shrubs, where it provides attractive dense cover. Its long trailing stems root freely and, in more open sites, it can quickly become invasive and smother smaller plants. Its foliage resembles that of a nettle in shape, and is dark green marbled with white. In early summer it produces 12 in high spikes of small yellow flowers. Planting distance is 24–36 in; propagation is by division.

Hedera canariensis 'Azorica'
Height: 6–9 in
A strong-growing ivy of carpeting habit that is tolerant of both deep shade and full sun. The leaves are large and dark green. 'Gloire de Marengo' (syn 'Variegata') has variegated white, grey and green leaves; it is a popular house plant but not reliably hardy in colder areas. Planting distance is 36–48 in; propagation is by division, layering or cuttings.

Hedera colchica
Height: 6–9 in
An ivy that grows well in both sun and deep shade. It is native to southwestern Asia and has large, thick, dark green leaves. The form 'Dentata' has larger, paler green leaves; 'Dentata Variegata' has creamy-yellow leaf margins; and the leaves of 'Sulphur Heart' have gold centres. Planting distance is 36–48 in; propagation is by division or cuttings.

Hedera helix (Common ivy)
Height: 6–12 in
A native species that grows strongly and takes root as it spreads. Its small yellow-green flowers are followed by fleshy black fruits. The dark-leaved Irish ivy (var hibernica) is the best form for dense, rapid cover. Many other varieties provide good cover but may need initial pinching to encourage branching. They include 'Silver Queen' and 'Glacier', which have white variegations on the leaves; 'Gold Heart', which has yellow variegations; and 'Caenwoodiana' and 'Green Ripple', which have attractive leaf shapes. All these varieties can be grown in full sun except in habitats that are naturally hot and dry. Green-leaved forms provide excellent cover in shade or under trees, but they should be kept clear of stems or trunks. Planting distance is 36–48 in (24–36 in for variegated forms); propagation is by division, layering or cuttings.

Group 1 characteristics
Evergreen; colonizers; high density
cover; rapid growth; possibly invasive
in fertile soils

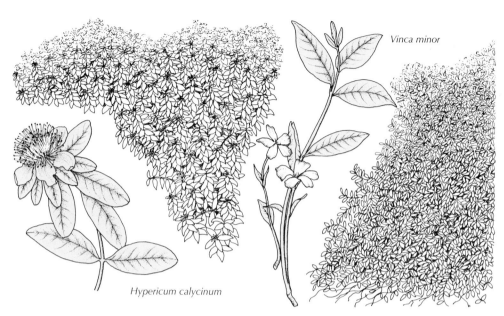

Vinca minor

Hypericum calycinum

Hypericum calycinum (St John's wort)
Height: 9–12 in
A low-growing shrub that spreads to form a
matted carpet of leafy suckering growths. It is
an excellent cover plant for sun or shade on
any well drained soil, and is particularly suitable for light, sandy soils. The large bright
yellow flowers are solitary and appear during
mid- to late summer. In colder winters some
foliage may be lost. To obtain the densest
cover trim this plant back annually in April.
Note that St John's wort can occasionally
become invasive in more fertile soils. Planting
distance is 15–18 in; propagation is by division, seeds or cuttings.

Vinca major (Larger periwinkle)
Height: 6–9 in
A shrubby carpeting or trailing plant that has
good shade tolerance and provides excellent
dense cover except on poorly drained soils
and very dry exposed habitats. Its star-shaped
flowers are blue or white and appear in
spring. 'Elegantissima' (syn 'Variegata') has
leaves with creamy-yellow margins and pale
green blotches; the flowers are pale purple. It
is slightly less vigorous than the parent. *V.
major* var *oxyloba*, on the other hand, is a
very vigorous sub-species that forms a dense

rampant cover. Planting distance is 18 in
(24 in for var *oxyloba*); propagation is by division, layering or stem cuttings.

Vinca minor (Lesser periwinkle)
Height: 4–6 in
A smaller-leaved species than *V. major* (see
above), but nevertheless a very effective
ground cover in similar conditions. It also
tolerates both deep shade and full sun. Its
flowers are blue; *V. minor alba* is a white-
flowered form. There are several other forms
with variegated foliage and single or double
flowers, for example 'Argentea Variegata'
and 'Variegata Aurea'. The plant may need
trimming back in April if it becomes untidy.
Planting distance is 15–18 in (less on very
poor soils); propagation is by division, layering or stem cuttings.

Waldsteinia ternata
Height: 3–4 in
A carpeting plant that grows equally well in
full sun or deep shade, on either moist or drier
soils. Its leaves are glossy and dark green, and
in late spring it carries small bright-yellow
flowers that resemble those of strawberries.
Planting distance is 12 in; propagation is by
division or seeds.

Specific plants: group two

Anthemis cupaniana
Height: 9 in
A hummock-forming, occasionally carpeting plant that needs a sunny, well drained site; it may not thrive during wet winters in areas that have high rainfall. The foliage is silvery-grey and finely divided; the flowers resemble daisies, both in colour and in shape. Planting distance is 18–24 in; propagation is by division or seeds.

Arabis albida (now *A. caucasica*)
Height: 5 in
An herbaceous plant that grows best on a sunny site with good soil; in shade or poorly drained areas it becomes sparse and straggly. It forms hummocks of loosely rosetted grey-green leaves, and in spring short-stemmed heads of white flowers appear. 'Flore Plena' has double flowers; 'Variegata' has cream margins to its leaves. Planting distance is 9–15 in; propagation is by division or cuttings.

Arctostaphylos uva-ursi
Height: 6 in
A spreading shrub that is suitable for acid soils only and should be grown in sun or light shade. The leaves are small, glossy and dark green. Tiny white bell-shaped flowers appear in spring, and are followed by small red berries. Its trailing branches will take root if the soil is moist and rich in humus. On sandy soils it needs careful planting but grows well once it has established. Planting distance is 15 in; propagation is by cuttings, division (which requires great care), layering or seeds.

Asarum europaeum
Height: 3–4 in
An herbaceous carpeting plant that is most suited to cool, moist, shady conditions. The leaves are dark and glossy and the flowers, which have no ornamental value, are almost always hidden by the foliage. *A. canadense*, *A. caudatum* and *A. shuttleworthii* are also good for ground cover, though they are not quite as dense. Planting distance is 9–12 in; propagation is by division or seeds.

Aubrieta deltoidea
Height: 3–4 in
A sun-loving plant that prefers well drained sites and an alkaline soil. It forms hummocks of densely matted stems which, in moist conditions, will take root if not cut back annually. In spring the soft grey-green leaves are hidden by numerous flowerheads. There are many varieties with red, carmine, pink, lilac or purple flowers. It is apt to become straggly unless trimmed back in spring after flowering. Planting distance is 12 in; propagation is by division or cuttings.

Aurinia saxatilis (syn *Alyssum saxatilis*)
Height: 9 in
A shrubby stemmed perennial that grows best in sunny, well drained sites. In spring, dense corymbs of golden-yellow flowers hide its long, narrow, grey-green leaves. In moist conditions it is inclined to become straggly if not cut back each spring after flowering. 'Citrina' has pale sulphur-yellow flowers. Planting distance is 15 in; propagation is by division, cuttings or seeds.

Ballota pseudodictamnus
Height: 9 in
A densely branched sub-shrub that needs full sun and a well drained site. The leaves are small, heart-shaped and woolly, and appear to be grey-white. In summer tubular white flowers with purple spots are borne in whorls. The branches may die back in colder winters; they should, in any case, be pruned back hard in spring. Planting distance is 15 in; propagation is by seeds, division or cuttings.

Bergenia spp and hybrids
Height: 6–12 in
A group of carpeting plants that are tolerant of sun or shade but are less satisfactory on drier soils or in deeper shade under trees. They spread slowly by means of woody rhizomes, and have large, often glossy, dark green leaves. Some develop purple tints in winter; the leaves of others, for example 'Ballawley' and *B. ciliata,* may be damaged in severe winters. Their long fleshy stems carry clusters of bell-shaped flowers in spring; these are rich pink on 'Morgenrote', mauve-crimson on *B. cordifolia* 'Purpurea', clear pink on *B.* x *schmidtii* and white on 'Silberlicht'. Planting distance is 9–24 in; propagation is by division.

Group 2 characteristics
Evergreen; hummock-forming or
colonizers; medium to high density
cover; slow to medium growth

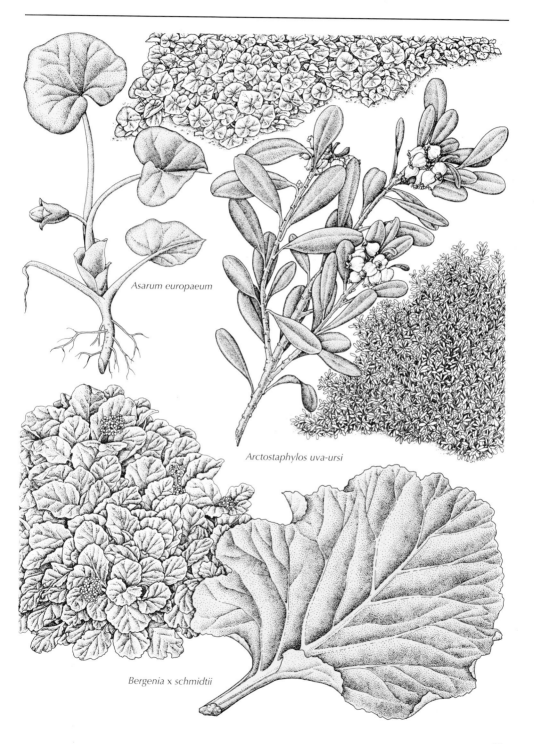

Asarum europaeum

Arctostaphylos uva-ursi

Bergenia x schmidtii

Specific plants: group two

Calluna vulgaris (Heather)
Height: 6–18 in
A hummock-forming shrub that provides a good dense cover in sunny or lightly shaded sites on acid soils. The spreading stems will take root if the soil conditions are rich and moist. There are many varieties, often with attractively coloured foliage. Erect flower spikes are borne in late summer. Clip the plant every spring to maintain a compact habit. Planting distance is 9–18 in; propagation is by division, layering or cuttings.

Ceanothus thyrsiflorus var. repens
Height: 36 in or more
One of the hardiest evergreen species of *Ceanothus*, and an attractive, densely spreading shrub for sunny banks or sites bordering walls. It has small dark green leaves, and pale to mid-blue flowers are borne in spring. Planting distance is 36–48 in; propagation is by cuttings.

Cerastium tomentosum
Height: 6 in
A rampant, invasive plant, but useful in sunny, dry situations. It forms dense mats of silvery foliage, and carries numerous small white flowers in early summer. Planting distance is 15 in; propagation is by cuttings, division or seeds.

Cistus spp
Height: 18–24 in
A hummock-forming group of shrubs, several of which are low-growing and provide a dense cover if planted in well drained soil in full sun. They may suffer winter damage in colder climates. Among the most reliable are *C. parviflorus, C. lusitanicus decumbens* and *C. salvifolius* 'Prostratus'. The pink or white flowers resemble single roses. Trim back straggly growth in April, but do not cut back into old wood. Planting distance is 24–30 in; propagation is by cuttings or seeds.

Convolvulus cneorum
Height: 18–24 in
A spreading shrub from southern Europe that needs full sun and good drainage. Its shoots and small lanceolate leaves are covered with silky hairs, which make the plant appear silver. The delicate flowers, which are pink in bud and white when open, are carried in terminal clusters. It may not survive in colder areas. Planting distance is 18–24 in; propagation is by cuttings or seeds.

Cotoneaster 'Gnom'
Height: 3–4 in
A rapidly growing prostrate plant and, with 'Skogholm', the best of the named ground-covering cotoneasters. Other cotoneasters include *C. congestus,* which is also 3–4 in high and dense but slower growing; *C. microphyllus,* which reaches 12–18 in, has a dense mounded growth and in good conditions will root; and *C. conspicuus* 'Decorus', which forms dense spreading hummocks up to 5 ft high. All are evergreen with small white flowers and red or crimson berries, and prefer a sunny or lightly shaded site. Planting distance is 18–24 in (72 in for 'Decorus'); propagation is by cuttings, seeds or division.

Cytisus × *kewensis*
Height: 12 in
A deciduous but densely stemmed shrub that requires full sun and a well drained soil. It has small grey-green leaves and small yellow flowers that are borne profusely in spring. Planting distance is 24 in; propagation is by cuttings.

Cytisus scoparius ssp *maritimus*
Height: 12–15 in
A vigorous, densely branched prostrate form of common broom. It requires the same conditions as *Cytisus* × *kewensis* (see above) and bears similar flowers. Planting distance is 36 in; propagation is by cuttings.

Daboecia cantabrica (Irish heath)
Height: 15–18 in
A fine-leaved but densely shrubby evergreen that requires full sun and grows best in moister, light soils that are acid and rich in humus. Its short spikes of bell-like flowers are borne during the summer months. 'Atropurpurea' has deep red-purple flowers; those of *alba* are white. Trim it back in spring before new growth begins. Planting distance is 15–18 in; propagation is by division, cuttings or layers.

Cotoneaster 'Gnom'

Ceanothus thyrsiflorus
var. repens

Daboecia cantabrica

Cytisus × kewensis

Specific plants: group two

Gaultheria shallon

Genista hispanica

Dryas octopetala

Erica herbacea
'Springwood White'

Dianthus spp
Height: 6–9 in
Mainly low-growing sub-shrubs that provide useful high-density cover. They flower freely in full sun on well drained alkaline soils. The best varieties for ground cover are 'Charles Musgrave', 'Dad's Favourite' and 'Mrs. Sinkins'. Planting distance is 9–12 in; propagation is by division or cuttings.

Dryas octopetala
Height: 2–3 in
A shrubby evergreen that needs full sun and a well drained soil. It forms a dense, though initially slow-growing, carpet of prostrate, rooting stems. The leaves are small and dark green, and its white flowers are followed by fluffy seedheads. Planting distance is 12–15 in; propagation is by cuttings, seeds or division, which requires care.

Erica spp
Height: 9–18 in
Good cover plants that grow best in open, sunny situations on lighter, acid soils that are high in humus, but some may tolerate partial shade and slight alkalinity if the soil is enriched with leaf-mould or peat. They have a dense branching shrubby growth, and many bear excellent flowers. *E. herbacea* (better known as *E. carnea*) is winter-flowering; quick-spreading varieties include 'Springwood White' and 'Springwood Pink'. *E.* × *darleyensis* also flowers in winter; the best varieties are 'Silberschmelze' and 'Furzey'. *E. vagans* is summer-flowering and requires acid soil; varieties include 'Diana Hornibrook', with pale rose-pink flowers; 'Mrs. D. F. Maxwell', with deep pink flowers; and 'St. Keverne' with bright pink flowers. Trim ericas in early spring to keep their growth compact. Planting distance is 12–15 in; propagation is by division, cuttings or layers.

Euonymus fortunei var *radicans*
Height: 9 in
A woody, carpeting evergreen that provides dense cover in sun or shade in all except poorly drained sites. It has small dark oval leaves and takes root from its stem. 'Kewensis' is a 3–4 in high, slower-growing variety. Planting distance is 12–18 in ('Kewensis' 9 in);

propagation is by either division or cuttings.

Euonymus fortunei f *carrierei*
Height: 24 in
A shrubby form of *E. fortunei* var *radicans* that has larger leaves and requires the same growing conditions (see above). The best varieties for ground cover are 'Coloratus', 'Emerald 'n' Gold', 'Silver Queen' and 'Variegatus'. Planting distance is 30 in; propagation is by cuttings.

× *Gaulnettya wisleyensis*
Height: 24–36 in
A suckering evergreen shrub that is a hybrid between *Gaultheria shallon* and *Pernettya mucronata*. It provides fairly dense cover in sun or shade and grows best in acid soils that are rich in humus. Small white bell-shaped flowers are borne in late spring, followed by purple fruits. Planting distance is 24 in; propagation is by division or cuttings.

Gaultheria shallon
Height: 36–48 in
A strong-growing, suckering, evergreen shrub that prefers an acid, humus-rich soil, though it is a useful cover plant for dry shaded areas under trees. The leaves are dark and glossy, and small clusters of pink bell-shaped flowers are borne in summer. Planting distance is 36 in; propagation is by division or cuttings.

Genista hispanica
Height: 24 in
A deciduous, densely branched and spiny shrub that bears numerous terminal clusters of small golden-yellow flowers in early summer. All genistas require full sun and a well drained soil. *G. lydia* is about 12 in high with low arching grey-green stems and linear leaves. *G. sagittalis* has winged stems and a prostrate or low arching habit. It forms a dense cover 9 in high. *G. delphinensis* is similar in appearance to *G. sagittalis* but smaller. *G. pilosa* is a shrubby, densely branched species that will tolerate light shade. It grows to a height of about 12 in and flowers profusely in early summer; the variety 'Procumbens' is a prostrate carpet-rooting form, 3–4 in high. Planting distance is 24 in for *G. hispanica*, 18 in for *G. lydia*, 12 in for

Specific plants: group two

G. sagittalis, 15 in for G. pilosa and G. pilosa 'Procumbens'. Propagation is by cuttings or seeds (by division for G. pilosa 'Procumbens').

× Halimiocistus sahucii
Height: 12 in

A low, spreading evergreen shrub that needs full sun and a well drained soil. The white flowers are similar in appearance to those of the dog rose but smaller, and are produced prolifically for a short period in summer. It is hardy except in very cold areas. Planting distance is 24 in; propagation is by cuttings.

Hebe albicans
Height: 12 in

An evergreen shrub that provides dense cover. It has grey foliage, and small spikes of white flowers appear in summer. 'Pewter Dome' is an attractive variety. Other hebes suitable for ground cover are H. rakaiensis and H. vernicosa, which are 18–24 in high, and H. pinguifolia 'Pagei', which grows 6–9 in high. 'Pagei' has small blue-grey leaves and white flowers and is carpet-rooting in richer, moist soils. These hebes need full sun and well drained soil, and are hardy except in very cold areas and severe winters. Planting distance is 18 in for H. albicans, 24 in for H. rakaiensis and H. vernicosa, and 15 in for 'Pagei'. Propagation is by cuttings, occasionally by seeds.

Helianthemum hybrids
Height: 6–9 in

A woody-stemmed, low-growing, spreading group of evergreens that require full sun and well drained soil. They have wiry stems and dark or grey-green foliage and provide good cover, particularly on sunny banks. The best varieties include 'Rhodanthe Carneum', 'Wisley Pink', 'Wisley Primrose' and H. nummularium 'Amy Baring', which is more prostrate and bears orange flowers. Planting distance is 18 in; propagation is by cuttings.

Hypericum cerastioides
Height: 3 in

A carpeting shrub that needs a sunny situation and well drained soil. It has grey leaves and yellow flowers. Planting distance is 12 in; propagation is by division or cuttings.

Hypericum × moseranum
Height: 18 in

A suckering shrub that provides good cover on all soils in sun or light shade. It has ovate, dark evergreen leaves and bears large single yellow flowers during the summer. It may be damaged by severe winters but regrows strongly from ground level. Planting distance is 18–21 in; propagation is by division or cuttings.

Iberis sempervirens
Height: 9–12 in

An evergreen shrub that provides good cover in sunny, well drained sites. It has small dark green leaves and arching, spreading stems, which root in moist conditions. Small heads of white flowers are borne in late spring. 'Snowflake' is a compact, densely leaved variety. Planting distance is 12–15 in; propagation is usually by cuttings.

Juniperus spp
Height: 6–9 in except where indicated

A group of evergreen, bushy trees and shrubs, several of which have arching mounded growth, or a low-spreading or prostrate habit. They grow best in full sun on well drained soils, particularly chalk. Suitable junipers include J. communis spp depressa; J. communis var jackii and the varieties 'Depressa Aurea', 'Effusa' and 'Repanda'. J. conferta provides rapid dense cover and is tolerant of light shade and sandy soils. J. horizontalis has a medium growth rate and is initially less dense than J. conferta; its varieties include 'Bar Harbor' and 'Glauca'. J. sabina var tamariscifolia forms a dense mounded bushy cover 15–18 in high. It is tolerant of light shade but is rather slow-growing. J. × media 'Pfitzeriana' forms dense cover 36 in high. It is tolerant of shade except in its golden variegated forms, which are less vigorous and require full sun. Planting distance is 18–24 in except for J. sabina var tamariscifolia (24–30 in) and J. × media 'Pfitzeriana', (48–72 in). Propagation is by cuttings or layering.

Leucothoe fontanesiana
Height: 36 in

An excellent cover plant in light or deep shade, on acid soils that are rich in humus.

Hebe pinguifolia 'Pagei'   Juniperus conferta

It has long arching stems and dark lustrous evergreen leaves. Pendulous white waxy flowers are produced on the undersides of the stems in June. The plant spreads by means of underground shoots. Planting distance is 36 in; propagation is usually by division or cuttings.

Lithodora diffusa (syn *Lithospermum diffusum*)
Height: 9 in
An evergreen shrub that grows best in full sun on good acid soils. It has small ovate dark green leaves, and deep blue flowers are borne in summer. Suitable varieties include 'Grace Ward', whose flowers are slightly larger, and 'Heavenly Blue'. Planting distance is 12 in; propagation is by cuttings.

Lonicera pileata
Height: 18 in
A small-leaved evergreen shrub with a strong horizontal branching habit that gives dense cover in sun or shade on any well drained soil. Inconspicuous yellow-green flowers are borne in spring. They are followed by attractive purple berries. The leaves are pale to mid-green, and some foliage may be lost in colder winters. Planting distance is 24 in; propagation is by cuttings, layering or seeds.

Mahonia aquifolium
Height: 24 in
An evergreen suckering shrub that will tolerate shade and drier soils if well mulched. It has glossy dark pinnate leaves, each with between five and nine spine-toothed leaflets. Dense clusters of small fragrant yellow flowers are borne in spring and are followed by blue-black berries. Cut the plant back annually in April to encourage denser growth. Planting distance is 24 in; propagation is by division, seeds or root cuttings.

Specific plants: group two

Pachysandra terminalis

Prunus laurocerasus

Pachysandra terminalis
Height: 3–4 in
An evergreen shrubby plant that provides excellent ground cover in dry shade and under trees in acid or alkaline soils. It spreads by underground stolons to form a low carpet of short densely leaved stems. Terminal spikes of small white flowers appear in spring. 'Variegata' is less vigorous and is more suitable for lighter shade. Planting distance is 12 in; propagation is by division or cuttings.

Pernettya mucronata
Height: 24–36 in
A densely leaved evergreen suckering shrub that requires acid soils and grows best in sun but will tolerate shade. It has small white axillary bell-shaped flowers followed by berries, which range in colour from white to dark purple. *P. prostrata* ssp *pentlandii* requires similar growing conditions but has denser,

lower growth. Planting distance is 24 in; propagation is by division or cuttings.

Phlomis fruticosa
Height: 36 in
An attractive evergreen shrub from the Mediterranean region that needs full sun, warm sheltered conditions and a well drained soil. It is particularly suitable for dry sunny banks. It has ovate grey-green woolly leaves, and whorls of yellow flowers appear on the upper stems in summer. Planting distance is 30 in; propagation is by cuttings or seeds.

Potentilla fruticosa
Height: 15–18 in
A deciduous shrub that grows well in any open sunny site, except those that are poorly drained or very dry. It has several varieties with a dense spreading habit suitable for ground cover. They include var *mandschurica*,

Potentilla fruticosa

var *farreri,* 'Beesii' and 'Longacre'. They have slender twiggy branches and small deeply cut leaves. White, cream or yellow flowers are produced singly but continuously throughout the summer. Planting distance is 24–30 in; propagation is by cuttings or layering.

Prunus laurocerasus
Height: 36 in
A dark glossy-leaved evergreen that provides good high cover in sun or shade on any soil, except where the drainage is very poor. There are three suitable varieties: 'Otto Luyken', which is dense and bushy; 'Zabeliana', which branches more horizontally; and 'Schipkaensis', which is similar to 'Zabeliana', but with narrow lanceolate leaves. They all produce attractive spikes of small white flowers in spring. Planting distance is 36 in; propagation is by cuttings.

Salvia officinalis (Common sage)
Height: 12–18 in
An evergreen shrub from southern Europe that forms a dense mounded cover in full sun and well drained soils. It has soft grey-green aromatic leaves and lavender-blue flowers. The plant should be trimmed back in April if growth is thin or straggly. Planting distance is 18–24 in; propagation is by division, layering, cuttings or seeds.

Senecio 'Sunshine'
Height: 36 in
An evergreen shrub of spreading mounded habit that forms dense high cover in full sun and well drained soils. It is better known to many gardeners as *S. laxifolius* or *S. greyi.* The foliage is grey, and large branching heads of yellow daisy-like flowers appear in early summer. Planting distance is 36 in; propagation is by cuttings or less often by layering.

Specific plants: group three

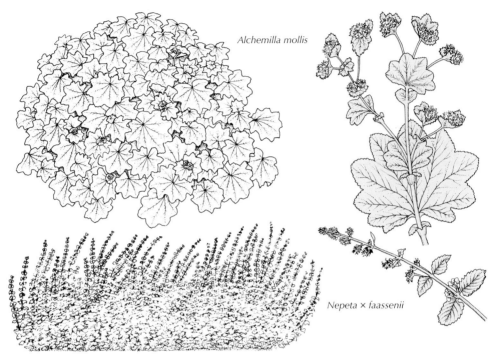

Alchemilla mollis

Nepeta × faassenii

Acanthus mollis 'Latifolius'
Height: 30–36 in
An herbaceous perennial that grows best in deep rich soil and is tolerant of sun or shade; in cold areas during winter it should be protected by a light leafy mulch. It forms an arching mound of deeply cut glossy dark green foliage, and spikes of purple and white flowers appear in late summer. Planting distance is 36 in; propagation is by division, root cuttings or seeds.

Alchemilla mollis
Height: 6–9 in
An herbaceous perennial that provides dense low summer cover in full sun or light shade in all except very dry soils. It has rounded green leaves, and yellow-green heads of small star-shaped flowers are borne in summer. Planting distance is 15 in; propagation is by division or seeds.

Brunnera macrophylla
Height: 12 in
An herbaceous perennial that forms dense summer cover in cool moist shady conditions. It is tolerant of drier shaded sites but should not be grown in full sun. The leaves are large and hairy, and bright blue panicles of flowers, similar to those of forget-me-not, are borne in spring. 'Variegata' has green and cream leaves. Planting distance is 15–18 in; propagation is by division or seeds.

Geranium spp
Height: 9–36 in
A group of herbaceous perennials, several of which are clump-forming. They provide good free-flowering summer cover and a winter cover of dead foliage, except on wet clays. The leaves are small, lobed or deeply cut and occasionally have attractive basal blotches. The following geraniums grow best in moist conditions and light shade but will tolerate full sun: *G. endressii* 'Wargrave Pink' (pink flowers); *G. psilostemon* (magenta) and *G. sylvaticum* (purple). Planting distance is 12–18 in; propagation is by division, although *G. psilostemon* and *G. sylvaticum* can also be propagated by seeds.

Group 3 characteristics
Deciduous (some retaining small
rosettes over winter); clump-forming;
medium to high density cover in
summer; slow to medium growth

Iris foetidissima

Geum × borisii
Height: 6–9 in
A clump-forming hybrid that is tolerant of sun
or light shade and grows best in rich, moist
soils. Branching heads of orange flowers
appear intermittently from early summer to
early autumn; they are borne above the
bright green rounded hairy leaves. Planting
distance is 12 in; propagation is by division.

Hemerocallis fulva
Height: 18–24 in
An herbaceous perennial with bright green,
grass-like arching foliage that provides dense
summer cover. The dead foliage is retained
over winter. Tall spikes of orange-red flowers
are borne in early summer. Most strong-
growing *Hemerocallis* species and hybrids
are also suitable. They all grow well in sun or
light shade and moist fertile soils. Planting distance is 18 in; propagation is by division.

Iris foetidissima
Height: 18 in
A rhizomatous perennial that is generally
useful, particularly in deeper shade and dry
conditions. It has dark green arching grass-
like foliage and dull mauve flowers. The seed
pods split open in autumn to reveal scarlet
seeds. The variety 'Citrina' has pale yellow
flowers and larger red seeds. Planting distance is 12 in; propagation is by division or
seeds (by division only for 'Citrina').

Liriope muscari
Height 9 in
An evergreen perennial that requires full sun
and is tolerant of dry conditions. It forms a
dense clump of dark green grass-like foliage
and bears spikes of small bell-shaped mauve-
pink flowers on long upright stems. They
appear in autumn. Planting distance is
9–12 in; propagation is by division or seeds.

Nepeta × faassenii (Catmint)
Height: 9 in
An herbaceous perennial that needs full sun
and a well drained soil. It has branching stems
and small grey-green leaves that are pun-
gently aromatic. Small lavender-blue flowers

91

Specific plants: group three

Origanum
vulgare

Pulmonaria
saccharata

are borne in whorls on the shoot tips in summer. Trim the plant back annually in spring to keep growth compact. Planting distance is 12 in; propagation is by division or cuttings.

Origanum vulgare (Marjoram)
Height: 6 in
An herbaceous perennial that provides good summer cover in sunny, well drained sites. It has branching stems that grow from over-wintering rosettes. The leaves are small, rounded, mid-green and aromatic. Tiny tubular rose-purple flowers are produced in dense terminal panicles in summer. 'Aureum' is an attractive variety with golden-yellow foliage. Planting distance is 12 in; propagation is by division or cuttings.

Polygonum campanulatum
Height: 18–24 in
An herbaceous perennial that requires moist or wet soils. Its trailing red-stemmed shoots grow from over-wintering rosettes and spread rapidly to form a dense leafy cover. Loose

clusters of white or pink flowers are borne in early summer. Planting distance is 18–24 in; propagation is by division or seeds.

Pulmonaria angustifolia
Height: 5–6 in
An herbaceous perennial that provides low cover in sun or shade on moist woodland soils or among shrubs. It dies back in the autumn to an over-wintering rosette. The leaves are long, ovate and hairy, and small heads of blue tubular flowers appear in spring. Recommended varieties include 'Azurea' and 'Mawson's Variety'. Other suitable species of *Pulmonaria* are *P. saccharata* (syn *P. picta*), which has silvery-white marbled leaves, and *P. officinalis,* whose leaves are spotted white. Both have flowers that are pink at first and then turn blue. They retain a greater proportion of foliage through the winter than does *P. angustifolia. P. rubra* has coral-red flowers and is almost evergreen. Its leaves are a lighter green than those of *P. angustifolia.* Planting distance is 12 in; propagation is by division.

HOSTAS SUITABLE FOR GROUND COVER

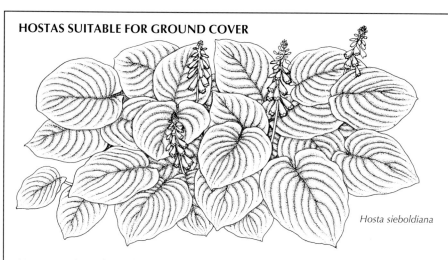

Hosta sieboldiana

Hostas are large-leaved herbaceous perennials, native to China and Japan. They provide good cover during the summer, although the leaves die down in the autumn and some hand-weeding of winter-germinating annuals may be needed. The leaves and flowers of most hostas are particularly ornamental. The flowers are borne on spikes and resemble those of lilies. They range in colour from white to rich violet-purple and are produced during July to September.

Hostas will grow in most soils but are less satisfactory on those that are chalky or strongly alkaline unless well enriched with humus. They prefer a deep rich loam or a sandy loam and can be grown in moist, sunny situations or shady, drier conditions but do not thrive in very dry areas. The following hostas are among the best for ground cover. Except where otherwise stated, the height and planting distance are 15–18 in.

Hosta crispula has long pointed spreading foliage. The leaves are dark green with broad white margins; the flowers are pale lavender. Height is 12 in.

Hosta decorata has broad white-margined leaves and violet flowers. Height is 9–12 in.

Hosta elata has large broad light green leaves with undulating margins and pale lilac to white flowers.

Hosta fortunei has lilac flowers. Among the best of the variegated forms are 'Albopicta', whose leaves are bright yellow, edged with green when new and becoming entirely green as the season advances; 'Obscura Marginata', which has green leaves with bright yellow edges; and 'Yellow Edge', which has deep green leaves with broad yellow margins. Among the best green-leaved forms are 'Obscura' and 'Hyacinthina'.

Hosta plantaginea has pale green, arching leaves, which are heart-shaped. The flowers are pure white and scented.

Hosta rectifolia has long, narrow mid-green leaves and violet flowers.

Hosta sieboldiana has very large, rounded, heavily veined, grey-green leaves. Var *elegans* has blue-grey leaves, and those of 'Francis Williams' are edged golden-yellow. They all have lilac and white flowers. Planting distance is 18–24 in.

Hosta undulata var *erromena* has long glossy green leaves; var *undulata* has smaller leaves, with a broad creamy-white central bar. Both have lilac flowers.

Hosta ventricosa has broad dark green leaves and rich violet-purple flowers. There are two variegated forms: 'Aureomaculata', which has yellow central stripes; and 'Variegata', which has broad, creamy-yellow leaf margins.

Specific plants: group four

Acaena novae-zelandiae
Height: 3–4 in
A semi-deciduous carpeting plant that requires full sun and a well drained soil. Its slender stems take root at the nodes and spread rapidly to form a fairly dense mat of soft, feathery foliage. The inconspicuous flowers are followed by small spiny red or russet-brown burrs. *A. caesiiglauca* and *A. buchananii* are similar in habit but less dense. All provide good out-of-season cover where bulbs have been planted. Planting distance is 15–18 in; propagation is by division. *A. novaezelandiae* is illustrated on page 125.

Ajuga reptans
Height: 2–5 in
A stoloniferous evergreen perennial that is tolerant of shade but needs moist conditions. It grows fairly rapidly to provide a dense low cover of evergreen foliage. There are also several varieties with attractively coloured foliage, including 'Atropurpurea', which has purple leaves, and 'Rainbow', whose leaves are variegated bronze, pink and yellow. All need full sun and a moist soil. Planting distance is 9–15 in; propagation is by division.

Antennaria dioica
Height: 1–2 in
An evergreen perennial that needs a light, well drained soil and full sun. It forms a fairly dense carpet of tiny silver-grey leaves, and bears small white flowers in summer. It is rather slow to establish, and is most suitable in sunny rockeries and for the edges of paths and paving. Planting distance is 9 in; propagation is by division.

Anthemis nobilis (Chamomile)
Height: 1–3 in
An evergreen perennial that forms a low carpet of leafy stems, which take root as they spread. It has finely divided aromatic leaves and white daisy-like flowers. It is tolerant of dry sunny conditions and can be grown as an alternative to grass, especially in small areas where the soil is dry and sandy. 'Treneague' is a non-flowering variety. Planting distance is 9–15 in; propagation is by division, stem cuttings or seeds. 'Treneague' is illustrated on page 125.

Artemisia stelleriana
Height: 12 in
A low-spreading, dense, suckering sub-shrub that needs full sun and a light, well drained soil. It is particularly tolerant of coastal conditions. The foliage is grey-white and aromatic. Planting distance is 18 in; propagation is by division, cuttings or seeds.

Asperula odorata (now *Galium odoratum*)
Height: 4–5 in
An herbaceous perennial that grows best in cool moist conditions and partial shade, such as under trees or between large shrubs. It spreads rapidly by means of slender rhizomes, giving a dense summer cover of ascending whorls of dark green leaves. The small white flowers are borne in terminal clusters in early summer. Planting distance is 24 in; propagation is by division.

Blechnum spicant
Height: 9–15 in
A hardy evergreen fern that grows best in moist humus-rich acid soils and shady sites, such as under trees and larger shrubs. It will, however, tolerate full sun if conditions are sufficiently moist. The lower fronds spread horizontally from a short rootstock but are slow to provide good cover. Planting distance is 12 in; propagation is by division.

Campanula portenschlagiana
Height: 3–4 in
An herbaceous perennial that grows best in rich soils in full sun, although it will tolerate light or partial shade. It spreads by underground shoots to form low leafy summer cover, which dies back in the winter. Small bell-shaped purple flowers are borne throughout the summer. *C. poscharskyana* is a more vigorous, evergreen species; it requires the same growing conditions as *C. portenschlagiana*. The flowers are lavender-blue and borne in small sprays. 'E. K. Toogood' is less vigorous but provides good cover. Planting distance is 12 in; propagation is by division, cuttings or seeds.

Centaurea 'John Coutts'
Height: 6 in
An herbaceous perennial that requires full sun

Group 4 characteristics
Deciduous or evergreen; colonizers;
medium to high density cover; medium
to rapid growth

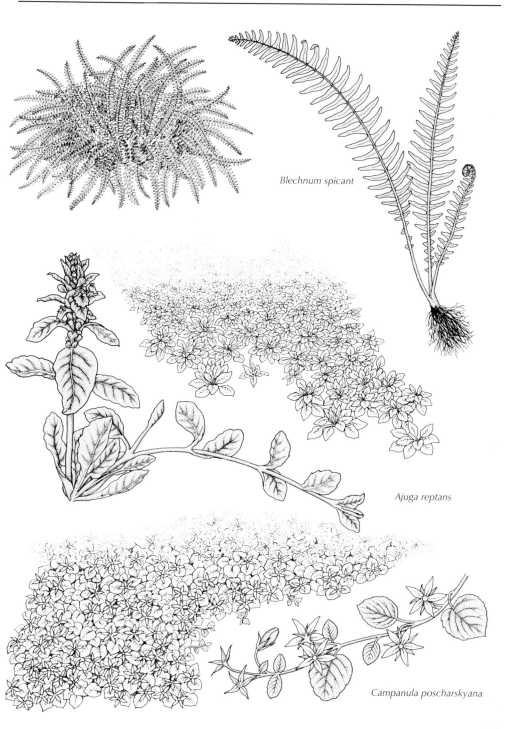

Blechnum spicant

Ajuga reptans

Campanula poscharskyana

Specific plants: group four

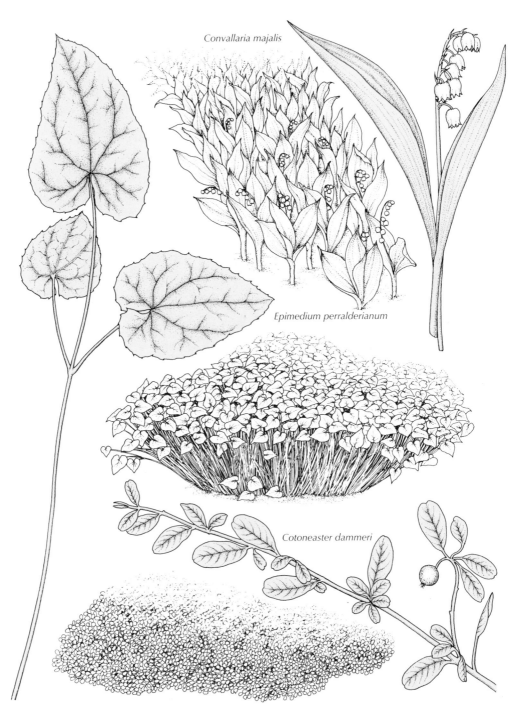

Convallaria majalis

Epimedium perralderianum

Cotoneaster dammeri

and a well drained soil. It has dissected, almost fern-like, grey-green foliage and, in summer, bears pink thistle-shaped flowers on long stems. Planting distance is 12–15 in; propagation is by division.

Convallaria majalis (Lily-of-the-valley)
Height: 9 in
An herbaceous perennial that grows from a fleshy creeping rhizome and spreads rapidly. It requires cool, moist humus-rich soil and partial or deep shade, such as under deciduous trees or shaded shrubberies. Pairs of large pointed oval leaves develop from each growing point in spring. The small fragrant white flowers are bell-shaped and borne on arching stems; they are followed by orange berries. Planting distance is 12–15 in; propagation is by division.

Cornus canadensis (syn *Chamaepericlymenum canadensis*)
Height: 4–6 in
A plant that requires an acid, fairly moist soil and partial shade. It is an herbaceous perennial, although it is often described as a subshrub. Short stems are produced annually from its creeping rootstock. They bear whorls of ovate leaves and, in early summer, dense heads of tiny yellow-green flowers appear, with each head surrounded by four white bracts. These are followed by clusters of bright red berries. Planting distance is 12 in; propagation is by division or seeds.

Cotoneaster dammeri
Height: 3–4 in
An attractive evergreen carpeting shrub that is rather slow to develop density but suitable for sun or shade in all soils. It has small glossy leaves and white flowers that are followed by bright red berries. The trailing stems root down in moist conditions. Planting distance is 24 in; propagation is by layers or cuttings.

Cotula squalida
Height: 1 in
A carpeting plant that is tolerant of sun or light shade in damp to fairly dry conditions. Its creeping stems make a useful cover for dwarf bulbs. The fern-like leaves are soft bronze-green, and in summer yellow

buttons of flowers appear. The plant tolerates light wear and is an attractive alternative to grass for small areas. Planting distance is 9 in; propagation is by division. The plant is illustrated on page 125.

Dicentra formosa
Height: 9 in
A stemless herbaceous plant that requires moist leafy soils and partial or deep shade. Each spring small clusters of fern-like leaves develop directly from the spreading underground rootstock. These are followed by long arching sprays of purple-pink flowers. Planting distance is 15 in; propagation is by division.

Duchesnea indica (syn *Fragaria indica*)
Height: 3 in
A rapidly growing and sometimes invasive plant that grows well in sun or shade on all but wet, heavy soils. It resembles the wild strawberry since its leaves have three leaflets, the flowers, though yellow, have the same shape, and it spreads by means of runners. The small red fruits are edible but have little flavour. Planting distance is 15 in; propagation is by division.

Epimedium spp
Height: 9–12 in
A genus of evergreen, semi-evergreen and deciduous plants that are noted for their attractive foliage. Although they are slow to spread, epimediums can provide good cover in sun or shade in any fertile and reasonably well drained soil. They grow best in light shade and moist, humus-rich soil. The leaves grow directly from the rhizomes and are composed of three to nine roughly heart-shaped leaflets. New leaves are often tinged red, bronze or pink, becoming green at maturity. In autumn they are either bronze or richly tinted with yellow or red. In early summer loose sprays of small red, yellow or white flowers appear. Among the best epimediums are *E. perralderianum*, *E.× perralchicum* and *E. pinnatum colchicum*, which are evergreen or semi-evergreen. Among deciduous epimediums, *E. × rubrum* and *E. × versicolor* provide good cover. Planting distance is 9–12 in; propagation is by division.

Specific plants: group four

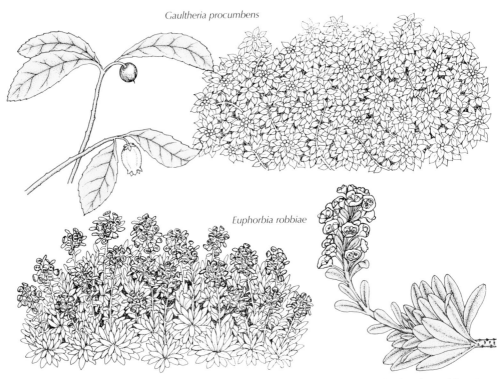

Gaultheria procumbens

Euphorbia robbiae

Euphorbia robbiae
Height: 15 in
A valuable evergreen plant since it grows well in either poor soils or dark corners where few other plants survive. It will also tolerate sunny sites. It spreads by means of fleshy rhizomes, and bears rosettes of dark green elongated leaves on tall firm stems. The flowers are small and yellow-green, each within a green bract, and are borne in loose terminal clusters. Planting distance is 18 in; propagation is by division or seeds.

Gaultheria procumbens
Height: 4–6 in
A low-growing shrubby evergreen that provides excellent cover for cool, moist shade on acid soils. It spreads by its creeping stems, which grow through the soil and occasionally on the surface. From them, short erect stems or suckers appear, bearing tufts of dark glossy green leathery leaves which are strongly aromatic when crushed. Small white bell-shaped flowers are carried singly in the leaf

axils; they are followed by bright red berries which are often hidden by the leaves. Planting distance is 12 in; propagation is by division or seeds.

Geranium spp
Height: 18–24 in except where stated
A group of summer-flowering herbaceous perennials, often with attractive leaves, which provide a good dense cover when well established. All can be grown in full sun or light shade and there are several that grow well in deep shade. Among the most effective as ground cover are *G. himalayense* (violet-blue flowers), *G.* 'Johnson's Blue' (pale violet-blue, height 15 in), *G. sanguineum* and its variety *lancastriense* (magenta to white, height 6 in), *G. macrorrhizum* (magenta to pink or white, height 12 in) and *G. procurrens* (dark silky mauve); these all spread by rhizomes and *G. macrorrhizum* is also stem-rooting. *G.* × *magnificum*, *G. ibericum* and *G. platypetalum* (shades of violet-blue), *G. phaeum* (maroon to white), *G. punctatum* (white) and *G. nodosum*

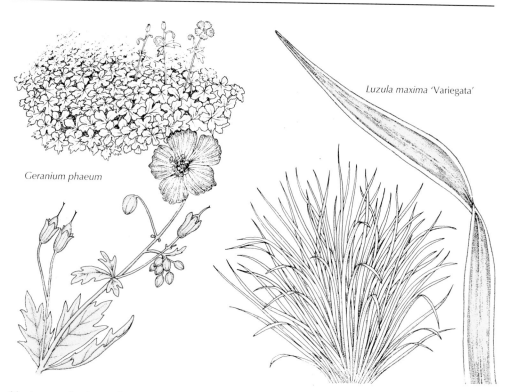

Geranium phaeum

Luzula maxima 'Variegata'

(lilac) are all clump-forming geraniums. G. 'Russell Pritchard' (pink) and G. wallichianum (violet-purple, height 6–9 in) are both clump-forming but have spreading stems that die back in the winter. Planting distance is 12–24 in; propagation is by division or seeds.

Glechoma hederacea (Ground ivy)
Height: 3–4 in

A vigorous stem-rooting perennial that tolerates both sun and light shade. Its serrated dark evergreen leaves are carried in pairs on slender stems. Whorls of small lilac-blue flowers are borne from the upper leaf axils in spring. Note that it can become a rampageous weed. The less vigorous 'Variegata' has white-margined leaves. It needs a good fertile soil and is slower to provide dense cover. Planting distance is 18 in; propagation is by division.

Lamium maculatum
Height: 3–4 in

A rapidly growing plant in partial or deep shade. Its stems are trailing and self-rooting. The leaves are dark green with a broad central white stripe; many of them are retained over winter. In early summer, whorls of magenta flowers appear. Album has white flowers and roseum is pink-flowered. 'Aureum', with bright yellow-green foliage, is rather slow-growing. Planting distance is 12 in; propagation is by division.

Luzula maxima (Woodrush)
Height: 12 in

A tough narrow-leaved evergreen that spreads rapidly by suckers to form a dense matted cover. It is suitable for banks, in dry or difficult situations, and in deeper shade. The slightly less vigorous 'Variegata' has its leaves edged cream. Planting distance is 15 in; propagation is by division.

Lysimachia nummularia (Creeping jenny)
Height: 1–2 in

An attractive ground cover for moist soils in sunny or partially shaded sites. It will also

Specific plants: group four

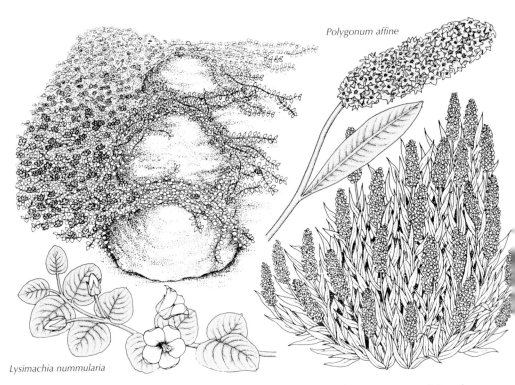

Polygonum affine

Lysimachia nummularia

grow in damp or poorly drained ground. Its numerous trailing stems take root at almost every leaf joint. It has small closely spaced leaves and buttercup-like yellow flowers, which are freely produced during the summer. The golden-leaved form 'Aurea' is less vigorous and may become scorched in dry sunny places. Planting distance is 12 in; propagation is by division.

Maianthemum bifolium
Height: 4–5 in
A good cover plant for growing in the shade of deciduous trees. It has smooth broad-bladed twin leaves and small spikes of creamy white flowers. It spreads by means of suckering underground shoots. Planting distance is 12 in; propagation is by division.

Muehlenbeckia axillaris
Height: 6–9 in
A low-growing deciduous shrub that needs full sun and a well drained soil. Its very small dark green leaves combine with the matted

network of slender stems to provide a dense, and sometimes invasive, cover. The flowers are tiny and green-brown. It spreads by suckering underground shoots. Planting distance is 18 in; propagation is by division.

Omphalodes cappadocica
Height: 6 in
A creeping, rhizomatous plant that grows best in moist, humus-rich soils in shade, though it will tolerate full sun if the soil is moist. It forms spreading clumps of long-stalked ovate leaves which die down in winter. In early summer it carries loose sprays of blue flowers that resemble those of forget-me-nots. The smaller-leaved *O. verna* spreads by surface runners. It has similar flowers and prefers a shady site. Planting distance is 12 in; propagation is by division.

Oxalis oregana
Height: 6 in
An attractive summer cover plant in woodland soils rich in leaf-mould. It spreads by

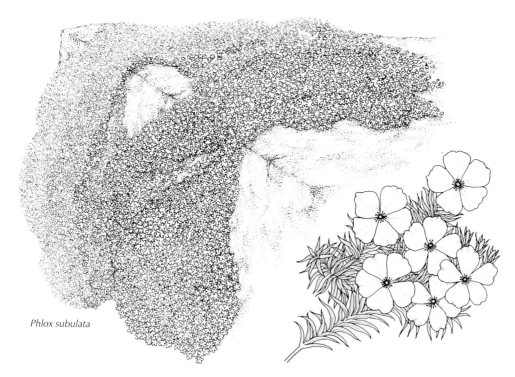

Phlox subulata

rhizomes, and has clover-like leaves and clusters of rose-purple, occasionally white, flowers; these appear in spring with the developing leaves. Planting distance is 9–12 in; propagation is by division or seeds.

Phlox spp
Height: 3–4 in
A group of herbaceous or sub-shrubby rock garden plants that form a dense low cover in full sun and on well drained soils. The stems are self-rooting and form an impenetrable mat. The leaves are small and narrow-bladed and, in late spring, clusters of brightly coloured starry flowers appear, which may completely cover the plant. *P. subulata* has white, pink or purple flowers; *P. douglasii* has pale lavender flowers. Among the best hybrids are 'Apple Blossom', 'Benita', 'Boothman's Variety', 'May Snow' and 'Temiscaming'. Older plants may die out in the centre, necessitating renovation from time to time. Planting distance is 9 in; propagation is by division or cuttings.

Polygonum affine
Height: 2–3 in
A mat-forming plant that is most effective in cool, moist soils in sun or partial shade. The dark green lanceolate leaves turn bronze-red in winter and are replaced by new foliage in spring. Numerous short erect tightly packed spikes of tiny flowers appear in early summer and are retained until late autumn. 'Darjeeling Red' (red flowers) and 'Superbum' (pink) are both good varieties. Planting distance is 9–12 in; propagation is by division.

Polygonum vacciniifolium
Height: 3–4 in
A good late-flowering plant that prefers cool, moist situations in full sun or partial shade, though it will also tolerate drier conditions. It forms a dense carpet of small glossy dark green leaves and slender twisting red-brown stems, which take root as they spread. The small rose-pink flowers are borne on short erect spikes. Planting distance is 9–12 in; propagation is by division, cuttings or seeds.

Specific plants: group four

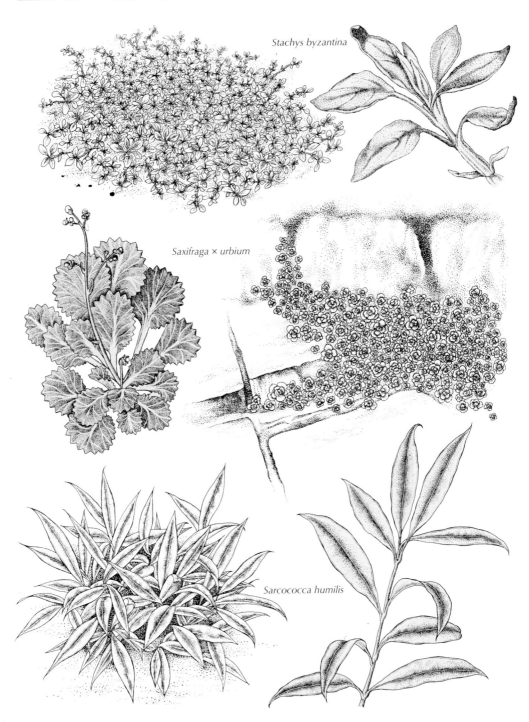

Stachys byzantina

Saxifraga × urbium

Sarcococca humilis

Potentilla alba
Height: 2–3 in
The best of the herbaceous potentillas for ground cover. It needs sun and a well drained soil, though it will tolerate light shade. It has deeply divided leaves, which are green above and grey beneath, and creeping stems that take root. The flowers are white with a small yellowish eye; they appear in spring and sometimes also in autumn. *P. calabra* has grey-white foliage and yellow flowers. Planting distance is 9–12 in; propagation is by division or seeds.

Prunella grandiflora
Height: 3–4 in
A good cover plant for moist conditions in sun or shade, though not hot, dry sites. It has small, evergreen leaves and procumbent stems that take root freely. In summer, short erect stems carry spikes of tubular rose-purple flowers. 'Loveliness' has pink flowers and *album* has white flowers. Seeds are freely produced, but named forms do not come true from them. Planting distance is 12 in; propagation is by division or seeds.

Rubus tricolor
Height: 12 in
An evergreen shrub that grows rapidly in sun or shade and in all but poorly drained soils. The leaves are roughly heart-shaped, dark green and glossy above, and white beneath. The leaf stalks and rooting stems are densely covered with bristly red hairs. Its white, axillary flowers are occasionally followed by bright scarlet fruits. Planting distance is 36 in; propagation is by division, cuttings or layers.

Rubus calycinoides (R. fockeanus of gardens)
Height: 2–3 in
A prostrate evergreen shrub that bears small dark green leaves having three to five lobes. The small white flowers are borne singly or in clusters during the summer. Planting distance is 12–15 in; propagation is by division, cuttings or layering.

Sarcococca humilis
Height: 9–15 in
A low suckering shrub that is effective in moister, humus-rich soils, but will tolerate

drier sites as long as they are shaded. It has glossy evergreen leaves, and produces small axillary clusters of inconspicuous fragrant white flowers in late winter. Planting distance is 12 in; propagation is by division or cuttings.

Saxifraga × urbium
Height: 2–3 in
A hybrid that provides useful cover on cool open sites. Many "mossy" hybrids of saxifrage provide neat low cover in fertile well drained soils on sunny or open, shaded sites. They all possess finely divided leaves and long stalks of white, cream or pink flowers, which are borne in early summer. Planting distance is 12 in; propagation is by division.

Sedum spathulifolium
Height: 2–3 in
A carpeting self-rooting plant that needs sun and a well drained soil. The leaves are grey-white, flushed with red or purple, and are borne in rosettes. The yellow star-shaped flowers are carried on flattened heads. 'Cappa Blanca' (syn 'Cape Blanco') has grey-white leaves and those of 'Purpureum' are strongly tinted red-purple. Planting distance is 9–12 in; propagation is by division or cuttings.

Sedum spurium
Height: 2–3 in
A densely carpeting plant that provides an attractive low cover for sun and good, well drained soils. Some older leaves are usually lost in winter; retained leaves develop a reddish tinge. Flattened heads of pink flowers appear in summer. Good varieties include *album* (white flowers), 'Green Mantle' (dense, non-flowering) and 'Schorbuser Blut' (dark red flowers). Planting distance is 9–12 in; propagation is by division or cuttings.

Stachys byzantina (Lamb's ear)
Height: 3–4 in
A creeping plant that needs full sun and a well drained soil. Its ovate evergreen leaves are densely covered with silvery-white woolly hairs, and the scattered tiny mauve flowers are borne on woolly stems. 'Silver Carpet', which rarely flowers, provides the best ground cover. Planting distance is 12 in; propagation is by division.

Specific plants: group four

Symphoricarpos × chenaultii 'Hancock'

Symphytum grandiflorum

Stephanandra incisa 'Crispa'
Height: 24 in
A hardy deciduous shrub that provides useful cover for banks or open sunny sites in all but poorly drained soils. Its slender arching branches take root when they touch the soil. The leaves turn a rich gold in autumn, and clusters of small pale green flowers are borne in panicles in early summer. Planting distance is 36 in; propagation is by division, cuttings or layering.

Symphoricarpos × chenaultii 'Hancock'
Height: 24 in
A deciduous suckering shrub that provides fairly dense cover in sun or moderate shade on all soils, except where the drainage is poor. It has small soft green leaves and arching or prostrate branches. Tiny green-yellow flowers are borne in terminal clusters and are followed by small pink or purple berries known as snowberries. It is particularly suit-

able for covering banks or larger areas of the garden. Planting distance is 36 in; propagation is by division, cuttings or layering.

Symphytum grandiflorum (Comfrey)
Height: 6 in
An herbaceous perennial that requires shade and grows best in cool moist conditions. It will, however, tolerate drier soils in deep shade. It spreads rapidly by rhizomes, and has ovate rough-textured leaves and small branched heads of creamy white, pink or blue flowers, which are short-lived and appear in spring. Planting distance is 12 in; propagation is by division.

Tellima grandiflora
Height: 6 in
An evergreen clump-forming perennial that grows well in sun or shade on all except poorly drained soils. It spreads quickly to form a dense cover of bright green rounded hairy

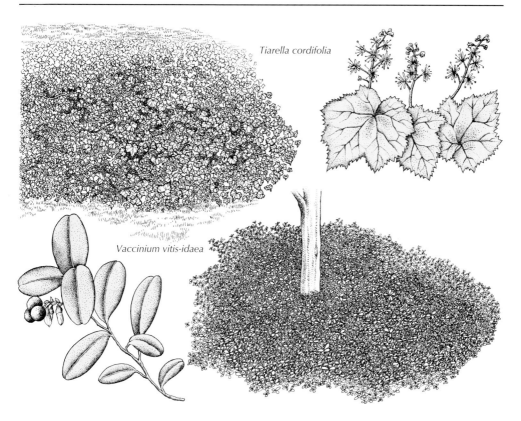

Tiarella cordifolia

Vaccinium vitis-idaea

leaves. A succession of small cream-yellow bell-shaped flowers are borne on tall spikes during late spring. The variety 'Purpurea' has pink flowers; its foliage resembles that of the species except that it turns purple-bronze in winter. Planting distance is 12 in; propagation is by division or seeds ('Purpurea' comes approximately true from seeds.)

Thymus serpyllum of gardens (Wild thyme)
Height: 1 in
An evergreen perennial that needs full sun and a well drained soil. Its tiny dark green leaves and matted branching prostrate stems form a dense low carpet of growth. Numerous small heads of lavender-pink flowers are borne in summer. The variety *albus* has white flowers, and 'Pink Chintz' has clear pink ones. Planting distance is 9 in; propagation is by division or cuttings, and also by seeds except for named varieties. 'Pink Chintz' is illustrated on page 125.

Tiarella cordifolia (Foam flower)
Height: 4–6 in
An evergreen perennial that requires cool moist humus-rich soils and partial or deep shade. It spreads by rhizomes, or sometimes stolons, to provide very dense cover. The leaves, which are similar in shape to maple leaves, turn bronze in winter. Spikes of creamy white flowers appear in spring. *T. wherryi* is a similar, but slower-growing, species. Planting distance is 12–15 in; propagation is by division.

Vaccinium vitis-idaea (Cowberry)
Height: 6 in
A low bushy evergreen shrub that requires humus-rich, acid soils and light or open shade. It has prostrate rooting branches and small shiny dark green leaves that may develop bronze tints in winter. Short racemes of white, often pink-tinted, bell-shaped flowers are borne in early summer, followed

Specific plants: group four

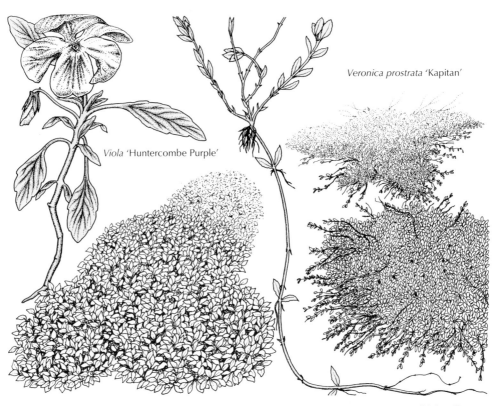

Veronica prostrata 'Kapitan'

Viola 'Huntercombe Purple'

by clusters of round red berries. Planting distance is 9–12 in; propagation is by division, cuttings or layering.

Vancouveria hexandra
Height: 6 in
A rhizomatous perennial that requires a humus-rich soil and a shady site, such as under deciduous trees or larger shrubs. The delicate long-stalked leaves are composed of nine slightly lobed rounded leaflets. They grow in clusters directly from the spreading rootstock and die down to ground level in winter. Long sprays of white flowers are borne in spring. Planting distance is 12 in; propagation is by division.

Veronica prostrata (*V. rupestris* of gardens)
Height: 1–2 in
An herbaceous plant that grows best on a well drained soil in full sun. It forms a dense low carpet of spreading rooting stems and narrow

serrated leaves. Numerous small blue flowers are borne in short racemes in summer. Suitable varieties include 'Kapitan' (bright blue flowers), 'Spode Blue' (clear, light blue) and 'Rosea' (pink). Planting distance is 9–12 in; propagation is by division.

Viola spp
Height: 2–4 in
A genus of herbaceous plants, several of which provide good dense low cover. They require cool open sites and well drained, but moist, soils. Among the most suitable are *V. cornuta* and the garden hybrids 'Connie', 'Haslemere', 'Huntercombe Purple' and 'Martin', which are all evergreen. *V. labradorica,* which is semi-evergreen, and *V. obliqua,* which is deciduous and less vigorous, will grow well in sun or shade and on all soils except those that are very dry or poorly drained. Planting distance is 9–12 in; propagation is by division, cuttings or seeds.

ROSES SUITABLE FOR GROUND COVER

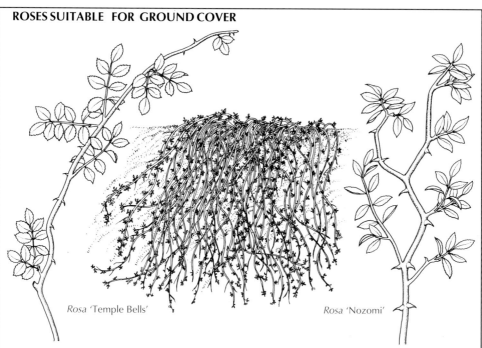

Rosa 'Temple Bells'   *Rosa* 'Nozomi'

There are several roses whose stems and leaves are sufficiently dense to be effective as ground cover.

Roses prefer a sunny site with a medium to heavy, well drained soil, although with good preparation and care after planting, they will grow quite satisfactorily on lighter soils. However, they do not grow well on wetter clay soils or those that are high in chalk. Plant ground cover roses in late autumn if the soil is light and well drained. On heavier wetter soils, do this in late winter. Weeds can be troublesome in the first two or three seasons until the branch canopy develops sufficient density, and seedlings of woody plants may occasionally be troublesome in later years. The following roses are well-tried as ground cover plants; numerous others are listed by rose nurserymen.

Rosa 'Max Graf' is stem-rooting in cool, moist sites and forms a fairly dense, thorny cover. Clusters of single bright pink flowers form in late summer. Height is 36 in; planting distance is 48–60 in.

Rosa 'Nozomi' is a hybrid that forms a low arching cover. It bears large clusters of small single white flowers during mid- to late summer. Height is 18–24 in; planting distance is 30–36 in.

Rosa × paulii is a large sprawling hybrid. Its numerous strong thorny stems form a dense mounded cover. Large single white flowers are borne throughout the summer. Height is 36–48 in; planting distance is 48–72 in.

Rosa 'Snow Carpet' is low-growing with double white flowers. Planting distance is 36–48 in.

Rosa 'Temple Bells' forms a dense arching cover and, in cool moist conditions, is stem-rooting. In summer, clusters of small white blooms appear. Height is 18–24 in; planting distance is 30–36 in.

Rosa wichuraiana is a strong-growing species whose stems form a dense low cover. Clusters of small single, fragrant white flowers are borne during mid- to late summer. Height is 12–18 in; planting distance is 60–72 in.

Preparing the site

Planning

The first step in preparing to plant ground cover is to draw a plan of the site. If the site is large, mark in any variations in soil conditions, exposure to wind and the degree of sun or shade. These can then be more easily taken into account when ground cover plants are being selected.

The choice of plants depends, in the first instance, on whether ground cover is needed to occupy a difficult site where little except weeds will grow, or whether it is needed because the site, though satisfactory, cannot be maintained to an acceptable level of appearance. In the former case the ornamental value of the ground cover is of less importance than its ability to grow satisfactorily under the conditions, and the choice may be confined to a single species, such as common ivy or St John's wort.

With the latter, the less stringent conditions usually allow a considerably wider choice of cover plants, and more emphasis can be placed on their ornamental qualities. Thus groups of plants with contrasting or complementing colours can be grown, for example, heathers that differ in both the colour of their foliage and of their flowers. Variations in height between adjoining groups can also be utilized, as can the contrast between leafy clump-forming plants and those that form a dense carpeting cover.

Weeding the site

The first step in preparing the site is to clear it of weeds. Established annual weeds are mostly shallow rooting and are easily removed when the site is forked over before planting. If the site has been neglected for a year or two, seedling growth after planting may be a problem, in which case a period of fallowing would be helpful.

Perennial weeds are a more serious problem, and it is essential to clear the site of all traces of such weeds before planting. If this is not done, strong-growing perennials such as bindweed, ground elder and couch grass will compete with the ground cover and weaken it. They will also be extremely difficult to eradicate once the ground cover is established. Do not plant until the site is completely free of perennial weeds, even if this means that

planting ground cover has to be delayed for a season or more.

To eliminate perennial weeds it is necessary to kill or remove the underground parts, such as rhizomes. If the weeds are to be dug out, this can be done at any time of the year, but weedkillers are only effective when the weeds are in active growth. The roots of some weeds, particularly bindweed and field horsetail, penetrate too deeply for them to be dug out completely. If they are present, it is better to leave infested plots unplanted for a full season and spray with glyphosate when the weeds are growing strongly. Even then there may be some regrowth later in the year, in which case, spray again. Field horsetail is very persistent, but control may be improved if the weed is crushed before spraying. For a more detailed discussion on clearing weeds from a neglected site, see pages 162–165.

Improving the soil

Irrespective of the nature of the site and the choice of plants, thorough and careful soil preparation is essential. The fact that some types of ground cover plant will grow in poor soils and difficult habitats does not mean that

Planning

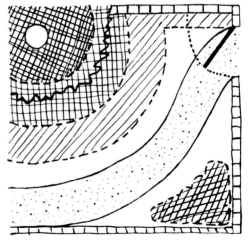

Draw a plan of the site, marking in any areas that are shaded or exposed to wind, and features such as walls, gates, paths, trees and shrubs.

they will provide effective cover if they are planted into unprepared soil. The site should be prepared as thoroughly as for any other kind of plant, since to obtain good cover the plants need to establish rapidly and remain healthy and effective for some years after being planted.

The texture of all types of soil will be improved by digging in a heavy dressing of organic matter or humus. Any type of decomposing vegetation can be used: garden compost, stable manure, leaf-mould or leaf litter, peat, pulverized bark or spent mushroom compost. However, the last of these is usually strongly alkaline and should not be used where acid-loving plants are to be grown. Use well decomposed materials on lighter soils. On heavier clay soils dig in coarser materials since they help to improve the aeration and drainage. A suitable quantity of dressing is roughly one heaped barrowload of manure for every 25 sq ft, dug in to a spade's depth.

Organic manures are rich in trace elements but contain relatively small amounts of major plant foods, and these foods are hardly present at all in peat and pulverized bark.

Therefore, to ensure that a sufficient supply of nutrients is available to encourage early growth, apply a general balanced fertilizer at 1–2 oz per square yard before planting, working it well into the top few inches of soil with a hoe or fork.

Another factor to take into account is the soil pH, although many ground cover plants are tolerant of all but extreme conditions. There are several soil testing kits on the market which will provide a good indication of the soil's acidity. Excessively acid conditions can be modified by dressings of lime, but the improvement is not immediate. Do not apply lime without establishing that it is needed. With alkaline or chalk soils, on the other hand, the pH cannot be reduced appreciably. Digging in acid peat or pulverized bark in quantity will improve the texture, but it will have little effect on the alkalinity. On some neutral or slightly alkaline soils the pH can be reduced by means of chemicals, but the process is slow and complicated. Whether the soil is acid or alkaline, it is simpler to choose plants that are tolerant of a particular type of soil than to attempt to change substantially the basic character of the soil.

Weeding the site

Improving the soil

Remove all traces of weed growth. Dig out shallow-rooted perennial weeds. Allow a full season for weed control, using glyphosate, if heavily infested.

Dig in organic matter to a spade's depth, at one heaped barrowload per 25 sq ft. Before planting, fork in a general balanced fertilizer at 1–2 oz per square yard.

Planting and spacing

Ground cover plants must be planted carefully and correctly, at the appropriate spacings and at the right time of year, to ensure that they grow away quickly and vigorously.

When to plant

The best period for planting is in late winter to early spring. At this time the soil is beginning to warm up and there is ample moisture available, both of which are conditions that encourage plants to produce new root growth quickly. They will also have a full growing season ahead in which to become well established and are, therefore, less likely to be damaged by severe winter conditions later on. Do not plant during hot, dry summer weather because such conditions may check their growth. Also avoid planting late in the year because the roots may not establish properly and the plants will deteriorate or even die during the winter.

Container-grown plants can be planted out at any time of the year as long as the soil conditions are suitable. The ground should not be heavy with recent rain, bone dry, frosted or covered with snow.

If planting has to be delayed because the soil or weather conditions are not right, the plants must be protected from hot sun and drying winds. Store plants with bare roots by heeling them in. To do this, dig out an angled trench in a cool position in friable soil. Insert the plants close together and cover the roots with earth to the level of the planting mark. This is the point on the stem where there is a slight colour change that indicates the depth at which they were planted. Store container-grown plants by plunging them to the rim in weathered ashes, grit or similar porous material. Alternatively, stand them in a cool, sheltered site and protect the containers with straw or bracken. Check their water requirements regularly.

Even if there is no delay to planting, always cover bare-rooted plants with damp sacking to protect them during site preparation.

How to plant

First, dig out a planting hole that is wide enough to take the roots when they are fully spread out. Where necessary, tease out the roots of container-grown plants that have become compacted. Ensure that the hole is deep enough to allow the plant to be inserted at the correct level. The soil level should be up to the planting mark on bare-rooted plants, or at the point where the roots and shoots meet if they are herbaceous. With

2 If planting is delayed, store bare-rooted plants by heeling them in up to the level of the planting mark.

3 To plant ground cover, first dig out a planting hole sufficiently deep and wide to accommodate the roots.

container-grown plants the soil level should be the same as it was in the container, or marginally deeper.

Insert the plant carefully. Return the soil around and between the roots and firm it well. Water in evergreen plants. Finally, lightly fork over the soil to give a smooth surface.

Planting distances

It is important to decide the correct planting distance for each kind of ground cover plant in order to achieve 75–100 per cent cover in one or two years. The planting distance is determined by a number of factors. The most important are the natural growth habit of the plant and the soil and climate conditions, all of which influence how quickly it will cover a given area and what its ultimate spread is likely to be.

The size of the plants should also be taken into account. Young, well rooted plants establish faster and grow more rapidly than larger, older plants, and will usually provide good cover by the end of the first season. However, more plants are required and this can be expensive.

The recommended planting distances for individual plants are included in the section on specific ground cover plants, pages 78–107.

Planting ground cover

1 Cover bare-rooted plants with damp sacking as soon as they have been lifted. This will protect the roots until they can be planted out.

4 Tease out the roots of plants if they were raised in a container, since they may have become compacted.

5 After inserting the plant, replace the soil and firm it down well. Then lightly fork over the surface.

Maintenance

One of the main factors to be considered when selecting ground cover plants is that they should not require a high degree of maintenance. However, a certain amount of work is necessary in the early stages to ensure that the plants establish successfully.

Weed control

During the first year after planting it is essential to keep weeds under control, otherwise they will compete with the plants for water, nutrients and light. Clear weed seedlings by hand-weeding or hoeing. Continue hand-weeding to kill weed seedlings as they appear and to remove any perennial weeds that have escaped treatment when the site was being prepared. Alternatively, spot-treat perennial weeds very carefully with glyphosate. An approach which can be adopted where planting a neglected site and a heavy "crop" of weed seedlings is anticipated, is to cover the site with black plastic sheeting, planting through slits made in the plastic.

For gardeners, however, an approach which is both effective in weed control and beneficial to plant establishment and growth is to apply a 2–3 in mulch of peat or pulverized bark. Well rotted garden compost or leaf-mould can also be used, but they may contain viable weed seeds. Apply the mulch between the plants, taking care not to cover the growing shoots if they are herbaceous. Carpeting plants require only a light sprinkling of mulch between the spreading shoots. The mulch suppresses most weed development and, as it breaks down, will provide nutrients for the plants. Mulching encourages carpeting plants to take root and give more rapid cover. It also helps to keep the soil cool and to conserve moisture. Renew mulches each spring until good cover has formed.

Fertilizers

Once the plants are established they should not be neglected completely. Feeding, though not essential, greatly improves their appearance and vigour. Feed every two years in early spring as new growth appears, applying either a balanced inorganic fertilizer or an organic one such as bone meal. Alternatively, use a slow release fertilizer; these are particularly suitable for ground cover plants since they release nutrients over a period of several months. Apply inorganic fertilizers carefully around the plants to avoid scorching the leaves.

Where plants have suffered a check, or where newly planted ground cover is slow to grow away, apply a foliar feed in late spring or early summer.

Pruning

As with feeding, pruning is not essential, but it does benefit the appearance and vigour of ground cover plants. Remove old flowering stems, dead twigs or damaged shoots when necessary, and examine all plants annually in late winter or early spring.

More severe pruning may be needed to prevent vigorously spreading plants from becoming invasive, and plants such as heathers and vincas from becoming straggly. Do this in January or February for deciduous woody plants, or in April for evergreens. Some young woody plants may need to be pruned back to encourage lower branching.

Tidy up deciduous herbaceous plants in late autumn when the foliage has died down. Cut back old flowering stems and remove dead leaves, but do not harm the crowns of plants that retain some foliage over winter.

Weeding

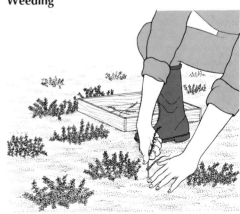

Hand-weed regularly to remove weed seedlings as they appear, and any perennial weeds that develop.

PROPAGATION

Many ground cover plants can be easily propagated, either by division, layering, taking cuttings or sowing seeds. Some general points concerning propagation are discussed below. For the methods of propagating a particular plant, see the appropriate entry on pages 78–107.

One of the simplest methods of propagating a plant is to divide and replant it, or to replant runners that have taken root. However, this inevitably disturbs the existing plant and can check its growth. A better method, though not always possible, is to peg down runners into pots of compost. Once they have taken root they can be severed from the parent and planted out. With clump-forming or suckering plants the only alternative to division is to grow several stock plants in a nursery bed and gradually build up the stock over several seasons.

Another method of propagation is to take cuttings. In most cases these will require two to three years to become sufficiently sturdy to be planted out. Most woody plants can be propagated from softwood cuttings taken in June or July; they will root satisfactorily if placed in a mist unit or a propagator with bottom heat. Others can be rooted from hardwood cuttings taken in autumn and planted in a cold frame or plastic tunnel. Certain herbaceous perennials can be propagated from leafy cuttings taken in late summer and planted under glass.

Many ground cover plants can also be raised from seed, but considerable attention is needed to produce well rooted plants within a few years of germination.

Feeding

Feed the plants every two or three years in early spring. Apply inorganic fertilizers carefully to avoid scorching the leaves.

Pruning

Examine plants annually in late winter or early spring, removing any dead foliage, damaged shoots or straggly growth.

Problem sites 1

One of the most common reasons for growing ground cover is to utilize those awkward sites in a garden where little other than weeds will grow. This section discusses these sites in turn, the difficulties that they present and points concerning site preparation and planting. For each site, a list of suitable ground cover plants is given, usually in tabular form. If only a few plants can be recommended, they are given within the text.

Shaded sites
One of the most important factors that limits the choice of plants for a particular site is the degree of shade present. Many plants grow poorly in shade and may become distorted by developing only towards the light. The soil conditions at the site may also be extreme, for example, under the canopy of larger trees the soil is often poor and dry, and there may be many tree roots near the surface. On the other hand, in low-lying poorly drained sites or open woodland, the soil may be perpetually moist.

To prepare the site, the first step is to mark out the extent of the shaded area; do this on a sunny day in spring or autumn. Decide on the degree of shade possessed by the site and the nature of the growing conditions there, then choose the appropriate plants accordingly. Plant the ground cover in the autumn because, if the plants are evergreen, they benefit from the moister winter conditions and may receive some winter sunshine. Also, many deciduous plants will begin growing in

spring well before the trees come into full leaf.

Prepare the site thoroughly and, after planting, water in evergreens to help their roots settle in the soil; if the weather is dry, water in deciduous plants as well. Mulch the plants in spring and, for at least the first season after planting, keep a close check on them to ensure that they have sufficient water.

If the plants are growing under large mature trees, there will be little change in the soil conditions from year to year. However, under young, rapidly growing trees both the extent and the degree of shade will increase annually. If, in the latter case, existing plants show signs of deterioration, replace them with plants that are more tolerant of the increasing shade and dryness. Where planting under young trees, anticipate the change in the shade as the trees mature by choosing plants that possess a greater tolerance to shade than is needed at the time.

Moist sites
With the exception of aquatics, few plants can survive prolonged wet or waterlogged conditions. Therefore, where possible, drain the site if the soil remains very wet or waterlogged for long periods, particularly if this occurs in winter.

Some plants, including a few with good ground cover qualities, can survive in moist to wet soils. Their roots have low oxygen requirements and they can establish and grow in conditions where those of many plants would rapidly decay.

DEGREE OF SHADE

In the section on specific ground cover plants (pages 78–107) the degree of shade that a plant needs, or tolerates, is indicated by the terms light shade, partial shade, moderate shade and deep shade.

Light shade usually refers to a site that is open to the sky, but is screened from direct sunlight by some obstacle such as a high wall or a group of trees.

Partial shade describes a site where the sun is excluded for all but two or three hours in a day, either early morning or late evening. Note that several hours of

sunlight in the middle of the day qualifies a site as sunny.

Moderate shade has little or no direct sun, but there is some reflected or transfused light. It often occurs in woodlands or larger shrubberies.

Deep shade is usually encountered under the canopy of larger deciduous trees that have low branches and dense foliage, for example, sycamore, beech and horse chestnut. This type of shade is also found under clumps of conifers or among overgrown shrubberies.

Shaded sites
A indicates a moist soil
B indicates an average soil
C indicates a dry soil
If a plant prefers one of these
conditions, then a letter in bold type is
used; a letter in normal type indicates
that the plant will tolerate these
conditions.

☆ indicates that the plant requires an
acid, lime-free soil.

PLANTS FOR SHADED SITES

Medium or deep shade

GROUP 1

Galeobdolon argentatum	A	**B**	C
Hedera canariensis		**B**	
Hedera colchica		**B**	
Hedera helix and var hibernica	A	**B**	C
Vinca spp	A	**B**	C
Waldsteinia ternata	A	B	**C**

GROUP 2

Asarum spp	**A**		
Euonymus fortunei var radicans			**C**
× Gaulnettya wisleyensis ☆	**A**	**B**	
Gaultheria shallon ☆		**B**	C
Leucothoe fontanesiana	**A**	**B**	
Lonicera pileata		**B**	
Mahonia aquifolium		**B**	C
Pachysandra terminalis		B	**C**
Prunus laurocerasus varieties		B	**C**

GROUP 3

Acanthus mollis 'Latifolius'		**B**	
Brunnera macrophylla	**A**	B	
Hosta spp	A	**B**	
Iris foetidissima		B	**C**
Pulmonaria spp	**A**		

GROUP 4

Asperula odorata		**B**	
Blechnum spicant	**A**		
Convallaria majalis	**A**	B	
Dicentra formosa	**A**		
Duchesnea indica		B	**C**
Euphorbia robbiae			**C**
Gaultheria procumbens		**B**	
Geranium nodosum	A	**B**	
Geranium phaeum	A	**B**	
Geranium punctatum	A	**B**	
Lamium maculatum	A	**B**	C
Luzula maxima		B	**C**
Maianthemum bifolium	**A**		
Omphalodes spp	**A**	B	
Oxalis oregana	**A**	B	
Rubus spp		B	**C**
Sarcococca humilis		B	**C**
Symphytum grandiflorum	**A**	B	
Tellima grandiflora	A	**B**	C

Tiarella spp	**A**	B	
Vancouveria hexandra	**A**	B	
Viola labradorica	A	**B**	C
Viola obliqua	A	**B**	C

Light or open shade

GROUP 2

Arctostaphylos uva-ursi ☆	**A**	B	
Bergenia spp and hybrids	**A**	B	
Cotoneaster spp	A	**B**	C
Cotoneaster 'Gnom'		**B**	C
Erica herbacea		**B**	
Euonymus fortunei f carrierei		**B**	
Hypericum × moseranum		**B**	C
Juniperus conferta		**B**	C
Juniperus × media 'Pfitzeriana'			**C**
Juniperus sabina var tamariscifolia		**B**	C

GROUP 3

Alchemilla mollis		**B**	
Geranium endressii 'Wargrave Pink'	**A**	B
Geranium psilostemon	**A**	B
Geranium sylvaticum	**A**	B
Geum × borisii		**B**	C
Hemerocallis spp	A	**B**
Polygonum campanulatum	**A**	

GROUP 4

Ajuga reptans	**A**		
Campanula spp		**B**	
Cornus canadensis ☆	**A**		
Cotula squalida		B	**C**
Epimedium spp		**B**	
Geranium ibericum	A	**B**	
Geranium macrorrhizum	A	**B**	
Geranium × magnificum	A	**B**	
Geranium platypetalum	A	**B**	
Geranium procurrens	A	**B**	
Glechoma hederacea	A	**B**	C
Lysimachia nummularia	**A**		
Potentilla alba	A	**B**	
Prunella grandiflora	A	**B**	
Vaccinium vitis-idaea ☆	A	**B**	
Viola cornuta		**B**	
Viola garden hybrids		**B**	

Problem sites 2

The roots of moisture-tolerant plants are usually rather fleshy, with the plants spreading by means of stolons or rhizomes to form a dense leafy cover. Some are plants of wet pasture or meadowland. Others are native to cool moist woodland or its fringes. They have large soft-textured leaves and pale delicate flowers; they come into growth and flower early in the year before the development of dense overhead leafy cover.

Plants with these qualities and characteristics can be used along the damp margins of streams and ditches where, for most of the year, conditions are too wet for other plants. They can also be used to provide good summer cover in poorly drained, low-lying areas and in damp woodland where deep leaf-mould provides a moist root run throughout the summer months.

Plant in the spring where possible. Autumn planting is acceptable, but even moisture-tolerant plants may deteriorate over winter in very wet conditions when their roots are not well established.

In suitably moist conditions there will be little need for summer watering except in very dry seasons, but, if the site is drier than anticipated, herbaceous plants may die down prematurely during the summer, giving a shorter season of good cover and the possibility of weeds establishing during the late summer or autumn. There may also be some leaf-fall from evergreens, reducing the density of cover and giving rise to similar problems of weed seedling development. In either case, water the plants to prevent this.

For the purposes of the table on this and the next page, a moist soil is defined as one that is uniformly moist, or relatively so, throughout the year. It may, however, become wet occasionally during periods of heavy and extended rainfall. Sites that are very wet in the spring and very dry during the summer do not come into this category. Few if any ground cover plants will provide satisfactory cover in such situations.

Cool, damp shade relates to sites both under trees and in open shade where the soil remains cool and moist throughout the year. Under trees, this is usually due to the presence of a good depth of moisture-retentive leaf-mould or humus.

PLANTS FOR MOIST SITES

GROUP 1

Galeobdolon argentatum		**B**	C
Vinca spp		**B**	
Waldsteinia ternata	A	**B**	C

GROUP 2

Arctostaphylos uva-ursi ☆		B	**C**
Asarum spp	**A**	B	
Bergenia spp and hybrids	A	**B**	C
Calluna vulgaris			**C**
Cotoneaster spp		B	C
Daboecia cantabrica			**C**
× Gaulnettya wisleyensis ☆		B	C
Leucothoe fontanesiana ☆		**B**	
Pachysandra terminalis		**B**	

GROUP 3

Brunnera macrophylla	**A**		
Geranium spp	A	**B**	C
Geum × borisii		**B**	C
Hemerocallis spp	A	**B**	C
Hosta spp	A	**B**	C
Polygonum campanulatum	A	**B**	**C**
Pulmonaria spp	**A**	B	C

GROUP 4

Ajuga reptans	**A**	B	C
Asperula odorata	**A**	**B**	
Campanula spp		B	**C**
Convallaria majalis	**A**	B	
Cornus canadensis ☆	**A**	B	C
Cotoneaster dammeri		**B**	C
Dicentra formosa	**A**	B	
Epimedium spp		**B**	
Gaultheria procumbens		**B**	
Geranium spp	A	**B**	C
Glechoma hederacea	*A*	**B**	C
Lamium maculatum	**A**	**B**	
Lysimachia nummularia	**A**	B	C
Maianthemum bifolium	**A**	**B**	
Oxalis oregana	**A**	**B**	
Potentilla alba		**B**	
Prunella grandiflora		B	C
Symphytum grandiflorum	**A**	**B**	
Tellima grandiflora		B	C
Tiarella spp	**A**	**B**	
Vaccinium vitis-idaea ☆	**A**	**B**	
Viola spp and hybrids	A	**B**	C

Moist sites
A indicates moist shade
B indicates cool, damp shade
C indicates a moist sunny site
If a plant prefers one of these
conditions, then a letter in bold type is
used; a letter in normal type indicates
that the plant will tolerate these
conditions.

☆ indicates that the plant requires an
acid, lime-free soil.

Hot, dry sites
☆ indicates that the plant requires an
acid, lime-free soil.

PLANTS FOR HOT, DRY SITES

GROUP 1
Hedera spp (not variegated varieties)
Hypericum calycinum
Vinca spp and varieties

GROUP 2
Anthemis cupaniana
Arabis albida
Aubrieta deltoidea
Aurinia saxatilis
Ballota pseudodictamnus
Cerastium tomentosum
Cistus parviflorus
Cotoneaster spp
Cytisus spp
Daboecia cantabrica (not on very dry sites)
Dianthus spp
Dryas octopetala
Erica herbacea (not on very dry sites)
Euonymus fortunei var *radicans*
Euonymus fortunei f *carrierei* and varieties
Genista spp
× *Halimiocistus sahucii*
Hebe spp
Helianthemum hybrids
Hypericum spp
Iberis sempervirens
Juniperus communis and varieties
Juniperus conferta
Juniperus horizontalis and varieties
Lithodora diffusa☆

Lonicera pileata
Phlomis fruticosa
Salvia officinalis
Senecio 'Sunshine'

GROUP 3
Liriope muscari
Nepeta × *faassenii*
Origanum vulgare

GROUP 4
Acaena novae-zelandiae
Antennaria dioica
Anthemis nobilis
Artemisia stelleriana
Centaurea 'John Coutts'
Cotoneaster dammeri
Geranium 'Russell Pritchard'
Muehlenbeckia axillaris
Phlox douglasii
Phlox subulata and hybrids
Potentilla alba
Potentilla calabra
Saxifraga "mossy" hybrids
Sedum spathulifolium
Sedum spurium
Stachys byzantina 'Silver Carpet'
Thymus serpyllum
Veronica prostrata
Viola labradorica
Viola obliqua

Hot, dry sites

There is a wide choice of plants for covering dry, sunny sites since there are many that grow naturally in such conditions. The main problem facing these plants is that they tend to lose more moisture through their leaves than they can absorb through their roots. Plants that are native to this type of habitat have had to adapt themselves to overcome this, for example, by having very small or narrow leaves and a dense system of branches, which help to shade the roots from the drying effects of the sun. Other plants have thick-skinned fleshy evergreen leaves, or leaf surfaces that are densely covered with fine hairs, making the plant appear silvery.

In many cases the root systems of such plants have also adapted, becoming extensive and deeply penetrating. This enables them to obtain sufficient moisture from the soil and allows their roots to escape the desiccating effects of summer heat on the upper soil layers. However, this places an important limitation on the type of site on which these plants will grow: it must be well drained throughout the year and, in particular, not become wet and heavy during the winter since much of the root system would die in such conditions. Plants with woolly or hairy leaves are particularly susceptible to this effect because, although they are perfectly hardy to frost, in their natural habitats the

Problem sites 3

climate is dry throughout the year. Thus, unless the soil is very well drained they may suffer or even die during a British winter, which typically has alternating periods of cold, frosty weather and mild, wet weather.

Before planting it is important to dig in a dressing of well rotted farm manure, garden compost, leaf-mould or peat, particularly if the soil is light. This is because the plants will have been raised in rich compost and kept well irrigated. They may, therefore, suffer a considerable check to growth and be slow to establish if they are planted into unimproved soil. By digging in a dressing, the ability of the soil to retain moisture will be increased temporarily, and so the risk of early losses will be reduced.

Planting should be done either in the spring or the autumn, when the soil is cool and moist. If possible, it is better to plant in the autumn, since this allows the roots to become well established before the following summer, when the site will become hot and dry. Mulch the plants in spring to help them conserve moisture during the summer.

Slopes and banks

Most slopes or banks are, by their nature, well drained, and those in full sun on lighter soils usually become quite dry in the summer. Therefore, when choosing plants, it is usually important to select those that are tolerant of drier, well drained soils.

Gentle slopes (those with an angle of less than 20 degrees) provide few problems and allow a wide choice of plants as there is usually little risk of surface erosion. However, if water drains on to the site from higher ground, choose stem-rooting or suckering plants rather than clump-forming plants.

On steeper slopes, grow either suckering shrubs or plants whose branches or stems take root as they spread, since they will consolidate loose surfaces and prevent erosion. Evergreen plants are also useful since they protect the surface from the impact of heavy winter rains, which can rapidly erode unprotected slopes. Common ivy is a valuable ground cover plant in deep shade where few other plants can survive.

Begin planting at the top of the site and

PLANTING ON SLOPES AND BANKS

On gentle slopes (a) plant in shallow hollows since this facilitates mulching and watering. On steeper slopes (b) create terraces, holding them in place with boards and pegs. On banks of porous rock, plant in pockets chipped from the rock face (c). If the rock is non-porous, either train plants up or trail them down the bank (d) or plant them through matting pegged to the rock (e).

Slopes and banks
A indicates a sunny site
B indicates a lightly shaded site
C indicates a deeply shaded site

☆ indicates that the plant requires an
acid, lime-free soil.

PLANTS FOR SLOPES AND BANKS

GROUP 1	Planting distance			
Hedera colchica	36–48 in	A	B	C
Hedera colchica varieties	36–48 in	A	B	
Hedera helix	36 in	A	B	C
Hedera helix variegated varieties	24–36 in	A	B	
Hedera helix var *hibernica*	36–48 in	A	B	C
Hypericum calycinum	15–18 in	A	B	C
Vinca major	18 in	A	B	C
Vinca major var *oxyloba*	24 in	A	B	C
Vinca minor	9–12 in	A	B	C
Also for milder climates:				
Hedera canariensis 'Azorica'	36–48 in	A	B	C
Hedera canariensis 'Gloire de Marengo'	36–48 in	A		

GROUP 2				
Arctostaphylos uva-ursi ☆	15 in	A	B	
Calluna vulgaris and varieties ☆	9–18 in	A	B	
Cotoneaster conspicuus 'Decorus'	72 in	A	B	
Cotoneaster 'Gnom'	18–24 in	A	B	
Cotoneaster microphyllus	18–24 in	A	B	
Cotoneaster 'Skogholm'	18–24 in	A	B	
Daboecia cantabrica and varieties	15–18 in	A		
Erica herbacea and varieties	12–15 in	A	B	
Erica vagans and varieties ☆	12–15 in	A		
Euonymus fortunei var *radicans*	12–18 in	A	B	C
Euonymus fortunei f *carrierei* 'Variegatus'	12–18 in	A	B	C
Gaultheria shallon	36–48 in	A	B	C
Genista hispanica	24 in	A		
Genista pilosa	15 in	A	B	
Helianthemum hybrids	18 in	A		
Juniperus communis, ssp *depressa* and varieties	24 in	A		
Juniperus horizontalis and varieties	18–24 in	A		
Juniperus × *media* 'Pfitzeriana'	48–72 in	A	B	C
Lonicera pileata	24 in	A	B	C
Also for milder climates:				
Ceanothus thyrsiflorus var. *repens*	36–48 in	A		
Juniperus conferta	24 in	A	B	
Phlomis fruticosa	30 in	A		

GROUP 4				
Cotoneaster dammeri	24 in	A	B	
Luzula maxima	15 in	A	B	C
Polygonum vacciniifolium	9–12 in	A		
Rubus tricolor	36 in	A	B	C
Stephanandra incisa 'Crispa'	36 in	A		
Symphoricarpos × *chenaultii* 'Hancock'	36 in	A	B	
Rosa spp and varieties	36–48 in	A		

Problem sites 4

work downwards. On gentle slopes dig a shallow hole for each plant with a trowel, drawing the soil forwards. Alternatively, dig a shallow trench across the slope. These holes will help the site to retain mulches and water. If the digging exposes sub-soil, or if the soil is poor, dig out larger planting holes and fill them with richer soil or work in some good planting compost.

On steeper slopes, construct small terraces by drawing soil forwards to create a series of levels. Hold the back of each terrace in place with boards and wooden stakes or pegs; after a year or two, when the plants are well established, these can be removed. Do not use logs to hold the terrace back because they will decay and may become infested with honey fungus, which will endanger woody plants in the garden.

On a newly cut bank where the soil is sandy there is considerable risk of erosion. Prevent this by firmly pegging down coconut matting or a similar, decomposable, material before planting so that the surface is held firm. Then make holes in the matting and plant through these with spreading, stem-rooting plants that will root down through the matting as it rots to provide good consolidation against erosion. Alternatively, if the underlying material is porous rock, chip pockets out of it and plant in these.

On very steep banks where erosion is likely to occur and it is virtually impossible to plant, the most satisfactory answer is to construct a retaining wall. Alternatively, plant sprawling climbers at the base of the slope and train them up the face, or plant them close to the crest of the slope to trail downwards. The strong-growing species of ivy are suitable for this, as are certain climbers which, though of little merit as ground cover in general, are very useful in this type of situation. They include *Clematis montana* 'Tetrarose', *Clematis orientalis*, *Lonicera henryi*, *Lonicera japonica* 'Halliana' and *Parthenocissus quinquefolia*.

Large areas

As the cost of maintaining a garden has escalated in recent years, the designs of many larger gardens have had to be modified. This has usually been done by increasing shrub plantings and putting down larger areas to grass. However, both methods have several disadvantages. Shrub plantings may take several years to develop into good cover and, in the interim period, will need regular weeding, mulching and pruning. Unless they are carefully selected and positioned, shrub plantings may grow to blot out attractive garden features. With grass there is the expense of fertilizers, weedkillers and mowing equipment. It also needs regular maintenance throughout the growing season.

A much more satisfactory solution to the problem of large areas is to plant ground cover, since it is visually pleasing and requires little maintenance.

As with any other kind of site, the choice of cover plants must be related to the nature of the site and its soil type, but where the planting is to replace a prominent garden feature, or will occupy a strategic position in a new garden, then strong emphasis should be placed on having attractive plants.

Apart from the ornamental aspects, the two most important factors when choosing plants are their height and planting distances. As stated above in connection with shrub plants, height may detract from other features in the garden. The planting distance will, of course, affect the cost of the ground cover. Before planting, measure the site carefully, then calculate the precise number of plants required by referring to the spacing recommendations. Where large numbers of plants are required, obtain quotations and, if the cost is too great, consider alternative selections. The planting distances may be slightly increased where the soil conditions are good, but this may delay the development of effective coverage for a season.

Exposed coastal gardens

Many plants do not grow well in coastal gardens because their shoots and leaves become badly scorched by the salt present in sea winds, even when they are growing some distance inland. There are, however, a number of plants that have become adapted to this type of habitat. For example, marram grass, sea holly and sea pink can be found close to the high-tide mark, where they are frequently drenched by sea spray during stormy weather. Similarly, gorse, Cornish

PLANTS FOR LARGE AREAS

GROUP 1	Height	Planting distance
Galeobdolon argentatum	6–9 in	24–36 in
Hedera canariensis 'Azorica'	6–9 in	36–48 in
Hedera canariensis 'Gloire de Marengo'	6–9 in	36–48 in
Hedera colchica and varieties	6–9 in	36–48 in
Hedera helix	6–9 in	24–36 in
Hedera helix var hibernica	9–12 in	36–48 in
Hypericum calycinum	9–12 in	15–18 in
Vinca major and var oxyloba	6–9 in	18–24 in
Waldsteinia ternata	3–4 in	12 in

GROUP 2		
Bergenia spp and hybrids	6–12 in	9–24 in
Calluna vulgaris varieties	6–18 in	9–18 in
Cotoneaster 'Gnom'	3–4 in	18–24 in
Daboecia cantabrica	15–18 in	15–18 in
Erica vagans and varieties	9–18 in	12–15 in
Euonymus fortunei f carrierei and varieties	24 in	30 in
Genista hispanica	24 in	24 in
Juniperus × media 'Pfitzeriana'	36 in	48–72 in
Juniperus sabina var tamariscifolia	15–18 in	24–30 in
Leucothoe fontanesiana	36 in	36 in
Lonicera pileata	18 in	24 in
Pachysandra terminalis	3–4 in	12 in
Prunus laurocerasus varieties	36 in	36 in
Senecio 'Sunshine'	36 in	36 in

GROUP 3		
Brunnera macrophylla	12 in	15–18 in
Geranium endressii 'Wargrave Pink'	18–21 in	12–18 in
Geranium psilostemon	30 in	12–18 in
Hemerocallis spp and hybrids	18–24 in	18 in
Hosta spp, particularly H. sieboldiana	12–18 in	15–24 in
Polygonum campanulatum	18–24 in	18–24 in

GROUP 4		
Asperula odorata	4–5 in	24 in
Geranium procurrens	18–24 in	18–24 in
Glechoma hederacea	3–4 in	18 in
Luzula maxima	12 in	15 in
Rosa 'Max Graf'	36 in	48–60 in
Rosa × paulii	36–48 in	48–72 in
Rosa 'Temple Bells'	18–24 in	30–36 in
Rosa wichuraiana	12–18 in	60–72 in
Rubus tricolor	12 in	36 in
Stephanandra incisa 'Crispa'	24 in	36 in
Symphoricarpos × chenaultii 'Hancock'	24 in	36 in
Tellima graniflora	6 in	12 in

Problem sites 5

PLANTS FOR COASTAL GARDENS

Fully exposed sites

GROUP 2		
Arctostaphylos uva-ursi ☆	A	B
Calluna vulgaris ☆	A	B
Cerastium tomentosum	**A**	B
Cistus spp	A	
Cotoneaster spp	A	B
Cotoneaster 'Gnom'		**B**
Cytisus spp	A	B
Daboecia cantabrica ☆	A	**B**
Dianthus spp	A	
Erica herbacea and varieties	A	B
Erica vagans and varieties ☆	A	B
Euonymus fortunei var *radicans*	A	B
Euonymus fortunei f *carrierei* and varieties	A	B
Genista spp	A	
x *Halimiocistus sahucii*	A	
Hebe spp	A	B
Juniperus communis and varieties	A	B
Juniperus conferta	A	B
Juniperus horizontalis and varieties	**A**	B
Potentilla fruticosa var *mandschurica*	A	**B**
Senecio 'Sunshine'	A	

GROUP 4		
Artemisia spp	A	
Cotoneaster dammeri	A	B
Potentilla spp	A	B
Rosa wichuraiana	A	
Sedum spp	**A**	B

Less exposed sites

GROUP 1		
Hedera spp	**A**	**B**
Hypericum spp (and Group 2)	**A**	**B**
Vinca spp and varieties	**A**	**B**

GROUP 2		
Arabis albida	A	B
Aurbrieta deltoidea	A	B
Bergenia spp and hybrids		**B**
Dryas octopetala	A	
Helianthemum hybrids	A	B
Lonicera pileata	A	B
Mahonia aquilolium		**B**

GROUP 3		
Alchemilla mollis		**B**
Geranium spp (and Group 4)		**B**
Hemerocallis spp		**B**
Polygonum spp (and Group 4)		**B**

GROUP 4		
Campanula spp		**B**
Euphorbia robbiae		**B**
Phlox spp and varieties	A	B
Rubus spp		**B**
Saxifraga "mossy" hybrids	A	B
Stachys byzantina	A	
Symphoricarpos × *chenaultii*		**B**
Thymus serpyllum	A	
Vaccinium vitis-idaea ☆		**B**

heath and thrift survive on sea cliffs, even though they are fully exposed to salt-laden gale-force winds.

Before selecting ground cover plants, study the site carefully and note whether any part of it is protected against the prevailing wind. Also take into account the soil type and growing conditions.

Prepare the site thoroughly before planting by digging in a dressing of well rotted farm manure, garden compost, leaf-mould or peat. This is particularly important on sand, silt or dry chalk soil. On drier soils, dig in fresh moist seaweed at up to 20 lb per square yard. This will increase temporarily the capacity of

the soil to hold moisture, and so reduce the risk of early losses and encourage quick establishment.

Plant in the spring to give the ground cover a full growing season ahead in which to become well established before there is any serious risk of exposure to severe weather conditions. After planting evergreens, water them in well to settle the roots. With all plants, whether deciduous or evergreen, apply a good surface mulch after planting.

Rose beds

Rose beds are very susceptible to weeds since the plants are spaced fairly far apart and

Exposed coastal gardens
A indicates a light sandy soil
B indicates a medium to medium-heavy soil
If a plant prefers one of these conditions, then a letter in bold type is used; a letter in normal type indicates that the plant will tolerate these conditions.

☆ indicates that the plant requires an acid, lime-free soil.

Exposed inland gardens
☆ indicates that the plant requires an acid, lime-free soil.

EXPOSED INLAND GARDENS

The following plants provide good ground cover in gardens that, although inland, are still exposed to severe weather, for example, northerly gardens. The same considerations apply to these plants as to those growing in coastal gardens.

GROUP 1
Hedera helix and var *hibernica*
Vinca major and var *oxyloba*
Vinca minor
Waldsteinia ternata

Iberis sempervirens
Juniperus communis and varieties
Juniperus horizontalis and varieties
Leucothoe fontanesiana☆
Pachysandra terminalis

GROUP 2
Arctostaphylos uva-ursi☆
Calluna vulgaris and varieties☆
Cotoneaster spp and varieties
Erica herbacea and varieties
Euonymus fortunei and varieties

GROUP 4
Cornus canadensis☆
Gaultheria procumbens☆
Sarcococca spp
Symphoricarpos × *chenaultii* 'Hancock'
Vaccinium vitis-idaea☆

---

are often rather gaunt and leafless towards the base. This problem can be overcome by using weedkillers (see pages 148–149), but an alternative approach is to grow ground cover. The use of ground cover does, however, have one serious drawback: it can interfere with pruning and feeding. Roses need feeding regularly in order to maintain their health and vigour. This can be done by using foliar nutrient sprays, but the best method is to apply mulches of farm manure or garden compost. However, these cannot be laid down effectively where ground cover has been planted. A compromise is to use ground cover plants of moderate vigour and height to provide a broad edging to rose beds without letting them encroach within the boundary defined by the stems of the outermost rose bushes. This will allow the roses to be mulched and pruned, while at the same time providing an attractive border.

Suitable plants for such ground cover include *Geranium sanguineum* var *lancastriense*, *Hebe pinguifolia* 'Pagei', *Helianthemum* hybrids, *Viola*, *Nepeta* × *faassenii* and "mossy" hybrids of *Saxifraga*.

If ground cover is to be planted throughout a rose bed, then the choice is limited to low-growing plants with some shade tolerance. On drier soils, suitable plants include *Lamium maculatum*, *Saxifraga* × *urbium* and *Campanula portenschlagiana*. On moister soils plant *Viola*, *Lysimachia nummularia* 'Aurea' or *Prunella grandiflora*.

Bulbs

In most gardens, bulbs are grown on sites that, for most of the year, are bare earth, for example, at the front of shrubberies or flower beds. This has the disadvantage that the site is readily colonized by weeds after the bulb foliage dies down in early summer. Some bulbs have to be grown in open ground since they need a high dormancy temperature, or "baking", to induce flower bud development, but others, particularly spring-flowering kinds, can be grown successfully under ground cover. The cover must not be so dense that it smothers the bulbs, yet it should be vigorous enough to suppress weed growth. The best plant to use for dwarf bulbs is *Cotula squalida*, which has a very low-spreading habit and gives medium density cover. It tolerates dry or moist conditions and full sun or light shade.

With taller, stronger-growing bulbous plants such as daffodils, *Muscari armeniacum* or bluebells, the density of cover is not so critical. Suitable plants for ground cover include *Ajuga*, *Pulmonaria*, *Viola*, *Glechoma hederacea* 'Variegata' and *Lysimachia nummularia* 'Aurea'.

123

Alternatives to grass

Ground cover plants can be observed growing naturally over large areas of uncultivated land; for example, in colder climates heathers and other low-growing evergreen shrubs frequently cononize land where the soil is poor and acidic. However, such plants cannot usually be used as substitutes for grass in the garden since they lack the resilience that grass possesses to continuous heavy usage. If an herbaceous plant were to be used in place of grass, then its broad leaves and fleshy stems would quickly become bruised and crushed if walked on. If, on the other hand, a shrub were used, then its woody stems would be easily splintered underfoot and the shoots be damaged. In both cases the plants are subsequently likely to be attacked by diseases.

There are, nevertheless, a few plants that can be grown as an alternative to grass, so long as wear is kept to a minimum, the most notable of these being chamomile. These plants all fulfil three necessary criteria: they will tolerate being walked on occasionally; they are neat and attractive throughout the year; and they are low-growing plants that form a cover sufficiently dense to keep the ground reasonably free of weeds. This last quality is particularly important since selective lawn weedkillers cannot be used on ground cover because they act by killing broad-leaved plants while leaving grass, which has narrow leaves, unharmed. Since the plants recommended on this page are all broad-leaved, they may be seriously damaged or even killed if weedkiller is used.

Anthemis nobilis (Chamomile)

Chamomile is a low-growing evergreen perennial with creeping stems that root as they spread. The dark green, finely divided leaves are aromatic when crushed underfoot; the flowers are small, white and daisy-like. The plant is tolerant of dry sunny sites and lighter soils, but it dislikes any degree of shade. It has a tendency to die out in patches and is not weed-proof, therefore hand-weeding is necessary from time to time. Trim chamomile with a mower or shears in late summer to remove dead flowerheads and the occasional ragged shoot. The best form for ground cover is 'Treneague', a non-flowering clone 1–2 in high.

Plants of the flowering form of chamomile are raised from seed. Sow these in early spring under glass, prick out the seedlings into boxes and then harden them off. Finally plant them out in late spring about 9 in apart in ground that has been well prepared and cleared of all perennial weeds. The form 'Treneague' does not produce seeds; it is propagated by division or cuttings and can be obtained only as plants.

Chamomile is a good ground cover plant for infrequently used paths or small areas that are difficult to mow. Chamomile lawns have been grown since Elizabethan times.

Thymus serpyllum (Wild thyme)

This is an evergreen perennial that has tiny dark green leaves and matted procumbent stems. Numerous small lavender-pink flowers appear in summer. Thyme needs full sun and a well drained site; it is less satisfactory on poor, light soils.

Thyme makes an attractive close cover for undulating surfaces where the soil is stony, and it can also be used to provide access to informally planted areas of low-growing plants; such areas are known as alpine lawns. There are several attractive variants, for example, albus and 'Pink Chintz'.

Cotula squalida

This is an attractive, fairly dense plant that forms a close carpet of creeping stems. It can be grown in sun or light shade and prefers reasonably moist conditions, although it is fairly tolerant of drier sites. The foliage is soft, fern-like and bronze-green. Yellow buttons of flowers appear in summer. It can be used for narrow borders next to walls and for planting occasional squares to break the formality of larger paved areas.

Acaena novae-zelandiae

This semi-evergreen sub-shrub is a useful grass substitute in sunny well drained sites. It forms a rather thick, 3–4 in high, carpet, has soft rich-green feathery leaves and spreads rapidly by means of slender rooting stems. It is a useful plant for sunny banks bordering driveways, or any area where grass is difficult to mow and the presence of taller plants would impede vision.

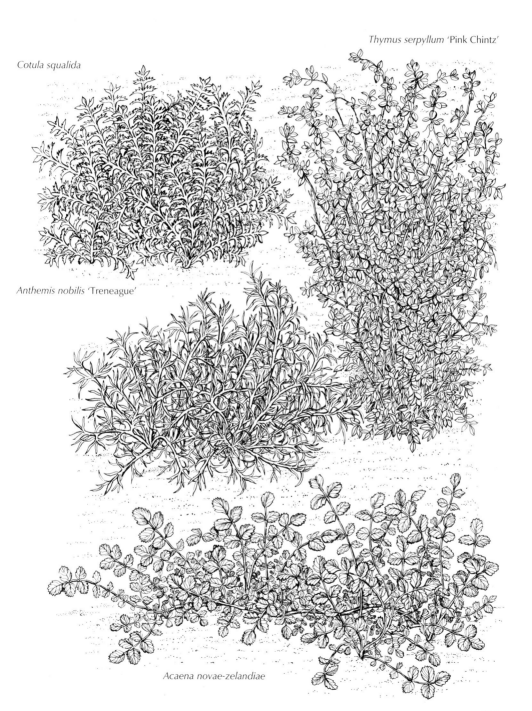

Thymus serpyllum 'Pink Chintz'

Cotula squalida

Anthemis nobilis 'Treneague'

Acaena novae-zelandiae

Introduction 1

In the broadest sense, any plant that appears where it is not wanted is a weed, though the term is usually applied only to those plants that are troublesome because they are most successful at competing with garden plants for soil and space.

Among the most common weeds in the United Kingdom are ground elder, horsetail, couch grass, bindweed, nettle and shepherd's purse, and in lawns, clover, dandelion, yarrow, daisy and speedwell. None of these plants was deliberately introduced into gardens, and they have become so widespread because they can readily adapt to different soils and situations. They grow strongly under adverse conditions, such as frequent mowing of lawns, and they reproduce efficiently. Many have a natural built-in resistance to weed-killers. Other weeds can survive weedkiller treatment because of the depth to which they penetrate the soil.

Obviously weeds are unsightly in ordered flower beds and shrubberies, and in the uniformity of a well kept lawn, but the most important reason for their elimination is that they compete strongly with garden plants for moisture, nutrients, light, air and growing space. Their presence is particularly detrimental to slowly germinating and developing vegetable crops such as onions and carrots, and weeds can substantially reduce crop-yield unless controlled from the earliest stages. Failure to control weed growth can result in low yields from tree and bush fruits and poor development and stunting of growth in woody plants of all kinds.

A further reason for control is that some weeds, if allowed to grow unchecked, can

Weed seedlings

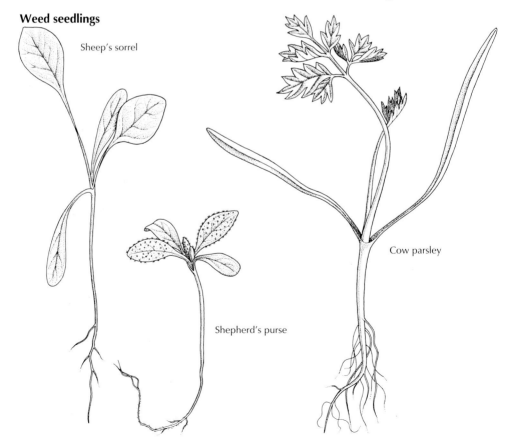

Sheep's sorrel

Shepherd's purse

Cow parsley

act as host plants for pests, viruses and fungal diseases. They can therefore be a source of reinfestation after garden or greenhouse plants have been sprayed. Weeds can also help pests and diseases survive periods of crop rotation and may harbour harmful creatures such as slugs and aphids.

Most troublesome weeds are native wild plants. Others such as creeping bellflower, Japanese knotweed and speedwell were originally introduced to this country as garden plants. They then "escaped" and became naturalized, transmitted as wind-blown seeds, or as small sections of underground stem or rhizome discarded with other plant material on waste land.

Native weeds can usually be identified by consulting one of the various reference works on the flora of the United Kingdom, such as W. Keble Martin's *The Concise British Flora*. Introduced weeds are often more difficult to identify since, by their nature, they are rarely illustrated in books on flora. The illustrations on pages 172-185 show the most troublesome weeds. The seedlings of these weeds often differ greatly from the mature weeds and are therefore illustrated on this and the next four pages.

Weeds may usefully be divided into annuals and perennials. Annual weeds are primarily weeds of cultivated areas, by virtue of their rapid growth, whereas perennial weeds tend to be weeds of neglected areas.

Annual weeds
Annual weeds complete their life cycle – germination, growth, flowering, development of seed, death – within a single season. They

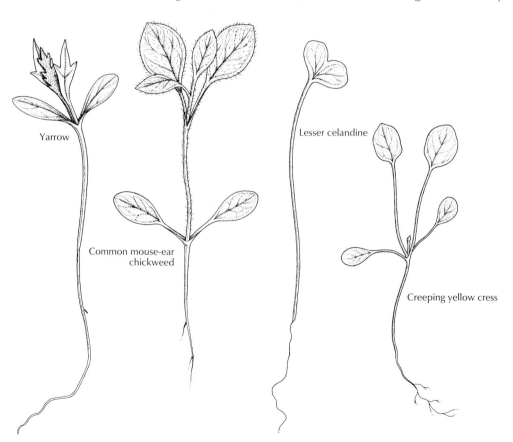

Yarrow

Common mouse-ear chickweed

Lesser celandine

Creeping yellow cress

Introduction 2

do not have storage organs such as rhizomes, tubers or bulbils by which they can survive over winter. Their survival depends on their ability to produce seeds freely, often under unfavourablel conditions and within a few weeks of germination.

In the garden annual weeds are usually most troublesome in areas that are frequently cultivated. Where annuals or bedding plants are grown, and in vegetable plots, the soil is dug and cultivated too frequently to allow perennial weeds to establish themselves. However, annual weeds can become a recurring problem. Once allowed to seed, annual weeds such as annual nettle or shepherd's purse may produce two or three generations in a season if neglected, shedding numerous seeds on to the soil. If the seeds are buried when lifting crops or digging, then they may remain viable in the soil for years, germinating only when brought close to the surface during site preparation or crop cultivation. From such a buried reservoir of seeds, weed seedlings may appear year after year.

Annual weeds are particularly troublesome in crops raised from seed sown *in situ* in the garden. Their vigour and rate of growth often far exceeds that of the crop plant. The seeds of the crop plant may germinate to find there is already strong competiton for moisture and nutrients, and unless the weeds are quickly eliminated the crop seedlings may become drawn and starved.

To control annual weeds first destroy all weeds by hoeing, hand-weeding or with contact weedkillers before they can set seed. Destroy any weed seedlings in the same way. Where past experience suggests that annual

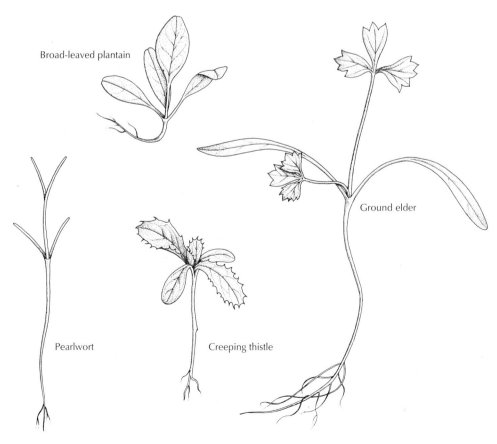

Broad-leaved plantain

Ground elder

Pearlwort

Creeping thistle

weeds may grow, use soil-acting residual weedkillers where possible to kill the weeds at germination. If the soil is infested with annual weeds, cultivate it frequently when it is free of crops to encourage germination of weed seeds. The seedlings can then be killed, thus using up the store of weed seeds in the soil. Apply only well rotted compost to the soil, discarding or re-composting the outer layers of the compost heap if it is only partially rotted or if weeds have been allowed to grow on it the previous season.

Perennial weeds

A perennial weed is one that grows from year to year, as distinct from an annual weed. They survive winter cold or seasonal drought in a state of dormancy, resuming growth with the return of more favourable conditions.

Perennial weeds survive because they are able to store food in organs such as fleshy roots, rhizomes, tubers or bulbs.

Herbaceous perennials have non-woody stems, dying back to ground level in late autumn or early winter. Typical of this group are perennial nettle, Japanese knotweed and field bindweed. Also included in this group are the stemless herbaceous perennials in which the leaves develop directly from roots or rhizomes, such as dandelion and oxalis.

Woody-stemmed perennials, such as blackberry and elder, do not have underground organs adapted for food storage and survive over winter by storing considerable amounts of food in stems and branches.

Perennial weeds are usually found in undisturbed soil, and rarely survive for long the frequent cultivations that are carried out in

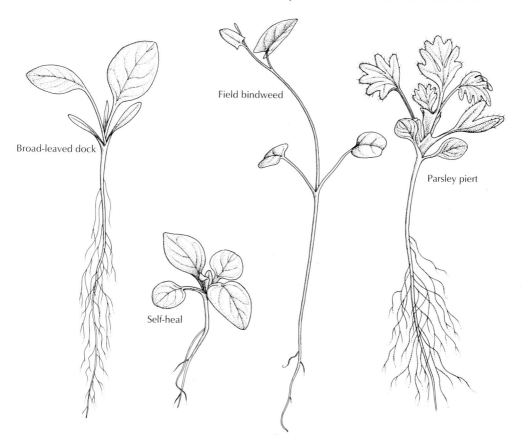

Broad-leaved dock

Field bindweed

Parsley piert

Self-heal

Introduction 3

vegetable plots and flower beds. They will, however, establish themselves in shrubberies, herbaceous borders and among fruit trees and bushes unless measures are taken to destroy these weed seedlings as soon as possible after they appear.

The extensive root systems of perennial weeds give them protection both against the gardener's fork and hoe, and against the effects of weedkillers. Many perennial weeds also have a natural tolerance to garden weedkillers.

These weeds can become established in the garden from seeds carried there by birds; bryony and blackberry being examples. Fireweed grows from wind-blown seeds. Others are brought in with leaf-mould or fresh soil. Some weeds such as couch grass, creeping thistle and ground elder produce few seeds but may often be introduced unwittingly into gardens as small sections of their fleshy underground stems or rhizomes.

To control perennial weeds first keep a watch for seedlings appearing, and destroy them before they reach the stage when tap roots start to develop.

Where possible fork out any small patches of perennial weeds, checking later in the season for signs of regrowth. If there are more extensive infestations of perennial weeds, use appropriate weedkillers if conditions permit. Check all imports of plants, manure and soil for traces of perennial weed stems, rhizomes or roots.

If perennial weeds are invading your garden or allotment from neighbouring land, consult the owner of the land and arrange to deal with the weeds on his ground.

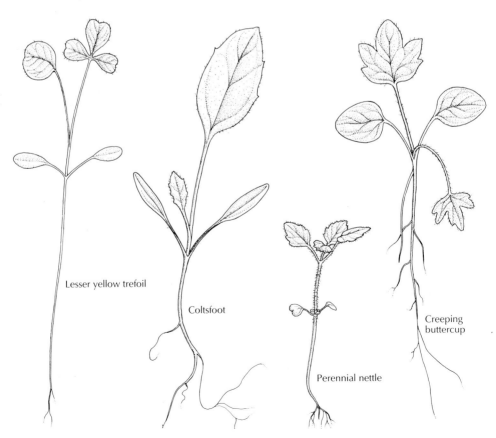

Lesser yellow trefoil

Coltsfoot

Perennial nettle

Creeping buttercup

PERENNIAL WEED STORAGE ORGANS

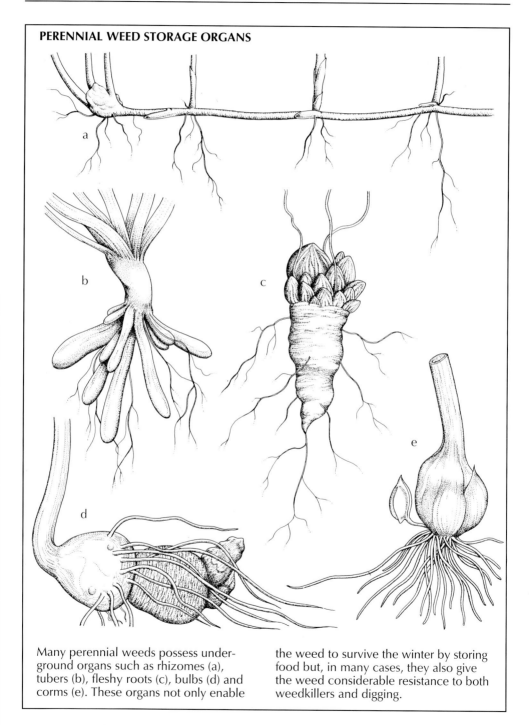

Many perennial weeds possess underground organs such as rhizomes (a), tubers (b), fleshy roots (c), bulbs (d) and corms (e). These organs not only enable the weed to survive the winter by storing food but, in many cases, they also give the weed considerable resistance to both weedkillers and digging.

Cultivation or weedkillers?

Weeds may occur anywhere in the garden. In some places it is obviously more practicable to remove weeds by hoeing, forking or by hand; in others, such as lawns, it is better to use weedkillers. In the small garden the various kinds of plants will be mixed. Woody-stemmed shrubs, herbaceous plants, bulbs, perhaps a few scattered fruit trees or bushes will all be grown close together. The different plants will have widely differing tolerances to weedkillers. Therefore, there may be very few situations in which weedkillers can be used effectively and safely. In extreme cases weedkillers may have to be limited to lawns and paths. In bigger gardens there is more scope for larger groupings of each type of plant and therefore more opportunity for the effective and safe use of weedkillers.

Occasions occur in any garden where either approach, cultivation or chemical, may seem equally viable to help the gardener decide, the advantages and disadvantages of these two approaches are listed below.

Advantages of cultivation
Weed control by cultivation uses simpler tools than does chemical control, and is much cheaper. Some cultivation techniques, such as the use of ground cover (see page 76)

can give permanent relief from previously recurring weed problems. Hoeing can provide a quick kill of seedling weeds in dry sunny conditions. It can also relieve compaction in the surface layers, improving moisture penetration and aeration.

Advantages of weedkillers
Chemical control leaves the soil undisturbed, encouraging crop root development nearer the surface and thus a quicker response to surface-applied nutrients. Weedkillers are effective over a long period, controlling weeds during wet summers when cultivation methods are relatively ineffective. They control all sizes and stages of weed growth. A single carefully timed application of weedkiller can give weed-free conditions for up to a full season. Weedkillers can kill an entire weed colony *in situ*, with no risk of accidental spread of infestation from weed rhizomes, bulbils, or sections of stem. In many situations weedkillers will act at the seed germination stage. This means that there is no resultant check to the crop from weed competition or from soil disturbance.

Disadvantages of cultivation
Hand-weeding row crops is impracticable until the seedling weeds are big enough to be

handled without excessive disturbance to the crop and can be removed with roots intact. During the time they take to reach this stage the weeds are in competition with the crop. The roots of crop seedlings are frequently damaged or disturbed when weeds are removed from the row by hand. Some crop seedlings may be lost, others may suffer a considerable check.

When weeds are pulled by hand, fresh soil is brought to the surface. Often it holds dormant weed seeds which then germinate to give further trouble. When hand-weeding perennials or maturing annuals, weed seeds or bulbils may be scattered over neighbouring areas and spread the infestation.

Forking out rhizomatous roots of weeds such as quack grass and wild chrysanthemum may be only partially successful and leave fragments to perpetuate the infestation. Weed rhizome fragments or bulbils may find their way to the compost heap, only to survive composting and be unwittingly re-introduced to the garden in compost dressings. The roots of the trees, shrubs and perennials may be damaged or disturbed by forking, resulting in a check to growth. Damage or disturbance may stimulate development of troublesome root suckers in some trees or shrubs, such as lilacs, roses, flowering cherries and flowering plums.

Hoeing may sever young plants or damage their roots, with a resultant check to growth. Frequent hoeing around trees, shrubs, fruit bushes and herbaceous perennials can destroy or inhibit development of near-surface feeding roots. it may also destroy soil structure and increase the rate of decomposition of organic matter in the soil. Hoeing in wet weather is frequently of little value, as many weeds will quickly re-establish themselves.

Disadvantages of weedkillers
The use of weedkillers demands time-consuming, laborious precautions. Weedkillers are expensive and must be handled carefully at all stages of preparation and application. Protective clothing should be worn when spraying, and all spraying equipment must be cleaned thoroughly after use. Spraying often depends upon the weather, and applications must be carefully timed for success. It also forms a potential danger to garden plants: inaccurate mixing or application, spray drift of foliar-acting weedkillers and leaching of highly soluble soil-acting weedkillers can all be fatal to plants. If spraying or watering equipment is used for purposes other than applying weedkillers it may be contaminated and cause considerable damage.

Weed control by cultivation 1

The more troublesome weeds are, by their nature, strong-growing and compete successfully with most garden plants. They often thrive in poor, dry or hungry soils in which many cultivated plants struggle. Evidence of this can be seen in any long-neglected garden. The weeds becomeing dominant and the cultivated plants consequently decline, both in vigour and in health.

It is therefore essential to take all possible steps by sound cultivation to ensure rapid establishment and strong healthy growth of cultivated plants, and to take the appropriate measures to reduce the possibility of weeds reappearing.

Site preparation
Thoroughly remove all traces of perennial weeds and their roots and rhizomes by hoeing or forking out. Where possible allow a period of fallowing. This enables weeds that are present as dormant seeds in the soil to develop and be destroyed.

Ensure good fertility before planting or sowing by digging in manure or compost during site preparation and by application of fertilizers beforehand.

Forking out weeds

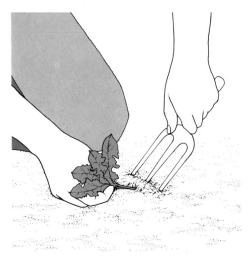

Before sowing, first remove all traces of perennial weeds by uprooting them with either a hand fork or a garden fork.

Choosing plants
Select plants and varieties that are suitable for local conditions and soils. Buy only sound, healthy, well rooted stock from reputable nurseries or suppliers. Ignore any weak, starved, unhealthy-looking plants, even at apparent "bargain" prices. These will be slow to grow away and be more susceptible to any competition from weeds. Good growing conditions enable vegetables, annuals and bedding plants to grow rapidly. With correct spacing their leaves will cover much more of the soil surface as they grow, suppressing weed germination and growth until a complete cover has developed.

Shrubs that have been fed regularly, mulched, pruned and sprayed to control pests and diseases will develop stronger growth and a denser leaf canopy than those that have been neglected. If a plant is neglected it may develop sparsely leaved branches, under which there is sufficient light and moisture for wing- or bird-carried seeds to germinate and grow. On the other hand, the denser canopy of healthy shrubs produces conditions that are unsuitable for weed development.

Feeding

Then dig in manure or compost and apply a general fertilizer.

Sowing seed

Sow vegetable and flower seeds at the recommended time of the year when conditions are right for rapid germination and early growth. Delay sowing if the weather is cold and wet, for bad weather will cause the seedlings to grow slowly.

Mulching

Organic mulches are very beneficial to plant growth, particularly on lighter, drier soils, since they conserve moisture and provide nutrients as the organic matter slowly breaks down. They also help in suppressing weed growth. The effectiveness of the combination of a good dense leaf canopy and a natural deep leaf-mulch can often be seen in mature deciduous woodland.

Apply mulches in spring when the soil is moist and before the onset of drier summer conditions, first removing any over-wintering weeds. Deep mulches of well rotted farm manure, leaf-mould, peat or processed bark will smother most weed seedlings and inhibit germination of weed seeds. Persistent perennial weeds will usually grow through the mulch, but they will soon root into it from

where they can be more easily removed. Wind- and bird-deposited weeds seeds germinating on the mulch can also be easily removed as seedlings. It should be noted that farm manures and garden compost, unless well rotted, may contain viable weed seeds.

Polythene as a mulch

Black polythene sheet is used extensively as a surface mulch. It effectively prevents weed seedling development and promotes growth in newly planted woody ornamentals, in tree and bush fruits and in strawberries. Perennial weeds can, however, come through between strips and through the holes provided for stems. It is important to remove all perennial weeds from the site before planting. The sheeting is put down after planting in spring when the soil is moist. Being impervious to moisture it stops evaporation, but rain can penetrate between overlapped strips. Black polythene promotes growth in young plants by up to 40 per cent over bare soil conditions. It is particularly useful in the critical first two or three years of establishing specimen ornaments. Apply it to an area 3–4 ft in radius from the stem.

Sowing indoors

Mulching

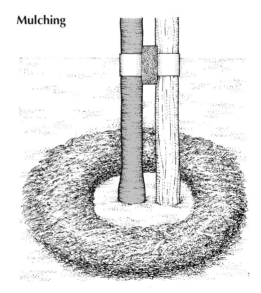

If the weather is cold and wet at sowing time, certain seedlings may be grown indoors in peat pots.

Mulching helps to suppress weed growth as well as conserving moisture and proving nutrients.

Weed control by cultivation 2

Clear polythene is less suitable since it transmits light and more heat than black polythene. Weeds may easily develop under it and, although some may be killed by increasing temperatures as the season advances, it is still often necessary to apply weedkillers. Brown plastic film that decomposes after one year has been successfully used around young herbaceous plants.

Ground cover plants
Some low-growing spreading plants are so dense that where they carpet the ground they suppress the germination of virtually all weed seeds. Such plants are called ground cover plants. Some will grow in damp or very dry, shady corners where few garden plants grow well but weeds thrive. Careful choice of such plants can eliminate various annual weeding problems while adding variety and interest to the garden. For further details, see the section on ground cover, pages 76–125.

Weed deterrent plants
Tagetes minuta is a tall, half-hardy annual that is occasionally suggested as a control for ground elder. However, there appears to be no reliable evidence to support claims that it will successfully control this or any other perennial weed. Gardeners wishing to test it may find it difficult to obtain seeds as it is seldom stocked by seedsmen.

Hand-weeding
In certain situations weeding by hand has advantages over both weedkillers and mechanical methods of control. It is often the only practicable method of dealing with weeds in flower borders since here the nature of the plants and their diversity precludes the use of weedkillers capable of killing established weeds. Hand-weeding can also be employed in various other parts of the garden where weedkillers cannot, by nature of the crop, be used. It may also be a better form of control than other cultural methods, for example between closely planted vegetable crops where injury would result from mechanical removal. Another advantage of hand-weeding is its thoroughness. Not only does it completely remove annual weeds, it also removes the leaves, stems and shoots of perennial weeds and gives them a considerable check.

Where hand-weeding, do so while the

Polythene mulch

Black polythene sheeting may be used as a mulch. Put it down when the soil is moist after planting in spring.

Hand-weeding

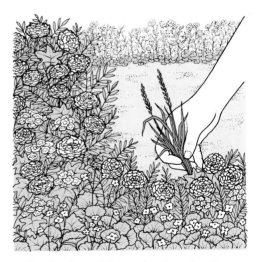

In closely planted flower borders, hand-weeding is very often the only practicable method of controlling weeds.

weeds are small, if possible before they provide any degree of competition for the garden plants and before they form seeds. Put all weeds into a trug or box as weeding progresses, and dispose of them by carefully composting or, if they are seeding, by burning. After weeding around seedlings or young plants irrigate the area well to settle any crop roots that have been disturbed.

Tools and techniques

The hand fork is an extremely useful tool, enabling the gardener to remove tap-rooted weeds in their entirety, as with dandelions in turf, and to ease out persistent weeds carefully from among clumps of garden plants or shrubs with minimum damage to the roots.

The garden fork is used to remove isolated clumps of spreading perennial weeds, such as couch grass, ground elder and perennial nettle. Do this, if possible, before they become too well established.

The hoe is a valuable tool when handled with care and is ideal for inter-row weed control, although it is less satisfactory for inter-plant use. There are various types, the most effec- tive for weed control being the two-bladed pull-push hoe which is angled to cut parallel with the soil surface. It is pushed or drawn through the soil just below the surface, severing and killing annual weeds and checking growth of perennials. Always keep the cutting blade clean and sharp.

Some types of hoe have a single cutting surface, others a serrated blade. There are several types of motorized rotary cultivators available; these can be fitted with various hoeing and cultivating attachments. The Dutch or draw hoe, with the blade meeting the earth almost at a right-angle, has little value in weed control since it lifts soil and weeds rather than severing cleanly.

Hoe in dry weather when severed weeds will quickly shrivel up and die. In wet, showery conditions many weeds may take root again to continue growth.

The flame gun may have some value on hard surface areas in burning off above-ground weed growth and destroying weed seeds, but as a method of weed control it has been largely superseded by modern weedkillers and is of little value in the garden.

Using a hand fork

In front of shrub borders, tap-rooted weeds such as dandelion are best removed with a hand fork.

Inter-row weeding

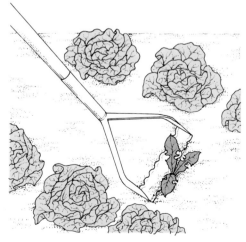

The two-bladed hoe is the most effective tool for inter-row weeding since it cuts parallel to the soil surface.

Weedkillers 1

How weedkillers work

The properties and modes of action of weed-killing chemicals vary considerably. Some are taken into the plant via the roots, others enter the plant both by root uptake and foliage absorption.

Mixtures of weedkillers with different properties are used to control different types of weed growing together. For example, lawn weedkillers often contain one chemical effective against broad-leaved weeds such as the daisy and another aimed at small-leaved, creeping weeds such as clovers.

There are three different ways in which weedkillers (or herbicides) work. Each varies in its effectiveness against certain types of plant and in the length of time that it remains active in the soil.

Contact action weedkillers destroy only the green parts of plants. They are most effective against annual weeds, usually killing them completely. They will also destroy the leaves and green stems of perennial weeds but have little or no effect on their underground parts. Fleshy-footed, bulbous or rhizomatous perennial weeds are usually only checked, and quickly resume growth. Contact action weedkillers usually have little or no residual effect on the soil.

Translocated weedkillers are absorbed into the weed, principally through leaves and stems, and then spread to all parts of it to kill rapidly. Most lawn weedkillers come into this category and are often termed selectives or growth regulators. They are most effective against broad-leaved weeds, which have a large leaf area to absorb the chemical. With narrow-leaved erect grasses and cereals there is little absorption, and thus little damage, but grasses can be harmed by strong concentrations. Some translocated weedkillers are particularly effective against woody-stemmed or shrubby weeds. The selectives usually remain in the soil for two to three

SAFETY

All garden weedkillers carry instructions on the pack, can or bottle label, or in an accompanying leaflet. However, there are certain commonsense precautions that may not be covered. These are listed below.

1 Use weedkillers only when and where necessary. Do not fill the sprayer with weedkiller, use perhaps half and then wander around the garden looking for somewhere to use it up. Plan spraying operations and use weedkillers economically. Never use up stocks unnecessarily.

2 Do not use weedkillers where small patches of weed can be forked out easily without damaging the roots of garden plants, or where scattered annual weeds can be easily hand-weeded or removed by hoeing.

3 Read the product label carefully before buying to ensure that the product does the required job. Never buy more than enough for immediate needs.

4 Keep all weedkillers out of reach of children and pets, preferably by storing them in a locked cupboard.

5 Check the label carefully immediately before use. Follow the manufacturer's instructions exactly.

6 Wear rubber gloves and old clothes when mixing and applying weedkillers.

7 Mix or prepare weedkillers in the open or in a garden shed, using an outside water supply. Never take weedkillers or spraying equipment into the kitchen for preparing or mixing.

8 Never leave packs or bottles open and unattended when spraying. Re-cork or reseal and return the container to safe storage before starting spraying.

9 Do not spray in windy weather because the spray may drift and cause damage to garden plants. During hot weather, spray in the cool of the evening.

months, after which it is safe to sow or plant crops. Glyphosate, however, though translocated in action, is non-selective and acts entirely through the leaves, leaving no residue in the soil.

Total weedkillers are usually soil-acting and in theory kill all vegetation, but in practice some regrowth may occur from a few very persistent, deeply penetrating perennial weeds. Most total weedkillers remain residual and active in the soil for several months. They can be divided into two sub-groups: long-term and short-term residuals.

Long-term residual weedkillers are relatively insoluble and when used at low rates remain residual in the top few inches of soil, killing germinating weed seedlings over a period of several months. Some will also control or check certain perennial weeds and grasses. Because the roots of most trees and shrubs penetrate well below the top few inches these weedkillers can be used at low rates to kill small and shallow-rooted weeds among certain ornamental trees and shrubs, roses and fruit bushes. Some woody plants are particularly susceptible, however, and can be damaged by weedkillers at even very low dosage rates. Others are shallow-rooting and do absorb some of the weedkiller but with no detrimental effect. Some herbaceous plants are tolerant of long-term residuals but many others may be damaged.

Short-term residuals are similar in action but they remain effective for only a few weeks. They are used mainly by nurseries and market gardeners to control weed seedlings in slow-developing crops, such as carrots and onions, where there is risk of strong competition from annual weeds during their critical early stages of growth. By the time the effects of the weedkiller have worn off, the crop is usually sufficiently advanced to be little troubled by further weed development. Their value in the small garden is limited.

10 Avoid contaminating ditches, streams, pools and ponds with spray.

11 Never store quantities of diluted but unused weedkiller solutions since, once diluted, their effectiveness may decline.

12 Never transfer weedkillers to other containers, particularly bottles. If weedkiller labels become detached always re-attach, firmly and immediately.

13 Thoroughly wash out sprayers and watering cans after use, with detergent and several rinses of clean water. Always have a separate can or sprayer for weedkillers. There have been numerous cases of crop damage, particularly to tomatoes, from minute traces of weedkillers remaining in watering cans after being used for weedkilling.

14 Wash hands thoroughly after weedkillers have been employed.

15 Dispose of all empty weedkiller containers with care. Always wash them out thoroughly, then compress or flatten metal containers before disposing of them with other refuse.

16 It is illegal to acquire quantities of commercial weedkillers from professional users. Some commercially used weedkillers can present a considerable health hazard to persons handling the concentrate, or even the diluted spray, unless full protective clothing is worn. All weedkillers are potentially dangerous when not in their original containers and when they are divorced from the manufacturer's pack and accompanying instructions for their handling.

17 If the hands or face become contaminated with weedkiller, wash it off at once with plenty of cold water.

18 Ingestion of weedkillers causes abdominal pains and vomiting. If these symptoms occur, take the victim to the nearest hospital immediately and inform the staff of the weedkiller responsible.

Weedkillers 2

Effectiveness
Weeds vary considerably in their reaction to weedkillers. Some weeds may be killed easily by a single treatment. Others may need two or more treatments at intervals of several weeks before being killed. A few may prove resistant to all attempts at chemical control. Garden plants also vary considerably in their reaction to weedkillers. There are many thousands of different plants in cultivation and with shrubs and herbaceous plants, for example, some may be killed or badly damaged by a single incautious application while others remain unharmed. The time of year, weather conditions, soil type and rate of application can all influence the degree of effectiveness and risk of damage to garden plants, and it is essential to study and follow carefully the manufacturer's recommendations that accompany the product.

Which weedkiller?
Described below are the more common weedkillers available to the amateur, grouped according to the weeds they work against.

General weeds
Dichlobenil provides total weed control in uncropped areas if applied at more concentrated rates. It is then residual for up to 12 months. At lower rates it controls germinating weed seeds, established annuals and certain perennial weeds where they occur among woody plants, though some woody plants are susceptible to dichlobenil. At lower rates it is residual for three to six months. Dichlobenil is a soil-acting weedkiller and should be used only when the soil is moist or rain is expected, otherwise residual action may be reduced.
Dichlorophen controls algal growths, mosses and liverworts on capillary matting, sand beds and the soil surface of pot and container plants. It also controls mosses and liverworts in lawns, frame-yards and on various hard surfaces. Apply it as a fine spray. Action is primarily by contact, though it remains residual for two to three months.
Glyphosate is foliar-acting, being translocated from the leaves to underground parts.

It controls both annual and perennial grasses, and broad-leaved weeds. Glyphosate rapidly becomes inactive on contact with the soil and there is no root uptake. Sowing or planting can be done as soon as weeds are dead. Liquid and gel formulations are available.
Paraquat/diquat is contact in action and effective against the green parts of all plants with the exception of mosses and liverworts. It kills annual weeds and checks the growth of perennials. Paraquat/diquat is available to the amateur in solid granular form only, to be dissolved and applied in water. It becomes inactive on contact with the soil, leaving no residues harmful to plant growth.
Propachlor is soil-acting, controlling many annual weeds at the seed germination stage in various ornamental plantings and amongst some vegetable crops. Persistence is for a few weeks only.
Simazine is used at higher rates for total weed control in uncropped areas and provides residual control for up to 12 months. At low rates it controls germinating weed seeds among most tree and bush fruits and many woody ornamentals, and is then residual for seven months or more. A soil-acting weedkiller, it is applied as an insoluble powder in water. When applying, agitate the solution constantly to ensure even distribution.

Weeds in lawns
Alloxydim-sodium controls couch grass and other perennial grass weeds. It is foliage-acting, non-residual and harmless to all non-grassy ornamentals.
Lawn sands are mixtures of sharp sand with calcined ferrous sulphate and sulphate of ammonia. Lawn mosses are killed by caustic action, the mixture being activated by moisture after application.
MCPA is translocated in action and used to control selectively various weeds.
Mecoprop/dicamba; 2,4-D/dichlorprop; 2,4-D/mecoprop; 2,4-D/dicamba; 2,4-D/fenoprop are all mixtures of translocated weedkillers, and are used to control established weeds. They are usually residual in the soil for between two and three months after application.

Woody weeds

Ammonium sulphamate is translocated and soil-acting. It is effective as a total weedkiller against a wide range of woody and herbaceous plants and is used particularly for killing tree stumps resistant to 2,4-D/dicamba mixtures. Store this weedkiller carefully since it is strongly corrosive to most metals and absorbs moisture from the air. Ammonium Sulphamate is residual in the soil for five to 12 weeks. After application to tree stumps allow at least three months before planting in the vicinity.

Some formulations of 2,4-D/dicamba, with mecoprop or MCPA, are effective in controlling woody weeds such as sycamore seedling, elder and bramble, can be used to kill smaller stumps of certain tree species, and in uncultivated areas can be used in the control of mixed woody and herbaceous weeds, such as ivy, nettle and bindweed. These weedkillers are usually residual in the soil for between two and three months.

Grassy weeds

Dalapon is used in the control of all grass weeds, particularly couch grass. A translocated weedkiller, it is applied as a foliage spray when grasses are in active growth. It can be used during winter months to control selectively grass weeds growing among tree and bush fruits, and is residual in the soil for between two to three months.

Weeds in uncropped areas

Sodium chlorate is a highly soluble crystalline weedkiller that is translocated and soil-acting. It can leach laterally through the soil to harm plants in untreated adjoining areas, particularly on sloping ground, and may also be taken up by tree or shrub roots. Therefore use it only for total weed control on uncropped areas. It is residual for six months or longer.

Use only formulations that contain a fire suppressant otherwise it renders treated vegetation highly inflammable. Do not use metal sprayers or equipment because sodium chlorate corrodes metal.

WEEDKILLERS FOR AMATEURS AND PROFESSIONALS

Since World War II many chemicals with weedkilling properties have been discovered and made available to professional users such as farmers, commercial growers, nurserymen and market gardeners. Over the years a number of these chemicals have been introduced on to the amateur market but, compared with the number of weedkilling chemicals that are available to the professional user, the amateur gardener still has relatively few at his disposal.

There are two basic reasons for this. Firstly, to be acceptable for amateur use a weedkilling chemical must be safe to handle and simple to prepare and apply. Some of the weedkillers widely used by professionals are toxic, and others need special handling and application techniques. They are therefore unsuitable for the amateur market. Occasionally however, manufacturers may find it possible to develop a formulation of a potentially hazardous chemical to meet the handling and safety requirements of the amateur. For example, paraquat is available to professionals as a liquid, but its toxicity prevents it from being allowed on to the amateur market in this form. However, paraquat is available to amateurs in a much safer, solid, form.

Secondly, to be considered for the amateur market a chemical weedkiller must have good sales potential. With the large areas of land involved in farming and commercial horticulture, a specialized weedkiller may still command large sales, whereas to be profitable on the amateur market it must have advantages over existing products, for example, by having a greater range of applications or improved efficiency. Often weedkillers appear on the amateur market, only to disappear after a few seasons because they have failed to achieve sufficient sales.

Weedkillers 3

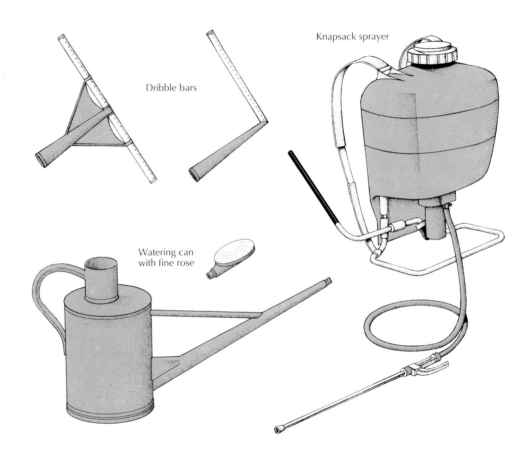

Knapsack sprayer

Dribble bars

Watering can
with fine rose

When applying weedkillers it is most important that they are distributed both accurately and uniformly. Not only does this ensure the safety of the crop but it is also the most effective and economical approach.

Where a specified amount of liquid weedkiller is to be applied to a given area, carry out trial applications with water to determine the area that can be treated with a full can or spray. Then adjust the concentration of the weedkiller or modify your pace of walking as necessary. Where feasible mark out strips a yard wide with garden twine and canes. This will act as a guide to minimize the risk of applying weedkiller to the same area twice. If this were to occur, any crops present

may be badly damaged by the excessively high concentration of weedkiller.

Liquid formulations
Most weedkillers available for amateur use are marketed as a concentrated liquid, to be diluted with water. They may be applied using any of the following methods.
Watering cans have either a fine rose or dribble bar attachment. A rose attachment provides concentrated applications of the weedkiller and is most effectively used where thorough wetting of dense weed foliage is required and the amount applied is not critical. A dribble bar is a hollow perforated tube with sealed ends. It is attached to the

142

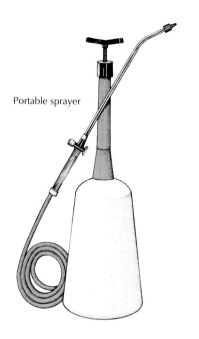

Portable sprayer

Hand sprayer

spout of the can with the bar parallel to the soil surface, the weedkiller solution being dribbled on to weeds or the soil. It is most effectively used for treating low weed growth on hard surfaces, lawns, between rows of crops, around tree and bush fruit, and ornamental shrubs.

The main drawbacks of using a watering can are firstly the weight of the can when full and the consequent difficulty in supporting it when treating taller plants. Secondly there is a risk of the can being used for watering when it has not been cleaned thoroughly after use. Always keep a separate watering can for weedkilling, and wash it out and store it immediately after use.

Portable sprayers have either a single spray nozzle or a multi-nozzle spray boom. There are numerous sprayers on the market and design features vary considerably. The main requirements for weed control are a satisfactory performance at low pressure (there is risk of drift damage if weedkillers are applied at high pressure) and a comfortable, adjustable support harness. The shape of the container holding the weedkiller is unimportant. The spray nozzle should be a flat fan since this directs the spray downwards. Where available, spray hoods give added protection against spray drift. Sprayers are of particular value where applying low concentrations of weedkiller to large area, but may have only

Weedkillers 4

Wheeled sprayer with
multi-nozzle spray boom

limited value in small gardens having a large number of plants. A hardboard square with a broom handle attached can be used to protect grass verges when spraying paths or paving gullies.

Wheeled sprayers have a multi-nozzle spray boom with a large capacity container, and are invaluable for weed control in large areas of turf. Some models are hand-propelled, others power-driven. In both cases the weedkiller is applied under pressure.

Roller sprayers consist of a container with a large roller mounted on the front instead of wheels. The weedkiller is trickled over the roller and applied to the weeds by direct roller contact. They are used only on lawns.

Where the turf is too short to record the roller's passage avoid overlapping by adding a trace of emulsion paint to the weedkiller solution.

Spot treatment is an effective method of controlling weeds growing in places where direct spraying is impossible. Application to herbaceous weeds of a non-drip gel formulation, by means of an applicator which accompanies the product, is often the only real deterrent approach where deep-rooted weeds such as field horsetail and field bindweed are established in beds, borders, rockeries and shrubberies.

Soluble solids

These may be applied using any of the

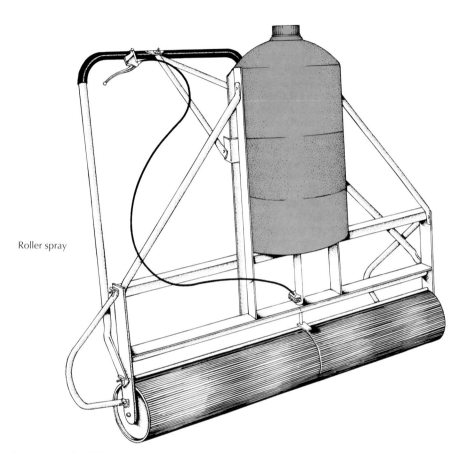

Roller spray

methods described for liquid formulations.

Wettable powders
These are applied as a suspension in water. Ensure that it is mixed thoroughly, and keep the suspension agitated during application.

Granular formulations
These are soil-acting and are applied direct to the soil surface. Accurate placing of the weed-killer and uniform coverage are essential, and various applicators are available for forestry, agricultural and industrial use. The gardener must, however, rely on a steady hand and keen eye. Apply with a shaker pack either to carefully calculated areas or with the aid of the manufacturer's visual distribution guide. Fertilizer drills are unsuitable for the application of granular weedkillers because of the low quantities of granules normally required and the need for accurate placing.

Aerosol formulations
This is a useful method of controlling scattered lawn weeds; some formulations include a foam marker which persists for some time to indicate where application has been made.

Solid formulation
Waxy formulations of selective weedkiller in "stick" form can be applied in individual large-leaved weeds in close-mown turf.

Weed control: trees and shrubs

In shrub borders annual weeds are usually troublesome in the early years following planting. As the trees and shrubs grow and the leaf canopy thickens, fewer annual weeds will germinate and survive, but at this stage perennial weeds may begin to appear.

Weed control techniques must take into account the habitat – shrub border, hedge or specimen plant – and the genus and species.

Cultural control

Promote strong, healthy growth at all stages of development of the shrubs. Encourage vigour in young trees and shrubs by thorough site preparation, careful planting and regular feeding and mulching as the nature of the soil dictates. Prune out older, worn-out wood from neglected shrubs, feeding and mulching to stimulate strong healthy new growth. Where there is bare soil under trees or beneath more upright-growing shrubs, plant low-growing evergreens of dense habit to inhibit weed development.

Use of weedkillers

If sites are thoroughly cleared of perennial weeds before planting, and beds and borders are kept well mulched afterwards, few problems will arise. But often there are limits to the amount of mulching that can be done, and then weedkillers must be considered.

Although the soil-acting weedkillers simazine and dichlobenil can be used at lower rates among established ornamental trees and shrubs, their use is restricted. Some trees and shrubs are tolerant of simazine or dichlobenil, while others may suffer damage (see Box). Tolerance to weedkillers may vary even between species within a genus and the tolerances of many of the more unusual kinds of trees and shrubs have yet to be reliably established. Therefore, before using either weedkiller in the vicinity of trees, shrubs or hedges, carefully check the manufacturer's latest recommendations on the pack label or in the accompanying instructions for use.

Simazine

After checking that the tree or shrub species is simazine-tolerant, choose a product recommended for use among ornamentals. Apply in February or March to weed-free moist soil to control nearly all weeds at the germinating stage. A few perennial weed seedlings may appear later from deeper levels. Do not use simazine around newly planted shrubs or very small specimens; it is safer to allow a season or two for the shrubs to become established and grow away strongly before simazine is used. Do not use simazine on light sandy soils, particularly those low in organic matter, because damage is more likely to occur in these conditions.

Dichlobenil

Low-strength dichlobenil can be used around quite a number of trees and shrubs provided they have been established for at least two years. It will control established annual weeds and germinating weed seeds, and control or check many perennial weeds. Apply in March or early April when the soil is moist and before growth begins. As with simazine the tolerances of many kinds of trees and shrubs have yet to be established.

Paraquat/diquat

This weedkiller can be applied at any time of the year to control annual weeds under or around trees and shrubs. Use in early spring to kill over-wintering annual weeds before applying simazine. Apply with care, avoiding shrub and tree foliage and the green stems of young plants, using a watering can and dribble bar. The spray will not harm mature bark but can damage soft younger wood. Use with particular care in the vicinity of shrubs, such as kerrias and forsythias, which freely produce new basal shoots or suckers.

Persistent perennial weeds

Carefully remove isolated weeds or small patches of weed with a hand or garden fork. Forking will, however, disturb and damage roots. With some trees and shrubs, such as lilacs, flowering cherries, flowering plums and shrub roses, forking may start troublesome suckering. Where there are weed species resistant to dichlobenil treat carefully with glyphosate or glyphosate gel. This weedkiller can be used in the vicinity of trees and shrubs because there is no risk of root uptake, but apply carefully as it can seriously damage or kill garden plants through leaves or green stems. Since it acts through the leaves, glyphosate is most effectively used in the spring and early summer when growth of perennial weeds is strong and vigorous. Caution is needed because this is also the growing period of trees and shrubs. Apply when weed growth is 4–6 in high, where necessary repeating when regrowth reaches 4–6 in.

When large shrub borders are being planned, select and group shrubs according to their weedkiller tolerances. Do not attempt to use simazine or dichlobenil in mixed borders where shrubs are growing in close association with herbaceous plants.

Specimen trees in turf

Development of specimen trees in turf can be seriously impeded if grass or weeds are allowed to grow closely around the tree in the early years after planting. Maintain a weed-free area around each tree, at least 4 ft in diameter, for two to three years after planting, longer if the tree is slow growing. Keep the area mulched to prevent annual weeds.

Annual weed growth can be suppressed by using black polythene sheeting around newly planted ornamental trees. Ensure that the soil is moist before sheeting is put down. Spread the sheeting across an area of 3–4 ft radius from the stem. Being impervious to moisture the sheeting also stops evaporation from the soil, promoting considerably faster growth than with bare soil or organic mulch methods (see page 135).

WHICH WEEDKILLER?

The following list gives the susceptibilities of certain trees and shrubs to simazine and dichlobenil.

Simazine

Strong risk of damage:
Betula pendula, Choisya ternata, Cornus (*alba* 'Spaethii'; *mas* 'Aurea'; *mas* 'Elegantissima'*) Cotoneaster* ('Cornubia'; *franchetii) Deutzia* spp, *Euonymus (alatus; hamiltonianus* var *sieboldianus) Exochorda* spp, *Forsythia* spp, *Fraxinus* spp, *Indigofera* spp, *Kolkowitzia* spp, *Poncirus* spp.
Some risk of damage:
Betula spp, *Cedrus* spp, *Cercis* spp, *Chaenomeles* spp, *Chamaecyparis* spp, *Cotoneaster* spp, *Diervilla* spp, *Euonymus* spp, *Ginkgo biloba, Halesia* spp, *Hebe* spp, *Hibiscus syriacus, Kerria* spp, *Laburnum* spp, *Larix* spp, *Leycesteria* spp, *Ligustrum* spp (privets), *Lonicera* spp, *Metasequoia glyptostroboides, Philadelphus* spp, *Prunus* spp, *Ribes* spp, *Robinia* spp, *Sambucus* spp, *Senecio* spp, *Spiraea* spp, *Syringa* spp, *Taxus* spp, *Thuja* spp, *Tilia* spp, *Viburnum* spp, *Weigela* spp.

Dichlobenil

Susceptible:
Larix spp, *Picea* spp, *Potentilla* spp, *Sambucus* spp.
Tolerant:
Aucuba spp, Azalea, Bamboo, *Berberis* spp, *Betula* spp, *Buddleia* spp, *Cornus* spp, *Cotoneaster* spp, *Crataegus* spp, *Deutzia* spp, *Erica* spp, *Escallonia* spp, *Euonymus* spp, *Fagus* spp, *Forsythia* spp, *Fraxinus* spp, *Hibiscus* spp, *Hydrangea* spp, *Ilex* spp, *Laburnum* spp, *Ligustrum* spp, *Malus* spp, *Pyrus* spp, Rhododendron, *Ribes* spp, *Salix* spp, *Sorbus* spp, *Spiraea* spp, *Syringa* spp, *Tamarix* spp, *Viburnum* spp, *Weigela* spp.

Weed control: roses

Most rose beds and borders are, once planted, likely to remain undisturbed for a number of years before being replaced. It is therefore essential to begin by planting on a site free of all traces of perennial weeds. The low, leafy growth of roses and the closeness of planting imposes considerable limitations on the range of weedkillers that can be used safely and effectively among them.

Newly planted roses
To control germinating weed seeds among newly planted roses, use only those simazine products that carry the manufacturer's recommendations for use with roses. Apply in spring after autumn or spring planting. Ensure that the soil is firm and moist before application. Simazine will control germinating weeds for up to seven months.

Established roses
The most satisfactory approach to weed control in rose beds is to establish an annual routine based on the use of simazine. Simazine is best applied in March, shortly before the weed seedlings are expected to appear. First remove by hand any over-wintering weeds or, if they are very small, hoe lightly or apply paraquat/diquat. Then prune and apply a rose fertilizer followed by simazine. Finally apply a mulch.

Annual feeding and mulching are essential to good rose cultivation since they assist weed control by encouraging strong, healthy growth and dense leaf cover, which help to suppress weeds growing from wind- or bird-carried seeds. In theory, the maintenance of a good thick rose bed mulch, renewed annually, should keep established roses almost free from weeds. With small numbers of roses it may be possible to dispense with the use of weedkillers after a year or two if they are kept well mulched. If there are larger areas to maintain and less material is available for mulching, a routine spring application of simazine is the better approach.

2 Use a watering can and dribble bar when applying paraquat/diquat. Frequently its use is impracticable except around the edge of the rose bed.

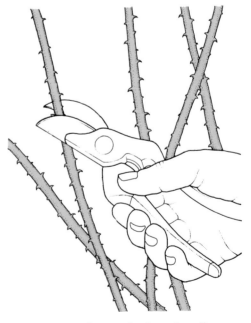

3 Then prune the rose bushes after all weeds have been killed or removed.

Perennial weeds in rose beds

If rose beds become infested with perennial weeds, dichlobenil can be applied in spring. However, dichlobenil should only be used on roses which have been established for at least two years. Apply before bud burst (before leaves begin to unfurl) when the soil is moist.

At the rates at which it can be used safely in roses, some perennial weeds are resistant to dichlobenil but others, such as couch grass and ground elder, can be checked or progressively controlled. Dichlobenil will control both germinating weed seeds and established annual weeds for three to six months, depending on soil conditions, the amount of moisture it contains and the temperature.

Use alloxydim-sodium as an overall spray where couch or other perennial grasses are troublesome. When all perennial weed growth has been eliminated return to annual treatment with simazine.

Weed control in established beds

1 First remove by hand any over-wintering weeds. If the weeds are very small hoe lightly or carefully apply paraquat/diquat.

4 Apply a good rose fertilizer followed by simazine after ensuring that the soil is firm and moist. This will control subsequent weeds. Do not use simazine on sandy soil.

5 Complete the programme by carefully applying a mulch of well rotted manure, peat or garden compost.

Weed control: flowers 1

Hardy annuals

Hardy annuals are sown outdoors in autumn or spring in the positions in which they are to flower. Therefore, it is important to sow in a site free from perennial weeds since no weedkiller can be used safely and effectively among young annuals.

On a site that is known to be infested with weeds prepare the ground early and apply the stale seedbed method. To do this prepare the seedbed some two weeks before sowing. Young seedling weeds will soon appear; kill them by spraying with paraquat/diquat or by hoeing. Then sow the seeds with as little disturbance to the soil as possible to reduce the possibility of further weeds emerging.

Since most annual plants are sown at fairly shallow depths, residual weedkillers cannot be used. Ensure that the crop plants establish quickly and grow away well by adhering to recommended sowing depths and dates (weather permitting), and by correct row spacing, early thinning where necessary and adequate irrigation at all times.

Half-hardy annuals

This is a term applied to certain ornamental plants of tropical or sub-tropical origin that are mostly perennial, but have little or no frost tolerance. Examples include lobelias, salvias, and nicotianas. They are grown as annuals from seed sown under glass, young plants being planted out in spring when danger of frost is past.

Before planting remove all traces of perennial weeds from the site, preparing it sufficiently in advance to allow weed seeds near the surface to germinate. Then kill them, either by light hoeing or by spraying them with paraquat/diquat.

Where problems with germinating annual weeds and grasses are anticipated apply propachlor within one to two days of planting out (but *not* with salvias). It is used as a granular formulation, sprinkled onto moist soil. It will control many annual weeds at the seed germination stage, but not established annuals. It is residual for about six weeks, by which time sturdy plants suitably spaced

should have grown together to suppress further weeds. If purchasing plants avoid those that are slow to grow away, for example plants that have been brought on in warm conditions and are consequently spindly and drawn, or plants starved and stunted from having been in pots or boxes for too long.

Hardy biennials

In raising hardy biennials from seed follow the treatment recommendations for hardy annuals. At final planting, if trouble is anticipated with germinating annual weeds and grasses, apply propachlor as recommended for half-hardy annuals.

Tender bedding plants

This is a group of ornamental tender perennials, often grown as summer bedding plants. They include woody-stemmed plants (heliotropes, pelargoniums), herbaceous plants (chrysanthemums, venidio-arctotis) and tuberous plants (begonias, dahlias). Weed control for this group of plants is the same as for half-hardy annuals.

Alpine and rock garden plants

Alpines are plants that are adapted to growing at high altitudes. Most rock gardens and alpine collections contain a great diversity of plants – shrubs, herbaceous plants, bulbs and so forth. With such variety growing in close association weedkillers cannot be used except as carefully applied spot treatments to individual well established perennial weeds that cannot be removed by hand. Where a rock garden becomes infested with the more persistent and troublesome weeds such as horsetail or field bindweed the only satisfactory approach is to lift all valuable plants then devote a season or more to eliminating weeds. Replant only when all traces of weed have been destroyed. Couch grass can, however, be eliminated from amongst rock garden plants by repeat spraying with alloxydim-sodium, which is harmless to non-grassy plants.

Some rock garden plants need a cool, moist habitat. This may also provide suitable conditions for moss and liverworts to grow on the soil surface. Deter these by top-dressing beds with grit or sharp coarse-grade sand.

Alternatively modify the soil texture by incorporating these materials. Where such growths persist carefully spray with a dichlorophen formulation which carries recommendations for use in the control of mosses and liverworts amongst ornamentals, repeating as necessary.

Herbaceous perennials

when planting herbaceous perennials it is important to select a site that is free from all perennial weeds and to use only clean, healthy stock. Before planting gifts of plant material, or plants of doubtful origin, their roots should be checked carefully and any traces of couch grass, ground elder or other perennial weeds should be removed. With fibrous-rooted plants, shake the roots clean and split them into single pieces to eliminate perennial weeds.

Annual weeds are controlled during the first season after planting by careful hoeing or hand-weeding between plants or clumps. If the site is known to be heavily infested with annual weed seeds apply propachlor after the spring planting. It may also be applied in early spring following the autumn planting after the ground has been hoed to kill over-wintering annual weeds. It gives control for about six weeks. Apply when the soil is moist, level and firm, taking care to avoid crop foliage and particularly the growing points. This weedkiller may also be applied directly after autumn planting.

Do not hoe from the second spring after planting because it may cause damage to near-surface roots. Plants should be sufficiently well established by then to suppress development of seedling weeds from late spring onwards, although in early spring there usually will be some over-wintering annual weeds to control. This may be done either by hoeing or by applying paraquat/diquat between the plants using a watering can and dribble bar attachment. Paraquat/diquat may also be applied as an overall spray if the plants have died down below ground level, however, this is extremely risky where plants have retained some foliage over winter. Mulching also helps to suppress annual weeds.

Since there are many different kinds of herbaceous perennials with varying growth habits all weedkillers pose some degree of risk. When using paraquat/diquat spring-flowering perennials such as pyrethrums may be particularly at risk.

Perennial weeds are best treated according to type. Where field bindweed or bellbind is troublesome carefully spot-treat with the foliage-acting weedkiller glyphosate gel. This is applied most effectively when the weeds are growing strongly. After treatment lay the wet twining shoots on a path or lawn to allow the weedkiller to be absorbed into their tissues.

In densely planted borders encourage the weed to climb up specially inserted canes or stakes where it can be more safely spot-treated.

When weeds such as couch grass and ground elder become troublesome lift, clean, split and replant herbaceous perennials. They should in any case be lifted and divided every three or four years.

Couch grass can, however, be eliminated from herbaceous borders by repeat spraying with alloxydim-sodium, which is harmless to non-grassy plants. Do not spray ornamental grasses such as pampas grass.

Bulbs

This term is used to cover both true bulbous plants (daffodils, snowdrops) and plants that grow from corms (crocus, gladioli). In the garden they are usually grown in small groups at the front of borders and shrubberies or naturalized in turf. Most have a relatively short period of growth and in border groups there is a long period when the bulbs are leafless. This provides an opportunity for wind- or bird-carried weed seeds to establish, or perennial weeds to encroach from surrounding areas.

When the bulbs are in growth, that is, the period between shoot emergence and dying down of foliage, hand-weeding or very careful hoeing are the only control measures that can be used safely.

Weedkillers can only be used when there is no bulb growth visible, except for alloxydim-sodium, which can be used to eliminate couch grass and other perennial grasses from plantings of bulbs, such as daffodils, bluebells, etc.

Weed control: flowers 2

Narcissus and daffodil, if newly planted, can be treated with propachlor if a large number of annual weeds is expected. It gives control at germination for a period of about six weeks. Apply when the soil is firm, level and moist, repeating if necessary. After the foliage has died down there are several possible control measures. To kill annual weeds and check perennials apply paraquat/diquat or hoe lightly. To kill both annual and perennial weeds apply glyphosate. Its effectiveness against perennial weeds may depend on the species, and its size and stage of development. In some instances regrowth may occur. Propachlor may also be applied following any of the above measures.

Before using paraquat/diquat or glyphosate ensure that dead foliage has been detached from the bulb, otherwise it may cause the weedkiller to channel down into the growing point of the bulb with risk of serious damage. Ensure also that the soil has been well raked over after removal of dead foliage. It is not advisable to use paraquat/diquat or glyphosate if the soil is very sandy.

Tulips and other bulbs are usually planted more shallowly than daffodils or narcissi. Consequently they have much less soil protection and there is increased risk of damage from weedkillers. Hand-weeding is the safest means of weed control but if care is taken the same chemical controls recommended for daffodils may be applied. If liverworts or similar growths are persistently troublesome improve surface drainage by top-dressing with porous, gritty soil or plant in raised beds with improved drainage.

Bulbs in turf can be harmed by translocated or growth-regulating lawn weedkillers, even when the bulbs are dormant, if the weedkiller reaches their growing points. However, if such weedkillers are used, the period of least risk to the bulbs is immediately after the bulb foliage is dead and has been detached. A safer approach is to fork out weeds as the bulb foliage is dying, when the position of the bulbs is still discernible and damage can be avoided. Where larger areas become heavily infested lift the bulbs as the foliage dies back, clean the site thoroughly, then replant and re-seed with grass in early autumn.

Path-sides

Around half-hardy annuals, when applying paraquat/diquat take care to avoid the foliage.

Narcissi and daffodils

Remove all dead foliage from narcissi and daffodils before applying weedkillers, otherwise the weedkillers may channel down to the bulb's growing point.

Rock garden

In rock gardens, mosses and liverworts can be deterred by applying a top dressing of sharp, coarse-grade sand or grit.

Herbaceous plants

Before replanting herbaceous plants, divide them into small sections and carefully examine them to ensure that they contain no traces of weeds.

Bulbs

If mosses or liverworts are troublesome around bulbs, replant the bulbs in raised beds since this will improve the surface drainage.

Weed control: strawberries

When cultivating strawberries it is important that the site has been prepared thoroughly and all traces of perennial weeds have been removed. Strawberries are intolerant of the weedkillers dalapon and dichlobenil, which are used to control perennial weeds in other fruit crops, and it would be hazardous to attempt inter-row application of the foliage-acting glyphosate because contact with the foliage or runners could lead to serious crop damage.

Strawberries are, however, a relatively short-term crop, usually replaced after the third year's fruit. With suitable site preparation there should be no problem with perennial weeds during the life of the crop.

Application of simazine will control virtaully all weed seeds at germination (see below). An occasional strong-growing perennial weed seedling may, however, appear from deeper levels. There may also be some

weed development from wind-carried seeds towards the end of the treatment stages as the residual effects of the simazine decline. Any such weeds are best removed by hand.

It is possible to use paraquat/diquat to control annual weeds, together with any unwanted runners, during the period from the end of picking to the start of flowering. It can also be used to kill annual weeds appearing during the period from planting until simazine can be used safely. On sandy soils where it is unsafe to use simazine, paraquat/diquat can be used between the rows. It should, however, be used only with great care as a carefully directed spray to avoid the strawberry plants. Any drift on to the plants will cause severe scorch and injury. Where this approach is adopted apply with a watering can and dribble bar, or as a coarse low-pressure spray using a sprayer with hood attachment to prevent drift.

Applying weedkillers

1 In December control germinating weed seeds by applying simazine products approved for use among strawberries. Apply to clean moist soil as an overall spray among plants that have been established for at least 12 months.

2 In July or August, after harvesting the crop, clear up the straw and fork out any unwanted runners between the rows. Next remove any existing weeds by hand and then apply simazine as an overall treatment to clean moist soil.

MULCHING

Mulching with straw

Mulching with circular mats

Mulching with black polythene

Not only does mulching help to prevent loss of moisture from the soil, it also effectively suppresses annual weeds. Straw is the traditional mulch for strawberries but nowadays inorganic materials are increasingly being used.

One such method is to use circular mats with a slit leading from the centre to the outside. These may be placed around strawberry plants as a mulch. Alternatively, black plastic sheeting may be employed.

To do this make rows of ridges 2 in high and set 3 ft apart. Black polythene strips 2½ ft wide are used. The strawberries are planted, through slits, along the ridges, rain and irrigation water being channelled into the 6 in strips of bare earth between each row. Control weeds that develop in the narrow inter-row strips by applying simazine or paraquat/diquat. If mats are being used, hoe or apply simazine or paraquat/diquat to suppress weeds.

Weed control: fruit

Tree and bush fruits are grown either as part of a general garden, often in or close to the vegetable plot, or in a special area in larger numbers and in a more orderly pattern. The arrangement of fruit trees and bushes affects the way the weeds are treated. When the plants are growing haphazardly, weedkillers can rarely be used safely, except possibly in very carefully directed spot treatments where perennial weeds become established. In the more formal fruit garden the orderly planting allows full scope for weed control programmes based on dalapon, dichlobenil, glyphosate, paraquat/diquat and simazine.

Apples and pears
If apple and pear trees are grown in an orderly arrangement then weedkillers may be used.
Before weeds appear apply simazine to bare, moist soil, preferably in February or March after killing over-wintering annual weeds. Simazine controls nearly all germinating weed seeds over a period of several months. The soil must be well firmed before applying around newly planted trees. Simazine may also be used at half-dosage in autumn if trouble is anticipated with autumn- and winter-germinating weeds.
After weeds appear apply paraquat/diquat as a directed spray on to established weeds at any time of the year. Repeated treatment will kill many perennial weeds. Paraquat/diquat will not penetrate mature bark, but avoid spraying the stems of trees that are less than three years old.
When perennial weeds appear apply dichlobenil in March or early April. It will also control established annuals and germinating weed seeds over a period of three to six months. Distribute the granules evenly over the soil surface. Do not apply within two years of planting the fruit trees.
Grass weeds such as couch may be killed by treating with dalapon. Apply as a directed spray during autumn or early spring when the grasses are growing actively. Use dalapon only where trees have been established for at least four years. Spray the grasses to wet thoroughly, but avoid excessive run-off.
Perennial weeds resistant to dichlobenil can be treated with glyphosate. Apply as a directed spray from November to bud burst.

It controls perennial broad-leaved weeds and perennial grasses, including couch. Apply glyphosate only where trees have been established for at least two years.

Gooseberries and currants
Care must be taken when using most weedkillers near bush fruit to ensure that the chemical does not touch either the foliage of stems.
Before weeds appear apply simazine to bare, moist soil, preferably in February or March, to control nearly all germinating weed seeds over a period of several months. The soil must be well firmed around newly planted bushes before applying. Do not use simazine if old bushes are to be replaced after fruiting unless the site is to be left fallow until the following year. It may also be used at half-dosage in autumn if trouble is anticipated with autumn- and winter-germinating weeds.
After weeds appear apply paraquat/diquat. It can be used at any time of the year, including immediately prior to using simazine, to kill established annual weeds and check the growth of perennials. Avoid wetting the foliage of bushes and the buds of black currant at any time otherwise damage will result.
When perennial weeds appear apply dichlobenil in March or early April to control many perennial weeds, including grasses, or in November for the control of couch. Dichlobenil also controls established annuals and germinating weed seeds over a period of three to six months. Distribute the granules evenly. Do not apply to bushes within two years of planting or in the first year of cropping, whichever is the later. Do not use on black currants of any age which have been cut down to soil level until at least one year after cutting back. Ensure the granules do not lodge within the buds or on leaves.
Grass may be controlled with dalapon. Apply it between leaf-fall and the end of December to control various weed grasses and, partially, couch. Apply as a directed spray on to the grass, avoiding excessive run-off into the soil. Use only where fruit bushes have been planted out for at least a year. Perennial weeds resistant to dichlobenil may be dealt with by very careful localized treatments, applying the weedkiller that is appropriate to

the weed's identity or habit of growth. For details of this, see the section on specific weeds, pages 172–185.

Cane fruits

Raspberries, loganberries and blackberries produce replacement canes each season, which fruit the following year.

Before weeds appear apply simazine to clean, moist soil, preferably in February or March to control nearly all germinating weed seeds. Firm the soil well around newly planted canes before application. Simazine may also be used at half-strength where trouble is anticipated with autumn- and winter-germinating weeds.

After weeds appear apply paraquat/diquat as a directed spray on to weeds at any time of the year to kill established annual weeds and check growth of perennials. During late winter, before bud burst, apply around the base of canes to control over-wintering weeds. Avoid wetting foliage or young re-placement canes. Suckers occurring between the rows can be controlled by repeated applications of paraquat/diquat.

When perennial weeds appear apply dichlo-benil in early spring before the first signs of bud movement. It controls many perennial weeds, established annual weeds and germinating weed seeds. Apply it only to canes planted for at least two years.

Plums and cherries

Simazine should not be used around plum and cherry trees, though other chemicals can be used to achieve weed control.

Treat established annual weeds with para-quat/diquat, applied as a directed spray at any time of the year. Repeated treatments will also gradually control perennial weeds. Avoid wetting the foliage, or the bark of trees less than three years old.

Treat established perennial weeds with gly-phosate, applied from November to bud burst as a carefully controlled spray. It will control couch grass, other perennial weeds and established annuals. Where there is not much foliage on perennial weeds there may be regrowth after treatment. Use glyphosate only where the trees have been established for at least two years.

RENOVATING TREES AND BUSHES

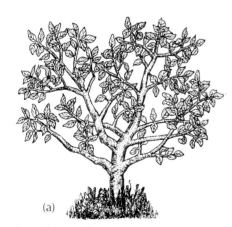
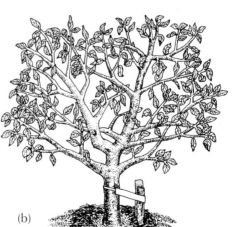

(a)　　(b)

If weeds are allowed to grow around fruit trees and bushes, they will compete strongly for moisture and nutrients and cause the plants to become stunted with low yields of fruit (a). After all weeds have been killed or removed, help the tree or bush to recover its vigour by staking it and applying a thick mulch of stable manure or compost (b). Water well and feed it with a general fertilizer in early spring.

Weed control: vegetables

Perennial vegetable crops
The most important vegetables to be grown as perennials are asparagus, globe artichoke, horseradish and rhubarb. Since these crops remain undisturbed from year to year perennial weeds can become troublesome if chance seedlings are allowed to establish. Therefore it is particularly important to plant only after sites have been thoroughly cleaned of all traces of perennial weed. Where the soil is known or suspected to contain numerous viable weed seeds, for example in a reclaimed allotment or neglected plot, apply chlorpropham/propham/diuron after planting.

Asparagus
Controlling weeds by close hoeing is possible only if the asparagus is planted in single rows. In other cases good control over weeds for the full life of the asparagus bed can be obtained by carefully applying the appropriate weedkillers.

Simazine will control almost all germinating weed seeds. Apply as a low-strength formulation after the final working of the bed in spring but before the spears emerge. Simazine will remain active in the soil for several months. Do not use it the first season after planting.

Paraquat/diquat is applied as an overall spray in spring before spears emerge or before mounding to control over-wintering annual weeds. Apply only where necessary as a carefully directed spray after the final cut.

Dalapon provides progressive control for couch grass and other grass weeds. Apply in spring before spears emerge, wetting the grass thoroughly. Repeat when cutting has finished, keeping spray contact with stems and foliage to a minimum.

Globe artichoke
Where trouble is anticipated from germinating weed seeds apply simazine as an overall spray in early spring. Take care to keep it away from young leafy basal growths.

Horseradish
In gardens horseradish is usually grown on a relatively small scale and, if it becomes infested with perennial weeds such as couch grass, the simplest approach is to establish a new bed elsewhere in the garden.

Rhubarb
The large broad leaves of rhubarb are very effective in suppressing the development of weed seedlings during the late spring and summer. Weeds may, however, become troublesome in the autumn and winter after the foliage has died down. Hoeing may damage the fleshy roots that lie near the surface and careful use of weedkillers is a more satisfactory means of control in larger beds of rhubarb.

Simazine can be applied to well established beds in autumn when the crop is dormant and the soil moist and weed-free.

Paraquat/diquat is used as an overall spray when the crop is completely dormant. It controls all established annual weeds and checks perennials that are still in active growth or in leaf.

Dalapon controls couch and other grasses. Apply as a diluted foliage spray during the autumn or early spring when the crop is dormant, avoiding rhubarb crowns and excessive run-off into the soil.

Annual vegetable crops
Annual vegetable plots are usually free of perennial weeds since they are cultivated frequently and thoroughly. Annual weeds can, however, be very troublesome. Weeds such as annual nettle and shepherd's purse mature rapidly, producing large numbers of seedlings which may stifle slow-germinating and developing crops. Hoeing and hand-weeding are effective methods of controlling annual weeds but they can cause damage to crops or check growth (see pages 132–137).

Although several weedkillers are available to commercial growers and market gardeners for use in annual vegetable crops very few reach the amateur market. Limited demand in a rather specialized field is probably the reason why most such products were available on the amateur market for a short time, only to be withdrawn. Therefore, the best means of weed control is good cultural practice, particularly in site preparation, feeding, irrigation and crop spacing. This encourages rapid establishment and growth of the crop to the stage where its foliage smothers most weed seedlings and inhibits further germination of weed seed. Weedkillers may, however, be usefully applied at the following times.

Before sowing use the stale seedbed method to remove weeds from infested sites. This will eliminate many weeds from the bed before sowing begins. Where conditions allow, prepare the seedbed 10–14 days before the planned sowing date. A few days later weed seeds lying at or near the surface will germinate. Kill these young seedlings by spraying with paraquat/diquat. Sowing can then proceed without delay since paraquat/diquat leaves no harmful residues in the soil. When sowing, the seedbed should be disturbed as little as possible to avoid bringing more weed seeds to the surface.

When planting out young crop plants may often be subjected to heavy competition from annual weeds in the critical early weeks of establishment.

Propachlor, a soil-acting weedkiller, can, however, be used within one to two days of planting out some vegetable crops. It is used as a granular formulation, sprinkled onto the moist soil. It will control many annual weeds at the seed-germination stage, including annual nettle, chickweed, grounsel, annual meadow grass, mayweeds and shepherd's purse. It does not control established annual weeds or perennial weeds.

Propachlor can be used after planting onion sets and shallots; also after planting out young onion and leek plants, and brassicae plants, including cabbage, cauliflower, brussels sprouts, broccoli and curly kale.

Propachlor is residual for around five to six weeks, when weed seedlings begin to reappear remove them by hand-weeding or hoeing them; if necessary, repeat the application. Often, however, the crop will be sufficiently well-established to make further application unnecessary.

The stale seedbed method

1 Rake the seedbed to a fine tilth. If the weather allows, do this 10–14 days before the planned date of sowing.

2 Weed seeds lying on or near the surface will germinate a few days later.

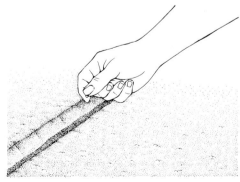

3 Hoe the seedbed thoroughly to kill these weed seedlings.

Weed control: paths

Preparing the site

Whenever a hard surface is to be laid down it is essential to begin by removing all traces of perennial weeds. Failure to clean thoroughly may result in the surface being quickly disrupted by weeds thrusting through.

Where deeply penetrating weeds, such as horsetail or field bindweed, are known to infest the site, spray with glyphosate in spring when the weeds are growing strongly. With horsetail, crush the shoots before spraying. Spot-treat if there is any subsequent regrowth; however, if the weeds are also controlled in neighbouring areas there should be little further trouble. Contractors usually apply very strong, persistent weedkillers before surfacing large areas. These weedkillers kill all weed growth but are unsuitable for garden use as they kill underlying roots and may contaminate neighbouring areas.

Gravelled areas

With gravelled areas depth and quality of surfacing materials are important factors in controlling weeds. On shallow surfaces and where materials are unwashed and contain a high percentage of sedimentary material, wind-blown or bird-carried weed seeds can easily take root and establish. Deep clean gravel remains drier and is therefore less hospitable to germinating weed seeds. Destroy any seedlings which do establish themselves by raking if the gravel is coarse or by hoeing if it is fine.

Weedd control may also be achieved by weedkillers. To kill weeds at germination apply simazine in March, having first destroyed any established weeds. If there are numerous annual weeds already established apply mixtures of simazine and paraquat/diquat. The paraquat/diquat kills the existing annual weeds and the simazine provides subsequent long-term control. Where perennial weeds are also established apply mixtures of simazine with aminotriazole, or with aminotriazole and MCPA, in March or April. The aminotriazole or aminotriazole/MCPA kills established annuals and most established perennials. Where horsetail is troublesome apply dichlobenil in March. For perennial weeds not controlled by the above treatments apply glyphosate when weed growth is vigorous. Treat with paraquat/diquat in autumn if annual weed seedlings appear due to the declining effectiveness of simazine.

Apply weedkillers with a watering can and dribble bar since they allow safe application right up to a path's edges. Apply in dry but dull weather so that it can readily be seen where the weedkiller has been applied by the wetness of the treated gravel.

Paved areas

Provided paving is laid on a weed-free site over firm deep foundations there may be little or no trouble from weeds for several years. In time, however, weeds will appear between the slabs. It is usually difficult to weed paving by hand satisfactorily because the weeds can neither be grasped easily nor removed with a trowel or hand fork. Therefore weedkillers must be used.

When isolated weeds appear spot-treat with simazine/aminotriazole or simazine/aminotriazole/MCPA mixtures. If the weeds are large and growing strongly apply glyphosate instead.

If weeds begin to appear in numbers apply

Weeds in gravel

If gravel becomes infested with weeds, remove them by either raking if the gravel is coarse, or hoeing if it is fine.

the following weedkillers. If the site is weed-free in March apply simazine; if there are over-wintering annual weeds use a simazine/paraquat/diquat mixture. If perennial weeds are present apply simazine/aminotriazole or simazine/aminotriazole/MCPA mixtures in March or April. If applying to crevices and between joints use a watering can with a shortened or partially blocked dribble bar attachment. Tread carefully, otherwise the weedkiller may be unwittingly transferred to grass verges or lawns on the soles of shoes. If horsetail is well established apply dichlobenil in March, carefully sprinkling it into all cracks and crevices. For perennial weeds not controlled by the above treatments apply glyphosate when weed growth is vigorous. If tap-rooted weeds such as docks and dandelions are well established, cut them off at the crown, then sprinkle the freshly cut surface with dichlobenil granules.

Stone and brickwork
Various mosses, lichens and algal growths can colonize stone or brickwork if the conditions are damp and shady. Some can be removed by scrubbing thoroughly. Dichlorophen is effective against many growths and it also controls liverworts.

There are proprietary formulations which carry recommendations for application to moss, algae, lichen and liverworts on paths, brickwork, walls, drives, fences and roots. In addition, formulations of phenols may be useful but there is risk of discoloration or staining of some kinds of paving or stonework and it is advisable to experiment before general use is made of such preparations.

Other hard surfaces
On hard tennis courts, tarmacadam drives and similar surfaces mosses, lichens and slime growths may develop. Chemical treatment may give temporary control but long-lasting control is unlikely unless basic site conditions can be improved – most such growths occur in cool, moist, shaded positions. Where possible, take steps to increase exposure to the sun and wind by pruning back overhanging branches, or by renovating or re-planning adjoining shrubberies.

Weeds in paving

If the crevices between paving develop weeds apply the appropriate weedkiller with a watering can and dribble bar.

Mosses on brickwork

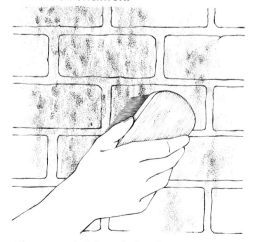

If stone or brickwork develops mosses or other growths, they can often be removed by vigorous scrubbing with hot water.

Weed control: neglected land 1

Cultural methods

The problems facing a gardener taking over a neglected garden vary according to the nature of the site and the length of time it has been neglected. If the site has been neglected for a full growing season or longer, much of the area will usually be colonized by annual weeds. Seedling or young perennials may also be present but in most cases will not be well established. At this stage of weed infestation reclamation of the site by cultural methods is the best approach since the main problem is the amount of weed seed present on the site.

One method is to dig the site, thus disposing of established annual weeds by burying them. Small patches of perennials can be removed by forking out. However this process will cause many weed seeds to be buried. These can remain viable in the soil for many years, germinating when brought to the surface by subsequent cultivations or harvesting of crops.

If the site is to be used for a permanent feature such as a lawn or shrubbery, this approach may be acceptable, but if it is to be cultivated and cropped regularly it is better to devote a season to removing all weed seeds before cropping begins. The method of doing this depends on the time of year that removal of weeds commences.

Winter and spring

If site reclamation is to begin in winter, weed seeds will have been dispersed by then. Therefore collect, remove and burn dead weed growth. Then wait for a period of fine weather in early spring when the soil surface is drying and the weather is settled. Hoe the site thoroughly to kill over-wintering annual weeds and leave the severed or dislodged weeds to die unless there is a change to wetter conditions, in which case remove the weeds and compost them. Hoe at frequent intervals as each fresh crop of weed seedlings appears. As the season progresses change to, or alternate hoeing with, a hand cultivator which will allow deeper penetration. This tool is particularly useful for dealing with small patches of recently established perennial weeds since it drags the roots or rhizomes to the surface for disposal. By the end of the summer the site should be almost completely free of weeds and in excellent condition for autumn sowing or planting.

Summer and autumn

In late spring or summer the first step is to deal with existing vegetation. This will consist mainly of low-growing annual weeds with possibly a few stronger-growing ones, such as fat hen. If there are weeds in the process of seeding hand-pull them as carefully as possible to minimize shedding and dispersal of seeds. Alternatively use a rotary mower to cut down the weed as close to soil level as is practical, first removing stones, bricks or other debris which may lie hidden among the weeds. Use a grass-box where possible, particularly if weeds are seeding. If weed growth is too dense for a grass-box to be used, allow the mowings to lie for a few days and collect them when they have lost much of their moisture content.

After cutting, begin cultivation by loosening the surface and dislodging weed roots with a hand cultivator, first working the plot lengthways, then crossways. If the weed roots are dense and matted and cover an extensive area, use a rotavator, but only at a very shallow setting. Rake off dead material then, with the site free of existing weeds, hoe or use a hand cultivator at frequent intervals to remove succeeding crops of weed seedlings during the remainder of the summer.

If the clearing programme does not begin until the latter part of summer or the early autumn it is advisable to adopt the stale seedbed method if vegetable or flower seeds are to be sown the following spring. First prepare the seedbed some two weeks before sowing. As the weed seedlings appear spray with paraquat/diquat or hoe to remove them. Then sow the seeds with as little disturbance to the soil as possible to prevent the emergence of further weeds.

Potatoes as a cleaning crop

In couch-infested plots main crop potatoes can be grown as a cleaning crop since the frequent cultivations involved – planting, earthing, hoeing – weaken and destroy much of the couch grass. Surviving rhizomes can be forked out when the crop is lifted.

Weedkillers

Where gardens or allotments have been neglected for several years earlier infestations of annual weeds often will have been superseded by stronger-growing perennial weeds. In suburban gardens there may be well established areas of couch grass, ground elder or perennial nettle encroaching from hedgerows or neighbouring property. In borders or beds many smaller plants may have already succumbed to perennial grasses, and areas of turf may be reduced to coarse grass, weeds and moss. In long neglected country gardens near woodland or heathland the weed population will often include creeping thistle, dock and bracken, together with tangles of blackberry and briar, and clumps of elder and thorn.

Reclamation is difficult after a long period of neglect; in beds and borders for example, few garden plants other than bulbs remain in sufficiently good condition to merit careful removal before dealing with weeds. If there is only a few square yards of infested ground then forking out the roots or rhizomes of perennial weeds is possible. Over larger areas this method is much too arduous except perhaps for the really dedicated gardener. Powered rotavators will cut easily through matted non-woody roots or rhizomes but inevitably it will cut them into small sections, which usually leads to dissemination rather than destruction.

The only effective approach is to use weedkillers. They will kill most if not all weed growth, both above and below ground, leaving the site ready for cultivation and planting. The most effective weedkillers in this situation are those which are non-selective or "total" in their action, killing all plant growth, although in practice a few deep-rooting weeds, such as horsetail may survive to reappear, usually much weakened, the following season. Weedkillers with these qualities are ammonium sulphamate, dichlobenil, glyphosate, simazine and sodium chlorate. Some are absorbed through the roots, others act through the foliage, but in all cases

Winter and spring programme

1 In winter, gather up and remove all dead weed growth. Then place it on the compost heap.

2 In early spring, during a period of dry settled weather, hoe the site thoroughly to control annual weeds.

Weed control: neglected land 2

weeds must be in active growth when application is made. Soil-acting weedkillers are applied most effectively in spring and early summer when there is a long period of active growth ahead; foliage-applied translocated weedkillers are best applied when there is strong active growth and a large area of leaf development.

Choice of weedkillers
The choice of weedkillers may be influenced by cost if the area is large, the length of time residues remain active in the soil and whether there are underlying tree and shrub roots in the treated area.
Ammonium sulphamate will kill a wide range of perennial broad-leaved weeds and grasses. Apply it to the foliage when growth is well advanced. It remains residual in the soil for up to 12 weeks but is very soluble and may have a shorter residual effect in wet seasons. Also, it can leach into neighbouring areas on sloping sites in wet conditions. Ammonium sulphamate is also effective against woody weeds such as blackberry and elder.

Sodium chlorate can be used as a total weedkiller but harmful residues may remain in the soil for six months or more. It is very soluble and should not be used on sloping sites that drain on to other areas nor where there are underlying tree or shrub roots.
Simazine and dichlobenil are both very stable in the soil, persisting for up to 12 months at the higher rates used for non-selective weed control in uncropped areas.
Glyphosate is foliage absorbed and translocated, and must be used with extreme care in the vicinity of garden plants. It acts quickly and is effective against almost all weeds, both broad and narrow leaved. There may, however, be regrowth from some of the most persistent and deeply penetrating perennials, such as horsetail, field bindweed and bellbind.

Glyphosate becomes inactive on contact with the soil and there is therefore no risk to underlying tree or shrub roots. Cultivation and planting or sowing seed can be carried

3 If the weather changes and becomes rainy, remove the weeds from the site and compost them.

4 As the season progresses kill new weed seedlings as they appear, using a hand cultivator or a hoe.

out as soon as treated weeds are dead and cleared from the site.

Dalapon is foliage absorbed and translocated, and effective against all grass weeds, including couch. However, where used to control couch in uncultivated areas, it is essential to plough or dig deeply not less than two weeks after spraying to bury as deeply as possible any surviving rhizomes. Dalapon is residual in the soil for two to three months.

After treatment

If any weed species survive treatment, or if regrowth occurs as the summer progresses, treat with glyphosate. If identification can be made see pages 172-185 for specific control recommendations. When all weed growth is dead, cut and clear it or, if sufficiently dense and the situation allows, burn it off. This also destroys weed seeds. In late autumn or early winter cultivate thoroughly, removing any traces of living weed roots or rhizomes that may have escaped the full effects of weed-killer treatment.

Summer and autumn programme

ROTAVATORS

Large plots of land that are heavily infested with annual weeds are best cleared with a rotavator (or rotary cultivator). Do not use these machines where there is heavy perennial weed growth since they will only disperse these weeds.

1 In early summer remove seeding weeds by hand-pulling them. If possible, do this before seeds have formed.

2 Cut back all other weeds, using a rotary mower or a scythe. Then rake up and remove all dead material.

Weed control: pools

A well kept garden pool is a desirable feature, attracting birds and providing interest with its diversity of water life. However, regular attention is needed to maintain a balanced pool community.

There are two approaches to the control of troublesome water plants: mechanical methods and the use of chemical weedkillers.

Before a weedkiller is acceptable for use in or near water, thorough tests are carried out to determine the risk to both people and wildlife. Very few weedkillers have received such clearance and none is approved for garden use.

It is important to note that, because of the danger of water pollution, the application of weedkillers in or near water is very carefully controlled. Consult the appropriate authorities before taking any action.

Submerged weeds

These weeds are rooted in mud and have all their stems and leaves below the surface with only the flowering shoots appearing above. Such weeds may increase rapidly and can quickly fill even quite large bodies of water with a dense mass of tangled growth, impeding fish movement and smothering more desirable water plants. Among the most troublesome of these weeds are Canadian pondweed (*Elodea canadensis*), curled pondweed (*Potamogeton crispus*) and water milfoil (*Myriophyllum* spp).

In small pools frequent thinning keeps growth in check. In larger shallow pools and lakes, weeds have to be cut by hand, the operator wearing waders and using a long-handled scythe or cutting tool. In deeper waters the operator must work from a boat. Rapidly growing water weeds may need cutting twice a year.

After cutting it is essential that as much cut weed as possible is removed from the water. If not, the weed decays, using up much of the dissolved oxygen in the water with a risk to fish through severe de-oxygenation. Also, many water weeds can grow again from small sections of cut stem.

Most water weeds float to the surface when cut and in larger pools and lakes, where there are any flow outlets, temporary booms should be constructed to catch and hold the floating weed, and prevent it from polluting downstream waters.

Draining, followed by dredging, is the most satisfactory way of dealing with heavily overgrown, silted pools and lakes. Draining alone is less satisfactory because rhizomatous weeds such as *Potamogeton* survive unless the soil is afterwards allowed to dry out thoroughly.

Floating-leaved weeds

Where there is no water flow, floating-leaved plants may completely cover the water surface, preventing sunlight from reaching submerged plants and causing de-oxygenation of the water. Among the more troublesome are the free-floating duckweeds (*Lemna* spp) and frogbit (*Hydrocharis morsus-ranae*), water lilies (particularly *Nuphar luteum* and *Nymphaea alba*), broad-leaved pondweed (*Potamogeton natans*) and amphibious bistort (*Polygonum amphibium*).

Where floating-leaved weeds are rooted into the bottom of lakes and pools, they can be cut and cleared the same way as submerged water weeds. Free-floating weeds require a different approach.

Duckweeds, particularly common duckweed (*Lemna minor*), although small as individual plants, can completely cover extensive areas if the water is still or slowly moving. Each plant consists of a single rounded leaf-like thallus floating on the surface, from which is suspended a slender root. The plant usually winters on the pool bottom, to surface again the following spring.

In smaller pools control lies in careful weed removal with a rake or net, particularly before winter dormancy. With larger pools a floating boom can be used to carefully sweep the pool from end to end. Stop-boards should be fitted at any upstream inlets to prevent duckweed entering pools and lakes.

Marginal or emergent weeds

Various members of the grass family are adapted to waterside conditions, growing in shallow water along pool and lake margins and increasing by means of spreading rhizomatous

Common water weeds

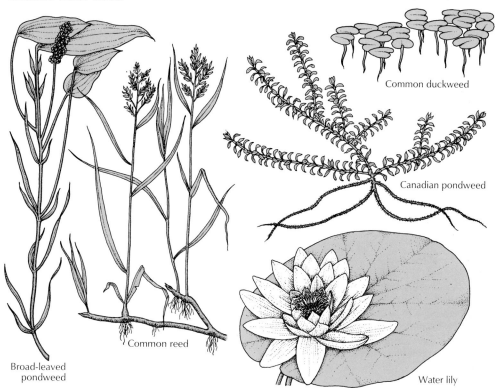

Common duckweed

Canadian pondweed

Common reed

Broad-leaved pondweed

Water lily

roots. Troublesome plants include common reed (*Phragmites communis*), sedges and yellow flag iris (*Iris pseudacorus*). In the small pool waders and a sharp knife will facilitate clearing, thinning and replanting. Do this at three- or four-year intervals as necessary.

Algae

There are various kinds of algae. Most familiar to gardeners are the minute free-floating kinds which increase rapidly in sunny, shallow pools during warm weather in late spring and early summer, clouding the water to a deep pea-green. The filamentous kinds are more troublesome. Examples include *Cladophora* and *Spirogyra* and are commonly known as blanket weed, hair weed or cott.

Algae proliferate both in new pools where pool-life is not fully established and in under-stocked pools. Encourage the quick establishment of a balanced pool-life by planting oxygenating plants, for example hornwort (*Ceratophyllum demersum*) and water crowfoot (*Ranunculus aquatilis*), adding fish two or three weeks later. Algae are much less of a problem if the pool has a minimum depth of 24 in. Encourage floating-leaved plants, such as water lilies, to provide up to 50 per cent surface coverage when in full growth.

Algae can be controlled chemically. Preparations of varying effectiveness are available for professional use. Some kill algal growth together with most pond weed; others are more limited in effect, some filamentous algae and water weeds being resistant or only partially controlled. Some provide only temporary control and others give slow-release control over a long period.

Killing tree stumps

Trees may have to be felled for a variety of reasons, but the remaining stump, whether living or dead, can become a source of trouble in the garden. Dead stumps can, as they decay, become hosts to honey fungus (*Armillaria Sp.*), a root parasite which can live for many years on slowly decaying stumps. It extends long, dark brown strands (called rhizomorphs) through the soil and these can attack and kill nearby trees and shrubs. The living stumps of some species may produce troublesome regrowth in the form of coppice shoots from around the base of the stump, or suckers may arise from the thicker roots, frequently several yards from the stump. Flowering cherry, flowering plum, poplar and sycamore are particularly troublesome in this respect.

It is therefore advisable to remove all stumps wherever possible and, with species prone to suckering, to kill the stump some time before it is removed in order to avoid regrowth of suckers from roots left in the soil.

Stumps may either be removed straight away, killed with weedkillers and allowed to decay naturally, or left for a year to allow roots to rot and then removed. It is not possible to hasten decay of the stump by the use of chemicals.

Killing stumps
To kill newly cut stumps apply a weedkiller based on 2,4-D/dicamba/mecoprop recommended by the manufacturer for stump-killing, using paraffin or another light oil as a mixing agent (see manufacturer's recommendations for the required proportions). It is best to treat stumps within 24 hours of felling, thoroughly soaking the freshly cut surface and bark to soil level. Do not apply the mixture when the stump is wet. The most effective period for treatment is January to March.

Older stumps with dried-out surfaces need a different technique. Using a sharp axe, make a series of overlapping cuts through the hard bark to expose the softer inner tissues, cutting completely around the stump to form a channel, known as a "frill-girdle". Introduce the weedkiller solution into this channel, which allows it to make direct contact with the inner tissues. The best time for treat-

ment of older stumps is late winter.

On stumps larger than about 10 in in diameter, for which 2,4-D/dicamba/mecoprop may be less effective, use ammonium sulphamate, applying it to freshly cut surfaces in the solid form or as a solution of 10 lb per gal of water. Use 6 oz of dissolved chemical per foot of stump diameter. For larger scale use, it can be applied using the frill-girdle technique as a solution of 4 lb per gal of water. Apply the solution in dry weather until the stump becomes saturated. Avoid run-off since this may damage surrounding plants.

Natural decay
Chemical treatment rapidly kills living stumps. But natural decay of the resulting dead wood is a relatively slow process and there is no chemical means of accelerating it. Where 2,4-D/dicamba/mecoprop has been used stumps are usually colonized by fungi which cause only a slow decay of the wood, whereas the use of ammonium sulphamate encourages other kinds of fungi which result in a more rapid rate of decay. Therefore in order to reduce the risk of a honey fungus colony becoming established and endangering nearby trees and shrubs, use ammonium sulphamate if it is not possible to remove a stump after the tree has been felled.

Stumps may have to be left in position, for example if the tree has been growing near the base of a wall. In such circumstances consider leaving the stump in place and soaking it with a proprietary wood preservative or creosote, which stops growth while at the same time preserving the stump. This reduces the risk of honey fungus becoming established. Further treatment will be necessary at least once every two years.

Removal of dead stumps
If the stump is large, winching is usually the most practical approach. If smaller stumps are killed, treated and left for a year or so, allowing the finer roots to rot, they can then be winched out fairly easily. Burning stumps is an approach occasionally advocated, thoroughly drenching the stumps with paraffin and setting them alight. This is only effective for stumps that are old and very dry.

Honey Fungus

Removal of tree stumps

1 Kill the stumps by making a series of overlapping axe cuts into the bark then applying the appropriate chemical to wet exposed tissues and bark to ground level.

2 A year later remove the stump by pulling it out with a hand winch. Greater leverage is obtained if 4–5 ft of stem is retained.

169

Controlling woody weeds

Tree seedlings

although many seeds from trees are gathered and eaten by rodents, some survive to appear as seedlings. Sycamore is particularly troublesome because its winged seeds are often carried by the wind for many yards. Oak and horse chestnut seeds may be carried and dropped by rodents or unwittingly introduced into shrub borders in leaf litter for mulching. Elder and hawthorn seeds are excreted by birds after digestion of their fleshy covering. Furthermore, tree seedlings quickly develop strong tap roots and, once a few inches high, may be very difficult to remove by hand.

Where oak, horse chestnut or sycamore shed seeds in quantity rake up all seeds periodically as they fall. If they are mixed with leaf litter carefully separate, composting the leaves but disposing of the seeds in a garden incinerator. Where large numbers of seedlings occur in uncultivated areas or hard surfaces well clear of garden plants, spray with 2,4-D/dicamba/mecoprop. Best period for treatment is June–September.

In the garden it is usually impractical to attempt overall spraying of young saplings. If practical, cut them back to about 18 in from the soil level then thoroughly wet the freshly cut surface and remaining stem to ground level, guarding against run-off into the soil wherever there is the possibility of underlying plant roots. Use ammonium sulphamate in solution where there is resistance fo 2,4-D/dicamba/mecoprop treatments. In most garden situations, however, garden plants will be too close to permit weedkiller to be watered onto cut-back saplings, or there will be underlying shrub or tree roots. In such situations one can only try digging up – if necessary temporarily moving garden plants to do so.

Tree suckers

Several common trees and shrubs produce suckers which will often appear from roots remaining in the ground after trees or living stumps have been removed. Among the most troublesome are sumach, lilac, poplar, wild cherry and myrobalan (a rootstock commonly used for flowering cherries, plums and almonds). Elm is also troublesome and root suckers may appear following removal of trees affected by Dutch elm disease. Suckers can appear many yards away from where a tree has been removed, often in situations where digging out is impracticable, such as rose beds or tarmacadam paths.

Sucker growths can be removed quite easily with a sharp knife, secateurs or small saw, but regrowth will usually occur later in the season or the following spring, sometimes several shoots appearing where only one had been removed. To prevent this, cut as close to the point of origin from the root as possible, if feasible excavating down to sever the shoot flush with the root.

To kill stump suckers, apply 2,4-D/dicamba/mecoprop as an overall spray where suckers are young and leafy, and where it is safe to do so. Where suckers appear among plants treat individually, it would not be safe to use this approach but smaller plants could be lifted and perhaps repositioned while attempts were made to deal with the troublesome sucker (or sapling) growth. Check shrubberies to ensure that no suckers escape detection.

Blackberry (bramble)

Blackberry can be very troublesome in country gardens and, in some soils and situations may be extremely difficult to dig out. Unless checked, its long scrambling thorny shoots spread relentlessly to form dense mounded thickets.

Spraying large, long-established clumps is impracticable because of the difficulty of covering them adequately. Before spraying large slumps, use a billhook to cut them back to within a few inches of soil level. Then drag the thorny shoots well clear and burn them. Grub out shoot tips that have rooted where they touch the ground. Parent stems often detach easily and plantlets can be easily over-looked. After clearing away the stems spray the freshly cut stumps with 2,4-D/dicamba/mecoprop, wetting thoroughly.

Where blackberries are encountered growing through shrubs or from the base of hedges, sever the stems a few inches from soil level. Then apply weedkiller to the remaining sections of stems, taking care to avoid any run-off into the soil.

Ivy

Ivy growing on walls does not harm sound brickwork and, indeed, can be useful in providing a degree of insulation, but it may in time damage gutterings if not kept in check. On trees, ivy climbs up the trunks and along larger limbs but usually only develops arboreal growth where the crowns of trees become thin from die-back or defoliation caused by disease or old age. It also has the advantage of providing a resting place for birds and cover for small animals. Ivy may,

however, hide dangerous cavities in a tree. It can also mar the appearance of specimen trees with attractive bark.

To clear ivy from walls or trees sever it close to the soil. The aerial shoots will soon die and after a time can be detached easily. In the event of regrowth from the stump treat with ammonium sulphamate. To kill ivy growing and rooting into banks or dry walls spray with 2,4-D/dicamba/mecoprop during the late winter or early spring before growth begins.

Bamboo

Bamboos can rapidly outgrow their allotted space in smaller gardens and overwhelm surrounding plants. Removal by digging out can be arduous, particularly on heavier soils. Instead, lift any valuable plants around the fringes of the bamboo in April and cut back the bamboo to near ground level. Then, when the new growth is growing strongly, spray with glyphosate or dalapon. Repeat if there is regrowth later in the season.

Suckers

To remove suckers excavate down as close to the root as is possible and cut the sucker with a sharp knife. Ideally, it should be cut flush with the root.

Unwanted bamboo clumps

Cut back unwanted bamboo clumps to near ground level in April. Then spray with glyphosate or dalapon when new growth is strong.

Specific weeds 1

Coltsfoot

Lesser celandine

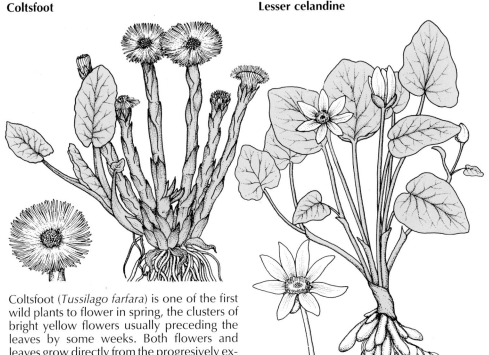

Coltsfoot (*Tussilago farfara*) is one of the first wild plants to flower in spring, the clusters of bright yellow flowers usually preceding the leaves by some weeks. Both flowers and leaves grow directly from the progresively extending system of underground stems. This often allows the weed to spread over several square yards, particularly on moist. heavier soils and on chalky clay. It reproduces primarily by seeds, which are freely produced and wind-dispersed. The weed can also regenerate from sections of underground stem unwittingly introduced to the garden in loam or manures, or among the roots of newly acquired plants.

It is best to eradicate large infestations with weedkillers since digging out, though possible, is arduous in heavier soils. In areas where there are underlying tree or shrub roots apply glyphosate during warm conditions in late spring when there is good leaf development and growth is vigorous. In uncultivated areas or where there are no underlying roots, use 2,4-D/dicamba/mecoprop mixtures or ammonium sulphamate. A single weedkiller application sometimes gives complete control but regrowth may occur, in which case repeat the treatment. Where there are underlying roots use paraquat/diquat.

Lesser celandine (*Ranunculus ficaria*) is a small clump-forming perennial bearing yellow, buttercup-like flowers. It grows in cool, moist places and spreads by means of seeds or bulbils.

It is difficult to eradicate by hand-weeding as its fleshy tuberous roots are easily detached and remain in the earth to form new plants. If it occurs in lawns improve the drainage, then spray at intervals with MCPA mixtures. Since lesser celandine has a relatively short period of growth before becoming dormant, treatment the following season is usually necessary. If it occurs in borders, it helps to maintain a good leaf-mulch since this reduces the possibility of the roots becoming detached. Where beds are heavily infested carefully lift any valuable plants in the autumn and plant them in temporary quarters. Then in spring, during warm weather when the weed is growing strongly, apply glyphosate or MCPA based lawn weedkiller mixtures with a watering can and dribble bar.

Bracken

Creeping thistle

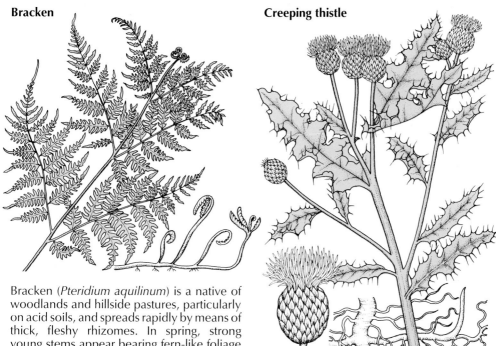

Bracken (*Pteridium aquilinum*) is a native of woodlands and hillside pastures, particularly on acid soils, and spreads rapidly by means of thick, fleshy rhizomes. In spring, strong young stems appear bearing fern-like foliage and eventually growing to a height of at least 6 ft. These die back to ground level in autumn but the dead stems can persist for much of the winter. Bracken may invade gardens from nearby woodland or pasture, or rhizomes may be brought in with coarse woodland leaf-mould or among the roots of plants.

Annual cutting or crushing when shoots are young and soft is a widely practised method of control in grassland. In the garden, tug out young stems as the fronds begin to unfurl, or cut back to ground level; however, this will stimulate growth of dormant buds along the rhizomes, necessitating further attention during the season. Infestations can be eliminated by annual attention if the weed is isolated but, if it is invasive, this method will only contain it. Glyphosate applied to the foliage in spring when growth is well advanced gives a good degree of control, but there is usually regrowth. If bracken is encroaching near established trees, bush fruits or woody ornamentals, a routine application of dichlobenil in spring will check its development.

Creeping thistle (*Cirsium arvense*) is a prickly-leaved perennial and a common weed of waste places and the fringes of cultivated land. It has a creeping rootstock with lateral roots extending from the main tap root to form a network of inter-connected growths. From these, aerial shoots develop, reaching a height of 3 ft or more. Viable seeds are seldom produced since plants of each sex must be near enough to each other to allow insects to transfer pollen.

On allotment sites or neglected borders dig deeply in winter, removing as much rootstock as possible. Leave the ground fallow and spray with glyphosate in late spring, when regrowth is well advanced. Repeat if necessary. Alternatively, spray during the spring and dig deeply the following autumn. 2,4-D/dicamba/mecoprop will check development but there will usually be strong regrowth. In the garden treat with glyphosate where possible, but among garden plants the only approach is to hand-weed repeatedly or remove valuable plants before applying control measures.

Specific weeds 2

Shepherd's purse

Japanese knotweed

Shepherd's purse (*Capsella bursa-pastoris*) is a small annual plant that is commonly encountered as a garden weed. It grows as a rosette of leaves with a tough, rather wiry tap root that produces a single leafy flowering shoot. The name covers a number of different forms or types, the leaves varying from entire to deeply lobed. There is also variation in the shape of the seed capsules. All forms produce large numbers of seed which may be shed over a period of several weeks. Some forms begin producing ripe seeds within six weeks or so of germination, thus giving rise to two or three generations a year.

In order to control the weed it is necessary to prevent seed development by destruction at the seedling stage. This can be effected in fruit plots by routine spring applications of the residual soil-acting weedkillers dichlobenil or simazine. In uncultivated or fallowed areas hoe or apply paraquat/diquat at frequent intervals. In vegetable plots or flower borders hoe regularly. Propachlor can be used amongst some flowering ornamentals and vegetable crops to control weeds at the seed germination stage, being particularly useful when applied following planting out of bedding plants and brassica seedlings.

Japanese knotweed (*Polygonum cuspidatum*) is a strong-growing perennial that dies back to ground level in autumn. It can grow to a height of more than 6 ft and has white flowers, red-brown stems and a stout, deeply penetrating, rhizomatous rootstock. Once established it spreads rapidly, engulfing all lesser plants in its path.

Digging out the rootstock is difficult, even in lighter soils, and virtually impossible on heavy clay soils. Repeated destruction of young growths by cutting at intervals during the growing season will progressively weaken the weed but it may take several years to clear large clumps. The most effective method of control is to apply glyphosate when growth is vigorous, for maximum effect applying in mid-summer or later. If there are valuable plants nearby which cannot be moved, erect temporary screening. The effectiveness of this treatment depends upon the vigour of the weed and its stage of development. If the weed is treated early in the season strong regrowth may occur.

Creeping yellow cress

Perennial nettle (stinging nettle)

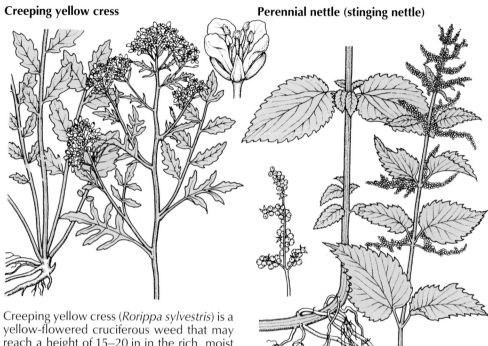

Creeping yellow cress (*Rorippa sylvestris*) is a yellow-flowered cruciferous weed that may reach a height of 15–20 in in the rich, moist conditions it prefers. Its troublesome nature as a garden weed lies in its ability to regenerate readily from sections of root left in the soil, even from the thinnest of its thread-like roots. Moreover, roots form at leaf-nodes wherever the prostrate stems press against the soil. Usually the weed is introduced unwittingly into the garden as pieces of root hidden among new plants or in well rotted manure.

Where the weed is troublesome in beds or in borders, lift valuable plants in autumn or spring, carefully checking for any traces of weed root before planting elsewhere. Then work through the infested area, carefully sifting the soil with a garden fork to remove as much weed root as possible. Repeat at intervals and do not plant in the site for a full season. Alternatively, where the situation allows apply glyphosate to the foliage in warm weather when weed growth is vigorous, taking great care if there are garden plants nearby. Where there are no underlying tree or shrub roots a solution of ammonium sulphamate can be watered on to the foliage in spring when growth is vigorous.

Perennial nettle (*Urtica dioica*) is a common weed occurring in hedgerows, open wood-land, waste land and neglected urban sites. It grows to a height of $4\frac{1}{2}$ ft or more, and thrives in loose, light, rich soils, spreading by means of underground stems and by surface-creeping stems which root at the nodes.

Fork out isolated clumps of perennial nettle in early spring when new growth is a few inches high, or later in the season after cutting back to near ground level. A few of the tough, deeply penetrating, yellow roots may be overlooked and these may produce further top growth. Check later in the season, forking out or treating with a weedkiller. With larger clumps it is better to apply weedkillers. Where there are underlying tree or shrub roots water-on glyphosate. On waste land or neglected sites apply glyphosate, 2,4-D/MCPA/dicamba, or ammonium sulphamate. Apply at flowering stage (early summer) or later. Check for signs of regrowth later in the season and, if present, repeat treatment as necessary.

Specific weeds 3

Ground elder

Cow parsley (keck)

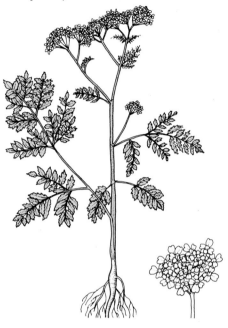

Ground elder (*Aegopodium podagraria*) is a common perennial weed bearing umbels of white flowers on stems 1½–3 ft high. It spreads by means of closely meshed white rhizomes. These are easily fragmented, consequently, although ground elder occasionally produces seed, it enters most gardens as small fragments of rhizome among the roots of acquired plants or in leaf-mould or manures.

Where ground elder becomes established among herbaceous perennials effective weedkillers cannot be used safely. Lift all valuable plants from infested areas in early autumn or spring, dividing clumps and discarding older sections. Remove all traces of rhizome from retained younger portions before replanting. To clean infested sites, fork out the rhizomes, then sift thoroughly for particles. Leave for a while to allow overlooked particles to produce new growth then fork over again or apply a weedkiller. Where there are roots that could be damaged by forking or by soil-acting weedkillers, use glyphosate, or paraquat/diquat repeated each time new growth appears. Use 2,4-D/dicamba/mecoprop or ammonium sulphamate in root-free areas away from valuable plants. Among tree and bush fruits, roses and some woody ornamentals, apply dichlobenil in early spring.

Cow parsley (*Anthriscus sylvestris*) is rarely encountered in well kept gardens. It is more familiar as a wayside weed thought it can be troublesome in orchards, paddocks, churchyards and similar grassed areas. A biennial, flowers in spring, bearing umbels of white flowers on 3–4 ft hollow stems. It may also persist as a perennial, developing offsets around the original plant.

At the seeding stage 2,4-D/dicamba/mecoprop will strongly check growth but well established plants are resistant to this and other weedkiller used in grassed areas. With established plants, however, try spraying April–May. Treatment after flowering is not effective. Physical removal is practicable where there is limited infestation; use a close-tine fork to lift out the weed by the roots in late spring when the flowering stem has developed sufficiently to provide good purchase. It is important to prevent the seed from developing. Where seed is known to have fallen on grassland spray with 2,4-D/mecoprop the following spring during the earliest stages of seedling development.

Couch grass (twitch)

Broad-leaved dock

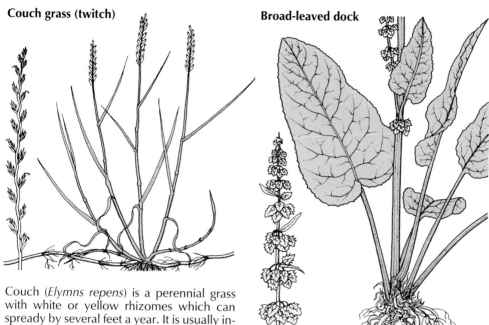

Couch (*Elymns repens*) is a perennial grass with white or yellow rhizomes which can spready by several feet a year. It is usually introduced into gardens unknowingly as small fragments of rhizome among the roots of plants. In heavily infested areas the rhizomes become densely matted and combine with the strong foliage growth to choke all but the toughest of garden plants.

Forking out localized infestations is practicable since few rhizomes penetrate deeply, but even small sections containing only a single leaf-joint and bud will, if overlooked, survive to perpetuate the infestation. In most situations glyphosate will give a rapid kill of couch grass. Apply in warm conditions when the couch has good leaf-cover and is growing strongly. Alternatively use dalapon or dichlobenil among fruit trees and bushes where there is risk of contact damage from glyphosate. Among herbaceous plants use the approach recommended for ground elder. In uncropped areas use glyphosate. Couch can, however, be eliminated from herbaceous borders and amongst other ornamentals (except ornamental grasses) by repeat spraying with alloxydim-sodium, harmless to nongrassy plants. Couch may appear in new lawns if the sites have not been thoroughly cleaned but it quickly succumbs to close regular mowing.

Broad-leaved dock (*Rumex obtusifolius*) is a strong-growing perennial with red-green flowers and thick, yellow-brown, branching tap roots which penetrate deeply. Curled dock (*Rumex crispus*) has narrower leaves with wavy margins, and the flowering stem has fewer branches. It too has a deeply penetrating tap root system.

The best means of control is to lift each plant carefully in order to remove as much of the root system as possible. Regrowth follows hoeing or cutting off at ground level but, if the top 4 in or more of rootstock is removed, further regrowth is unlikely. Regeneration can occur from small pieces of the upper rootstock. Therefore do not use mechanical cultivators. Seedling docks in lawns can be controlled by spraying with lawn weedkiller mixtures which include 2,4-D, but established docks are strongly resistant. Where local infestations cannot be dug out apply glyphosate when growth is vigorous, if possible at the flowering stage or later.

Specific weeds 4

Mind-your-own business

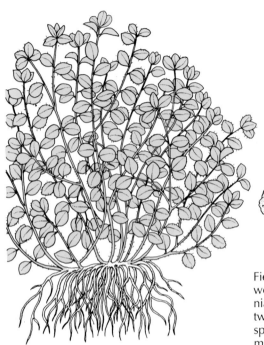

Field bindweed

Mind-your-own-business (*Soleirolia soleirolii*, syn *Helxine soleirolii*) is a creeping perennial that bears minute flowers and forms dense, slowly spreading mats of bright green foliage. The thin, fleshy, much-branched stems root as they slowly spread. It is often grown in the greenhouse or rock garden but can become invasive, spreading into borders and the lawn. It may also colonize dry stone walls.

If conditions are dry, control this weed by hoeing. If damp, hoeing may only spread the weed since it roots readily from small sections of stem. In borders use a hand fork to lift out patches of weed. Where it has settled in paving or walls apply dichlobenil granules or glyphosate with a watering can and dribble bar attachment. Helxine is resistant to lawn weedkillers, therefore if it occurs in lawns, strip off infested turf and re-turf in late autumn, or re-seed in September. On larger areas apply a tar oil wash in late winter. Use at ¼ pt in 2 gal of water applied to 20 sq yd.

Field bindweed (*Convolvulus arvensis*) is a weak-stemmed scrambling or twining perennial. Its stems, which grow to 2½ ft or more, twine around and strangle weaker plants. It spreads by means of fleshy rhizomes which may be found 6 ft or more into the soil. Small white or pink trumpet-shaped flowers are produced throughout the summer. *Calystegia sepium* (bellbind or greater bindweed) is similar to field bindweed, but has larger, white flowers. It is a much stronger plant and is capable of passing through hedges. Both species reproduce from seed or rhizomes.

Control these weeds by repeated forking out of all shoot growths over three or four seasons. This stimulates new shoot growth from dormant buds on the rhizomes, which exhausts the rootstock. However, if the weed is encroaching from neighbouring land it will remain a problem. In uncultivated areas well clear of garden plants apply glyphosate when the shoots are growing strongly and are about to flower or later, but before die-back in autumn. In tree and bush fruits, roses and some woody ornamentals dichlobenil will also provide a check, but with all weedkillers repeated treatment is usually necessary. Where these weeds occur among garden plants, spraying is too hazardous, but use of glyphosate gel may be possible, with care.

Horsetail

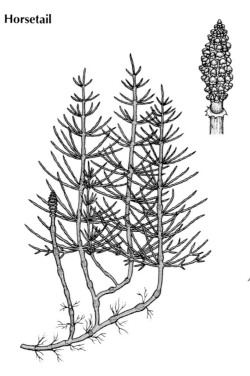

Oxalis

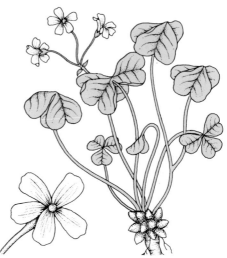

Field horsetail (*Equisetum arvensis*) is a perennial leafless plant with dark, wide-spreading rhizomes which may penetrate 6 ft or more into the soil. It has green, branching stems that function as leaves. They are preceded in early spring by white unbranched stems terminating in cone-like structures that produce the spores by which it propagates.

Forking out clears rhizomes from the upper soil layers but there will be regrowth from deeper-sited rhizomes and dislodged tubers. Where possible use foliage-absorbed, translocated weedkillers as these will provide a substantial check. Apply in spring when growth is vigorous. Glyphosate or 2,4-D/dicamba/mecoprop can be used in uncultivated areas; apply only glyphosate where there are underlying tree or shrub roots; the effectiveness of glyphosate may be increased if the stems are crushed before applying this weedkiller. Dichlobenil can be used if the weed occurs among certain fruit crops, woody ornamentals and roses and prior to laying paving.

Oxalis corymbosa is a perennial weed with pink flowers. It spreads either by seed or by its numerous tiny bulbils which develop around the soft fleshy tuberous roots.

To clear oxalis from heavily infested beds or borders first lift any valuable plants during autumn or spring. Carefully remove all soil from the roots and examine them closely for oxalis before replanting in a weed-free site. Then allow the weed to develop a strong growth of foliage before applying glyphosate in June or later, using watering can and dribble bar, or a low-pressure sprayer where well clear of garden plants. Apply in warm weather when the soil is moist and the weed is growing strongly. Repeat the treatment should any regrowth occur. Glyphosate can also be used to control oxalis around trees and shrubs where branches are well clear of the ground. Where growth is dense or low, as in rose beds or shrubberies, remove as much weed as possible by lifting out carefully with a hand fork to prevent bulbils from scattering. The best time for this is spring when the developing bulbils are still firmly attached to the parent plant. Subsequently maintain a good deep mulch. This encourages the oxalis to develop in the mulch from where it can be more easily removed. Other introduced species of oxalis are often locally troublesome; control is as for *Oxalis corymbosa*.

179

Specific lawn weeds 1

Yarrow

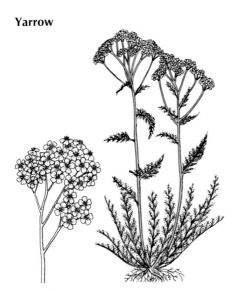

Parsley piert

Yarrow (*Achillea millefolium*) is a perennial weed that produces large flat-topped heads of white flowers on 1–2 ft stems. With regular lawn mowing it does not flower and can then be recognized by its pinnate and finely divided leaves, which have a soft, almost mossy, texture and are fragrant when crushed. Yarrow has prostrate, branching stems which root at the nodes, and is a widespread weed, particularly in turf that is poor, dry and undernourished. Large areas can be colonized from a single seed deposited by a bird or present in unsterilized top-dressing materials. The weed can also reproduce from small stem sections severed and scattered by the mower in spring.

Control yarrow by encouraging turf grasses to compete with it. Feed and top-dress the lawn with nitrogen-rich fertilizers, watering in when necessary. Use a hand fork on small areas, but sections of stem will remain to grow again unless forking is very thorough. Rake with a wire-toothed rake before mowing. This lifts up trailing ends so that they can be severed by the mower, which weakens the weed by defoliation. Lawn weedkillers containing mecoprop or 2,4-D/dicamba mixtures can be applied at four or five week intervals in spring when the weed is growing strongly, however, spraying may be necessary for two or more seasons.

Parsley piert (*Aphanes arvensis*) is widespread and often troublesome on lighter, drier soils where the turf is weak. It is an annual of low, spreading, branched growth, forming small hummocks of three-lobed, bright green leaves. It flowers and seeds freely throughout the spring and summer months. The yellow-green flowers are, however, hard to see. Reproduction is by seed, which is freely produced. Many seeds germinate in mild autumns, the seedlings over-wintering to form numerous small cushions by the spring. Their bright green colouring is particularly noticeable when the turf is sparse and weak through disease or following drought.

Control parsley piert by encouraging vigour in the turf by feeding and top-dressing, and by irrigating thoroughly during dry periods. Do not close-mow. Parsley piert is fairly resistant to lawn weedkillers, therefore, apply 2,4-D/mecoprop in mild conditions when growth is vigorous. Repeat as necessary at four or five week intervals and check regularly for signs of fresh seedling growth.

Field woodrush

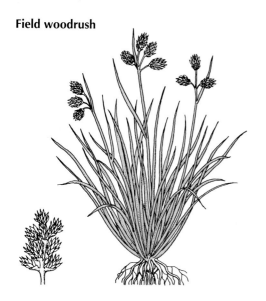

Mouse-ear hawkweed

Field woodrush (*Luzula campestris*) is often mistaken for a lawn grass until the stalked clusters of chestnut-brown flowers appear in spring. The leaves of field woodrush are similar to those of finer lawn grasses but are broader, darker green and thinly fringed with long pale, silky hairs. In dull weather patches of the weed appear darker than the surround turf; in angled sunlight the silky hairs give the patches a silvery sheen. Field woodrush is a perennial of short-stemmed, loosely tufted habit, spreading slowly by means of short creeping shoots. It is particularly common on poor light acid soils with low nutrient reserves. Infestation may arise from seeds or it may be introduced unnoticed in poor quality turf.

To counter field woodrush, feed and top-dress regularly to encourage vigour in the turf. On light, very acid soils, apply a light winter dressing of ground chalk or ground limestone at not more than 2 oz per square yard, or a spring dressing of nitro-chalk at 2 oz per square yard. This will stimulate grass growth and lessen the chances of the weed seedlings surviving. Begin mowing in spring before the stage of seed development. Repeated use of mecoprop may check growth but only in association with liming to reduce acidity.

Mouse-ear hawkweed (*Hieraceum pilosella*) is one of a number of plants of the Compositae (or daisy) family that are common as lawn weeds. Others in this family include dandelion (*Taraxacum officinalis*), cat's ear (*Hypochaeris radicata*) and hawk's beard (*Crepis capillaris*, syn *C. virens*). Of these, mouse-ear hawkweed is among the most troublesome when well established. A perennial, it over-winters as a rosette of small hairy leaves. In spring, shoots known as stolons appear from the base of the plants, each terminating in a new rosette. These root on contact with the soil and rapidly form a dense mat, stifling and suppressing the grass. The pale yellow, short-stemmed flowers appear in early summer. Mouse-ear hawkweed is common on light soils, particularly on drier soils where turf growth is weak.

In spring lift stolons with a wire-toothed rake, then cut with a mower. Chemical control is by 2,4-D with mecoprop or dicamba in spring when growth is vigorous, if necessary repeating after four or five weeks.

Specific lawn weeds 2

Creeping buttercup

Sheep's sorrel

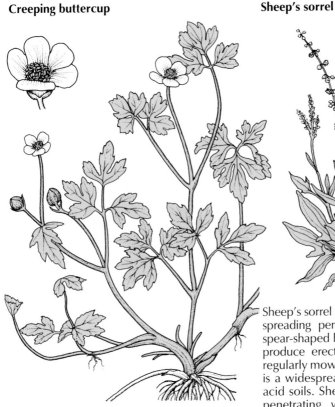

Sheep's sorrel (*Rumex acetosella*) is a creeping spreading perennial that has approximately spear-shaped leaves. Where unchecked it will produce erect 12 in flowering stems but in regularly mown lawns it remains flowerless. It is a widespread weed, particularly in sandy acid soils. Sheep's sorrel develops a deeply penetrating wiry tap root, spreading by means of a network of fine surface roots and rhizomes. Tufted shoots appear from these to colonize the turf densely. The weed may be introduced as seeds brought in by birds or in soil adhering to footwear or tools. Small sections of viable rhizome can be introduced in unsterilized top dressing materials.

Creeping buttercup (*Ranunculus repens*) is a perennial weed that is most troublesome in moister soils where it grows strongly and roots deeply. It spreads by means of long runners: strong, white, deeply penetrating roots that branch from each leaf node. Sublateral runners develop to form a vigorous, firmly anchored network of stems. The erect flowering stems appear in spring carrying large, glossy yellow flowers. Reproduction is usually from seeds but in moist conditions small nodal sections of stems may become established if severed and scattered when roots are beginning to form.

In spring, before mowing use a wire-toothed rake to lift the developing runners so that they can be cut by the mower. Chemical control is by the application of 2,4-D/mecoprop in spring when growth is vigorous. Repeat if necessary. Most lawn weedkillers will control creeping buttercup.

To control, feed and top-dress the lawn regularly to encourage more competition from the turf grasses. On light, very acid soils apply a winter dressing of ground chalk or ground limestone at not more than 2 oz per square yard. This will stimulate the grass and lessen the chances of any weed surviving weedkiller treatment. Hand-weeding checks sheep's sorrel but many of the finer thread-like rhizomatous shoots may remain to perpetuate the infestation. Apply 2,4-D/dicamba after feeding in spring when growth is vigorous. If necessary repeat four to five weeks later.

Pearlwort

Lesser yellow trefoil

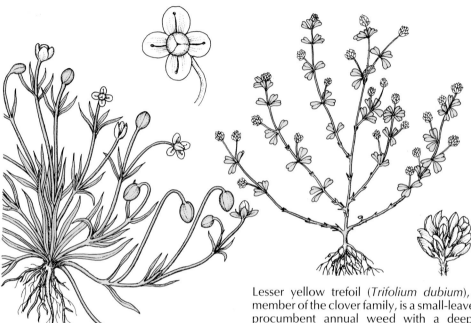

Lesser yellow trefoil (*Trifolium dubium*), a member of the clover family, is a small-leaved procumbent annual weed with a deeply penetrating tap root. It forms a flattened, roughly circular mat of interlaced thin wiry stems, with tiny trifoliate leaves. Many small multiple heads of pale yellow flowers are produced throughout the summer months. It seeds freely and, if scattered plants are ignored, large colonies can quickly form.

Pearlwort (*Sagina procumbens*) is a tufted perennial weed having prostrate, needle-like leaves on side-shoots that spread from a central rosette. The flowers are very small, often without petals. It may reach 2 in or more in height but it is usually much lower and in lawns it is often mistaken for moss. On paths it often has a very flattened habit. Pearlwort is a common weed where the soil is poor and light and the grass undernourished and weak, often surviving where grasses have succumbed to heavy wear. Reproduction is by very small seeds which are freely produced and can be carried considerable distances by the wind.

Feed and top-dress the lawn regularly to encourage vigour and density in the turf. Avoid close mowing. For chemical control apply 2,4-D/mecoprop or 2,4-D/dicamba mixtures after feeding in spring when grass growth is at it s most vigorous.

Hand-weed isolated specimens or lift them carefully with a hand fork. Clovers thrive where the turf is weak and poorly fed, therefore feed the lawn at intervals during the spring and early summer with nitrogen-rich fertilizers such as sulphate of ammonia, or high-nitrogen liquid feeds. On strongly acid soils use nitro-chalk. Top-dress in the autumn. Always use a grass-box on the mower to minimize seed dispersal. Where the weed is widespread, rake the turf and lift stems before mowing. 2,4-D/mecoprop mixtures can be applied one to two weeks after feeding in spring, when weeds and grasses are growing strongly. Repeat weedkiller and fertilizer applications, suitably spaced, at four to six week intervals as necessary from May to August, continuing the treatment the following spring to control any further seedlings.

Specific lawn weeds 3

Broad-leaved plantain

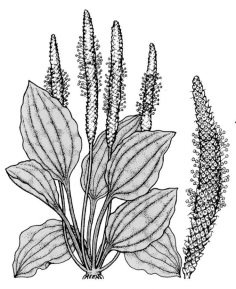

Common mouse-ear chickweed

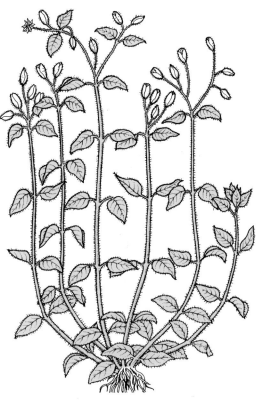

Broad-leaved plantain (*Plantago major*) is the largest leaved of the plantain species, and the most common on lawns. Other plantains may also be troublesome. Stag's or buck's horn plantain (*P. coronopus*) is most frequently encountered on lighter, drier soils and by the sea. Its leaves are usually very narrow and may be either lobed or toothed. Hoary plantain (*P. media*) is more common on chalk and limestone. It has more oval, hairy leaves. Black plantain or ribwort (*P. lanceolata*) is widespread, with leaves varying from strong-growing and erect in rich grassland to short and flattened on poor soils. All plantains are perennial rosetted weeds and produce erect spikes of tiny green or brown flowers, followed by numerous seeds, which may spread to nearby lawns unless controlled.

Carefully use a hand fork to lift out scattered specimens, but do this only in spring, when the grass is growing vigorously. If attempted when grass growth is slow the resulting bare patches may be colonized by moss or seedling weeds. Most lawn weedkillers will kill plantains. Apply in spring, feeding the lawn prior to treatment to ensure that the grass quickly covers the bare patches left as the weeds die. Apply as spot treatments to individual weeds.

Common mouse-ear chickweed (*Cerastium holosteoides*, syn *C. vulgatum*) is the only species frequently found as a lawn weed. A perennial, it has slender, hairy stems and lance-shaped leaves. The small white flowers are produced throughout the summer. It is prostrate and mat-forming in short or close-mown turf. In rougher grass it is more straggly in habit. Mouse-ear chickweed seeds heavily and is therefore a widespread lawn and grassland weed.

To control it feed and top-dress the lawn to encourage vigour and density in the turf. Before mowing use a wire-toothed rake to disturb patches of the weed so that they can be cut by the mower's blades. Chemical control is by 2,4-D/mecoprop or 2,4-D/dicamba, which should be applied after feeding the turf in the spring and when growth is vigorous, repeating at 4 or 5 week intervals.

Slender speedwell

Self-heal

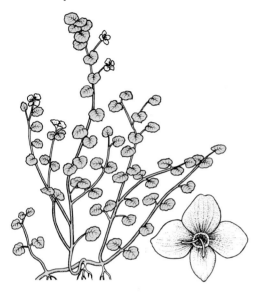

Slender speedwell (*Veronica filiformis*) was introduced into gardens during the early 19th century, and was much grown as a rock plant until gardeners realized how invasive it could be. It is now widely naturalized in many parts of the country and is a common and troublesome lawn weed. Speedwell is a perennial plant, producing numerous slender, branched stems, creeping and rooting at the nodes as they spread to form a dense weed carpet. The bright blue, long-stemmed flowers are produced early in the year but are rarely followed by seeds as the plants are self-sterile and most appear to be from the same clone. Speedwell can, however, reproduce from stem-sections scattered by the mower. Mowings put on the compost heap may spread the weed to other lawns when used as top dressings if incompletely decomposed.

Raking out will remove much of the weed, but usually numerous small-rooted sections will remain. Speedwell is extremely difficult to eradicate, being resistant to all lawn weed-killers. Tar oil winter washes applied in late winter to individual patches will usually control heavy infestations, though grasses may partially be temporarily scorched. Use at ¼ pt in 2 gal of water applied to 20 sq yd.

Self-heal (*Prunella vulgaris*) is a perennial weed and particularly widespread on chalk soils. It has a branching prostrate stem that roots strongly as it spreads. The oval leaves are carried in pairs and the short, leafy, flowering shoots appear in early summer. They carry whorls of purple-margined green bracts and violet to blue flowers. Self-heal reproduces itself both from seeds and by means of runners.

Carefully use a hand fork to lift small patches of self-heal. Large patches are often deeply anchored and cannot be removed without considerable disturbance and damage to the turf. Self-heal is fairly resistant to lawn weedkillers, the most effective being mecoprop and 2,4-D/dicamba. Apply in spring after feeding the turf, when growth is vigorous. Repeat treatment at four or five week intervals.

Index 1

Index 2

Index 3/Acknowledgements

Before using any weedkiller, it is important to read the relevant parts of the Introduction on page 3 and the points on safety listed on page 138.

The Royal Horticultural Society and the Publishers can accept no liability either for failure to control weeds and lawn pests and diseases by the methods recommended, or for any consequences of these methods. We specifically draw the readers, attention to the necessity of carefully reading and following the manufacturer's recommendations on any product.

Acknowledgements
The Publishers wish to thank the following companies and individuals for supplying illustration references: Allen Power Equipment Ltd., ASL Airflow Ltd., CeKa Works Ltd., Ciba-Geigy Ltd., Haltrac Ltd., Hills Industries Ltd., Kress and Kastner U.K. Ltd., Melnor N.V., T. Parker and Sons (Turf Management) Ltd., Poly-Gard Products Ltd., S. Ross-Craig,. Shell International Petroleum Co. Ltd., SISIS Equipment (Macclesfield) Ltd., Templar Tillers Ltd., Tudor Garden Products Ltd., Westwood Engineering Ltd., Wolseley Webb Ltd. The illustrations of weed seedlings on pages 126-130 were based on *Seedlings of the North-western European Lowland* by Dr F. M. Muller (1978), with the kind permission of the publishers, Dr W. Junk B.V. Publishers and the Centre for Agricultural Publishing and Documentation, the Netherlands. The Publishers also wish to acknowledge the help given by the Ministry of Agriculture, Fisheries and Food's Advisory Committee on Pesticides.

Artists: Lindsay Blow, Charles Chambers, Pamela Dowson, Edwina Keene, Sandra Pond, Ed Roberts, Paul Stafford, Lorna Turpin, John Woodcock.

Typesetting by SX Composing Ltd, Rayleigh, Essex
Origination by M&E Reproductions Ltd, North Fambridge, Essex

THE R.H.S. ENCYCLOPEDIA OF PRACTICAL GARDENING

EDITOR-IN-CHIEF: CHRISTOPHER BRICKELL

A complete range of titles in this series is available from all good bookshops or by mail order direct from the publisher. Payment can be made by credit card or cheque/postal order in the following ways:

BY PHONE   Phone through your order on our special CREDIT CARD HOTLINE on 0933 410511; speak to our customer service team during office hours (9am to 5pm) or leave a message on the answer machine, quoting your full credit card number plus expiry date and your full name and address. Please also quote the reference number shown at the top of this form.

BY POST   Simply fill out the order form below (it can be photocopied) and send it with your payment to: REED BOOK SERVICES LTD, PO BOX 5, RUSHDEN, NORTHANTS, NN10 6YX.

SPECIAL OFFER: **FREE POSTAGE AND PACKING** (UK ONLY)

ISBN	TITLE	PRICE	QUANTITY	TOTAL
1 85732 976 7	GARDENING TECHNIQUES	£7.99		
1 85732 974 0	WATER GARDENING	£7.99		
1 85732 900 7	CONTAINER GARDENING	£7.99		
1 85732 901 5	GARDEN STRUCTURES	£7.99		
1 85732 902 3	PRUNING	£7.99		
1 85732 903 1	PLANT PROPAGATION	£7.99		
1 85732 905 8	FRUIT	£7.99		
1 85732 904 X	VEGETABLES	£7.99		
1 85732 908 2	GROWING UNDER GLASS	£7.99		
1 85732 907 4	LAWNS, WEEDS & GROUND COVER	£7.99		
1 85732 906 6	GARDEN PESTS AND DISEASES	£7.99		
		POSTAGE & PACKING		FREE
		GRAND TOTAL		

Name .... (BLOCK CAPITALS)

Address..

.... Postcode ....

I enclose a cheque/postal order for £ .... made payable to Reed Book Services Ltd, or:

Please debit my: Access ☐ Visa ☐ AmEx ☐ Diners ☐ account

by £.......................... Expiry date ....

Account no ☐☐☐☐☐☐☐☐☐☐☐☐☐☐☐☐

Signature ....

Whilst every effort is made to keep our prices low, the publisher reserves the right to increase the price at short notice.

Your order will be dispatched within 28 days, subject to availability. Free postage and packing offer applies to UK only. Please call 0933 410511 for details of export postage and packing charges

Registered office: Michelin House, 81 Fulham Road, London SW3 6RB. Registered in England no 1974080.

THIS FORM MAY BE PHOTOCOPIED.